THE LEVY FAMILY'S EPIC QUEST

TO RESCUE THE HOUSE

THAT JEFFERSON BUILT

SAVING
MONTICELLO

MARC LEEPSON

THE FREE PRESS

NEW YORK LONDON TORONTO

SYDNEY SINGAPORE

fP

THE FREE PRESS
A Division of Simon & Schuster, Inc.
1230 Avenue of the Americas
New York, NY 10020

For information regarding special discounts for bulk purchases,
please contact Simon & Schuster Special Sales:
1-800-456-6798 or business@simonandschuster.com

Designed by Jeanette Olender
Manufactured in the United States of America

1   3   5   7   9   10   8   6   4   2

Library of Congress Cataloging-in-Publication Data
Leepson, Marc.
Saving Monticello: the Levy family's epic quest to rescue the house
that Jefferson built / Marc Leepson.
p.   cm.
Includes bibliographical references and index.
1. Monticello (Va.)—History. 2. Jefferson, Thomas, 1743–1826—Homes and haunts—
Virginia—Albemarle County. 3. Historic sites—Conservation and restoration—Virginia—Albe-
marle County. 4. Historic buildings—Virginia—Albemarle County—Design and construction.
5. Levy, Uriah Phillips, 1792–1862. 6. Levy family. 7. Historic preservation—United
States—Case studies. 8. Antisemitism—United States—Case studies. I. Title.
E332.74 .L44 2001
975.5'482—dc21   2001033195
ISBN 0-7432-0106-X

TO THE MEMORY OF LEE SHERMAN

CONTENTS

SAVING MONTICELLO

Jefferson's House

On July 4, 1776, the day the Second Continental Congress adopted the Declaration of Independence marking the beginning of the end of the British empire, King George III wrote in his diary: "Nothing of importance happened today."

On July 4, 1826, as people across the United States joyously celebrated the young nation's Independence Day Jubilee, several matters of great importance took place. Early that afternoon, Thomas Jefferson, the author of the Declaration of Independence, died in his bed at Monticello, his beloved home in Central Virginia's Blue Ridge Mountains. The nation's third president was eighty-three years old.

Later that day, in one of the more remarkable coincidences of history, Jefferson's fellow founding father John Adams died in Massachusetts. The nation's second president's last words were: "Thomas Jefferson still survives."

Thomas Jefferson rarely was sick during his long, productive life. But in the spring of 1825 he had developed dysuria, a painful discharge of urine, probably caused by an enlarged prostate gland. The condition weakened him considerably and he was under a physician's care all that summer.

"My own health is very low, not having been able to leave the house for three months," Jefferson wrote on August 7. "At the age of 82, with one foot in the grave, and the other uplifted to follow it, I do not permit myself to take part in any new enterprises."

Jefferson suffered greatly until his death the following summer. His physical suffering was made worse by mental anguish. In his last year,

Jefferson was tormented by thoughts about the fate of his only surviving daughter, Martha Jefferson Randolph, who was then fifty-three, and her children after his death.

"It is agony to leave her in the situation she is now in," Jefferson said to his grandson Thomas Jefferson Randolph (Martha's oldest son) two weeks before he died. "She is sinking every day under the suffering she now endures; she is literally dying before my eyes."

Plagued by large debts, failed farming and other business ventures, constant extended visits from friends and family, and by his own often profligate spending habits, Jefferson knew that Martha would inherit only debts. He also knew that she would be forced to sell all of his property—including Monticello, the neoclassical mansion Jefferson called his "essay in architecture"—to satisfy his creditors.

On June 24, 1826, Jefferson called for his physician, the British-born Dr. Robley Dunglison of Charlottesville, who came up to Monticello and stayed there, attending the dying Jefferson during the last weeks of his life. Martha sat at her father's bedside during the day. Her oldest son (known to the family as "Jeff"), then thirty-three, and Nicholas Trist, her son-in-law, took over at night, aided by several household slaves, including Burwell Culbert, Joe Fossett, and John Hemings.

Jefferson seemed to become calmer as death drew near. He lost consciousness on the night of July 2. He awoke briefly on the morning of Monday, July 3. At least once that day he asked if the Fourth of July had come. Dr. Dunglison told him the day would soon be upon them. Nicholas Trist nodded in assent. He and his brother-in-law Jeff sweated out the last hours of July 3, staring at Jefferson's bedside clock as midnight approached, silently hoping he would keep breathing until the Fourth of July. He did.

Jefferson awoke around 4:00 in the morning on July 4 and called to his slaves—whom Jefferson referred to as "servants"—in what those around him said was a clear voice. He then lapsed into unconsciousness for the last time. Jefferson died in his sleep at 12:50 in the afternoon.

Church bells began tolling soon thereafter in Charlottesville. The next day was a day of mourning in that university town. The fifty-year-old nation began grieving soon thereafter. Jefferson was buried at Monticello on July 5.

When Jefferson died, Monticello, his idyllic mountaintop home, was in the early stages of physical decay. Due to his fiscal troubles, from the time Jefferson stepped down from the presidency in 1809 and retired to Monticello, he could not afford the upkeep on the mansion he had lovingly designed and created.

Monticello was an unbearable burden for Martha Randolph and her son, who was named executor of Jefferson's estate. They were forced to put Monticello on the market to try to raise cash to pay off Jefferson's $100,000-plus debts. The Randolphs soon discovered, however, that no one wanted Monticello, which today is recognized worldwide as a priceless architectural masterpiece. No one wanted what today has become an iconic structure revered by millions—a house whose image has graced the back of the Jefferson-head nickel since 1938 and was engraved on the back of the two-dollar bill for a half century.

In 1827, at Monticello the Randolphs auctioned off Thomas Jefferson's slaves, household furniture and furnishings, supplies, grain, and farm equipment. Then they sold or gave to relatives nearly all of his priceless collection of artwork, along with thousands of acres of land he owned in Virginia.

That left Monticello bereft of furniture and furnishings. Martha Randolph fled the decaying, almost-empty mansion. When the Randolphs put the house itself and its surrounding acreage on the market, there were no takers for years. The house sat virtually neglected until 1831 when James Turner Barclay, a Charlottesville druggist, bought Monticello and 552 acres for $7,000.

Barclay and his family lasted less than three years in the house before they sold Monticello to a most unlikely buyer: U.S. Navy Lieutenant Uriah Phillips Levy, a colorful, brash, controversial man who was an ardent Jefferson admirer. Levy, the first Jewish American to make a career as a U.S. naval officer, had amassed a fortune in real estate. He immediately set about making much-needed repairs at Monticello.

Uriah Levy, by all accounts, saved Monticello from physical ruin. Although he did not live there, Levy opened Jefferson's mountaintop home to visitors who showed up to pay homage to his memory. Later, during the Civil War when the South seized Monticello because it was owned by a Northerner, another period of physical decline set in.

Uriah Levy died childless in 1862. He left a strange, convoluted will that did not sit well with his family heirs, who challenged it in court. Seventeen years of legal wrangling ensued, during which time Monticello again fell into near ruin.

In 1879, Uriah Levy's nephew—the strangely but aptly named Jefferson Monroe Levy—gained title to Monticello. Jefferson Levy was a big-time New York City lawyer, flamboyant stock speculator, real estate wheeler-dealer, and three-term U.S. congressman. When the lifelong bachelor took title to Monticello the building was falling apart. He immediately began spending what soon amounted to a small fortune to repair and restore Monticello and its grounds.

Like his uncle, J. M. Levy was a New York City resident, although he spent many summer weekends at Monticello. He allowed visitors to roam the grounds and permitted some to tour the house. Like his uncle, he was a great admirer of Jefferson. He served as host to one president (Theodore Roosevelt), countless members of Congress, ambassadors, and other officials and dignitaries who flocked to Monticello out of respect and admiration for Thomas Jefferson.

Jefferson Levy's proud ownership of Monticello came under attack in 1911. A national movement to wrest control of the estate from him was led by Maud Littleton, a New York socialite. The goal of her well-organized and well-funded effort was to turn the house over to the federal government to be used as a shrine to Jefferson.

In 1912, Congressman Jefferson Levy had the singular misfortune of having to defend his ownership of Monticello in the House of Representatives as Congress debated legislation aimed at confiscating the mansion. That legislation was defeated, but in 1914 Jefferson Levy— who once vowed that he never would sell the place—bowed to public pressure and offered to sell Monticello to the government. His asking price was $500,000, about half the amount he estimated he had put into the property.

Congress balked at Levy's asking price. In 1919, in the throes of a deep personal financial crisis, Levy put Monticello on the market. There were no takers until 1923 when the newly formed private, non-profit Thomas Jefferson Memorial Foundation agreed to Levy's price. In December of that year the foundation purchased the property. Levy died less than three months later.

The Levy family owned Monticello for eighty-nine years—far longer than the Jefferson family owned it. Uriah Levy and Jefferson Levy (who pronounced the name "Leh-vee," rhyming with "bevy") took control of Monticello at critical periods in the history of that historic house; in each case it was on the verge of physical ruin. A case can be made that Uriah Levy was the first American to act upon the idea of preserving a historic dwelling. His restoration of Monticello took place two decades before the first efforts to preserve George Washington's Virginia home, Mount Vernon.

This book offers the first close look at the post-Jefferson history of Monticello and the crucial roles played by Uriah Phillips Levy and Jefferson Monroe Levy in saving and restoring Monticello. The story is filled with memorable, larger-than-life characters, beginning with Jefferson himself and including James Turner Barclay, a messianic visionary; Uriah Phillips Levy—six times court-martialed—and his teen-aged wife; the colorful Confederate colonel Benjamin Franklin Ficklin who owned Monticello during the Civil War; the eccentric, high-living, deal-making egoist, Jefferson Monroe Levy; and the single-minded Mrs. Littleton.

The story is filled with mysteries and controversies. What happened at Monticello from 1826 to 1923 has been one of best-kept secrets in the history of American preservation.

Until now.

CHAPTER ONE

Stealing Monticello

I am happy no where else and in no other society, and all my wishes end, where I hope my days will end, at Monticello.
THOMAS JEFFERSON, AUGUST 12, 1787

Description: Brick, Flemish bond; two stories disguised to look as one; porticos front and rear, with octagonal dome on roof. Plan complicated by additions made to original building by Jefferson after his return from France. Much fine interior woodwork.
HISTORIC AMERICAN BUILDINGS SURVEY FOR MONTICELLO,
NOVEMBER 2, 1940

Thomas Jefferson, the original American Renaissance man, began clearing the land atop a small mountaintop to build the house of his dreams in 1768. He was twenty-five years old. The heavily wooded land three miles outside of Charlottesville in Albemarle County, Virginia, in the foothills of the Blue Ridge Mountains was part of the thousands of acres of land he had inherited in 1764 from his father, Peter Jefferson, a self-made cartographer, surveyor, landowner, and prominent citizen of Albemarle who married into one of the most powerful colonial American families, the Randolphs of Virginia.

Thomas Jefferson was born on April 13, 1743, at Shadwell, his father's Albemarle County plantation. Since childhood Jefferson had dreamed of building a house on top of a nearby 560-foot mountain—a radical idea at a time when most Virginia plantation homes were built in the low-lying, tobacco-growing Tidewater region. The name he selected for the site was "Monticello," Italian for hillock or small mountain. Jefferson designed the building based on his study of ancient—particularly Roman—architecture, and on the ideas of the great Italian Renaissance architect Andrea Palladio (1508–1580).

Construction of Monticello began in 1769. A team of masons, carpenters, and joiners did the work. Some were white; others were Jefferson's slaves (he referred to them as "servants") who lived on the site along what became known as Mulberry Row. Jefferson himself moved to the small mountain in 1770 after Shadwell burned to the ground in a fire.

Some of the bricks and nails the workers used were forged on the mountaintop. The wood and stone used for the cellars and the columns on the East front and the limestone to make mortar came from Jefferson's own extensive estates. The window glass was imported from Europe.

Jefferson spent many years fine tuning the design for the house. In 1796 he tore up his original plans, and created new ones incorporating architectural ideas he was exposed to during the four years (1784–1789) he spent in Paris, first as American trade commissioner, and later as Minister to the Court of Louis XVI. By 1809, at the end of his second term as president when he came home from Washington to live full time at Monticello, the mansion was essentially complete.

The result was a 10,660-square-foot, twenty-room Roman neoclassical building with distinctly Jeffersonian touches. "The influence was Palladian, the immediate example was French, but viewed from any possible position Monticello was Jeffersonian," said longtime Monticello curator James A. Bear, Jr. Jefferson shaped every aspect of the house, inside and out, from the window draperies to the Windsor chairs. Jefferson packed the place with an impressive art collection, a library of books that grew to nearly seven thousand volumes in seven languages, and an enormous amount of household objects and fittings.

Most of the interior furnishings came from France in a shipment of 86 crates of furniture, silverware, glassware, china, wall paper, fabrics, books, portraits and other works of art, and household goods. As Monticello's curator Susan Stein says, during his years in France, Jefferson "shopped for a lifetime."

Included in this shipment of treasures were sixty-three paintings by different artists and seven terra-cotta plaster busts by the foremost French sculptor of the day, Jean-Antoine Houdon. Jefferson's European treasure trove also contained four dozen chairs, two sofas, six mirrors, assorted tables, four marble tabletops, and four full-length mirrors. Jefferson added more to this auspicious collection—including eighteen chairs, six mirrors, several beds and tables—from the top craftsmen in Williamsburg, New York, Philadelphia, and London.

Jefferson crammed Monticello's rooms with artwork, sculpture, archeological specimens, musical and scientific instruments, Indian artifacts, and *objets d'art* of all kinds. He designed features found in few homes in eighteenth-century America: two-story high ceilings, a dome —the first on an American house—beds tucked in alcoves, skylights, indoor "privies," extremely narrow staircases. Other one-of-a-kind interior touches included a dumbwaiter to carry wine from the cellar to the dining room and the enormous seven-day great clock framing the door of the entrance hall.

Jefferson—the nation's third president and the man who wrote the Declaration of Independence—was described by the Marquis de Chastellux in 1782 as a "Musician, Draftsman, Surveyor, Astronomer, Natural Philosopher, Jurist and Statesman." Jefferson was that and much more.

He also studied botany, agriculture, forestry, viticulture, and landscape architecture. Monticello's grounds—which have been likened to an "ornamental working farm"—were extremely well planned. Jefferson turned the wild hardwood forest on the mountaintop into a park with broad lawns and flowerbeds, and carved out an ornamental forest he called the Grove. He divided the surrounding three hundred acres into seven fields, each of which he planted in a different crop, rotating the crops annually. They were pleasingly and practically separated with rows of peach trees, numbering in the hundreds.

He selected many more fruit and shade trees, shrubs, and other plants at Main's nursery near Washington and personally laid out the flower beds surrounding the house. He imported seeds from Italy, from the Jardin des Plantes in Paris, and from the top nurseries in Virginia,

Philadelphia, Washington, and South Carolina. He planted dozens of varieties of fruit trees, including peaches, apples, cherries, apricots, nectarines, quinces, plums, and pears. He cultivated Seville orange trees, which he brought indoors during the winter, and imported olive trees from Italy and southern France.

Jefferson built a thousand-foot-long, three-terraced "kitchen" vegetable garden, with twenty-four beds divided into "Fruits, Roots, and Leaves." There he grew some 250 varieties of vegetables, including beans and corn from seeds brought to him by Lewis and Clark, seventeen kinds of peas, white eggplant, and purple broccoli.

Monticello was "an artistic achievement of the first order," in the words of Jefferson scholar Merrill D. Peterson, but it was a seriously flawed achievement. All was not well when the nation's third president came to live at Monticello full time on March 15, 1809. The debts he had accumulated before becoming president in 1801 still weighed heavily. While Jefferson had managed to pay off many of his pre-Revolutionary debts to British firms out of his not-insignificant $25,000 annual presidential salary, the interest that had accumulated on the remaining debts was crippling.

Jefferson owed his creditors about $11,000 when he bid farewell to Washington, D.C., and headed home. That amount was not troubling to him, even though there was no presidential pension plan. Jefferson believed that he could easily repay what he owed from the income he would earn from his farming operations at Monticello and his other Virginia properties, which included the nearby farms of Shadwell, Tufton, and Lego in Albemarle County and Poplar Forest in Bedford County.

There was reason to be optimistic. Jefferson owned a total of some 10,000 acres, about half of it in Albemarle County and the remainder in nearby Bedford County, including his country retreat at the Poplar Forest plantation. He also owned the 157-acre Natural Bridge to the west in Rockbridge County in Virginia's Shenandoah Valley. Jefferson had bought that scenic property from King George III for twenty shillings in 1774. The plan was to earn money from travelers who came there to see the spectacular natural rock bridge formation. Jefferson took the first step in that direction in 1803 by building a two-room log cabin on the site. He also owned several building lots, including one in Richmond. He expected to reap further dividends from the two gristmills he owned on the Rivanna River, which he expected to produce more than a thousand dollars in income a year.

But Jefferson's financial problems worsened after he moved to Monticello. His farming operations rarely did anything but lose money due to periodic droughts, crop failures, and depressed crop prices. The mills were poorly managed and their hoped-for revenues never materialized. Jefferson's debts mounted, augmented by growing sums he owed to Charlottesville-area merchants from whom he bought everything from tea and coffee for his household to salt fish and "Negro cloth" for the more than two hundred slaves he owned.

He was also burdened financially by his generous hospitality and family responsibilities. Jefferson's wife Martha had died in 1782, but his adult children, his grandchildren, his sisters and their children, and various other relatives and friends spent long periods of time in residence at Monticello, especially after 1815. By all accounts, Jefferson was hospitable to other visitors as well, some who venerated the man, and others who sought him out for favors. They included artists and writers, traveling merchants, would-be biographers, adventurers, and the just plain curious. The list included noted figures such as Daniel Webster, the Marquis de Lafayette, James Madison, and Jefferson's Albemarle County neighbor, James Monroe. The well-heeled came with horses, servants, and family members. Sometimes he found himself hosting as many as fifty guests at a time.

The domestic manager of the sprawling household during Jefferson's post-presidency retirement was his eldest daughter, Martha Jefferson Randolph, whom Jefferson called "Patsy." Martha had joined the household in 1809, with her children and her husband, Col. Thomas Mann Randolph—a notoriously inept businessman who was constantly in financial straits. There she continued her role as hostess and female household head that she had begun in Washington.

Jefferson's financial situation deteriorated further after the War of 1812. His expenses continued to outstrip his income and he was forced to take on additional loans, while continuing to make interest payments. In 1815, his farming operations were particularly hard hit by a severe drought. That spring, Jefferson turned the management of his Albemarle County farms over to Thomas Jefferson Randolph, his eldest and favorite grandson. By all accounts Jeff Randolph was trustworthy and extremely competent in business matters, especially compared to his dissolute father.

But even with the good management of his grandson, Jefferson's financial woes continued. He experienced some relief in 1815 when Congress, after a spirited debate and by a small majority, agreed to buy his library of 6,487 books for $23,950. Jefferson had offered the books—the largest personal collection in the country—to the nation in September soon after he learned that British troops had burned the congressional library in Washington a month earlier. Because of his generous offer to expand the library, Jefferson has been known as the father of the Library of Congress, which had started in 1800 and had consisted of some three thousand volumes before the disastrous fire. A Library of Congress exhibit on Jefferson in 2000 included a re-creation of the library Jefferson sold to the nation in 1815. It filled twenty twelve-foot-high bookcases.

This large congressional cash infusion did little to stem Jefferson's fiscal woes. He continued to lay out lavish sums to maintain his large household. With his farms and mills providing little or no relief Jefferson was forced to borrow further and his debts mounted.

In January 1826, five months before his death, the eighty-two-year-old Jefferson came up with a plan that he believed would pay off all his debts: a state lottery. In part, the lottery idea was a reaction to his failed effort to sell off large parcels of land at a time when land prices were severely depressed. When he proposed the idea to the Virginia legislature in Richmond, Jefferson received a lukewarm reception, although several legislators floated a plan to provide him an $80,000 interest-free loan.

After the Virginia legislature's debate over the lottery made the newspapers, Jefferson's financial plight became known throughout the country. He received many letters of support, including one from James Monroe (1758–1831), the nation's fifth president who owned a large amount of land in the state and was in similar land-rich, cash-poor financial difficulties.

The publicity over Jefferson's misfortunes resulted in several unsolicited contributions, including a bank note for $7,500 from a group of admirers in New York.

But Jefferson pinned his hopes on the lottery. He let it be known that if the lottery did not work, he was prepared to sell Monticello and his mills and move to his property in Bedford County. As he put it in a February 17 letter to Madison: "If refused, I must sell everything here, perhaps considerably in Bedford, move thither with my family, where I have not even a log hut to put my head into."

A lottery bill was passed by the Virginia legislature on February 20, one in which Monticello essentially was the prize. The plan was to sell at least 11,000 lottery tickets at ten dollars each. Under the plan, Jefferson would keep Monticello for the rest of his life, but it would go to the lottery winner after his death. His daughter Martha, the head of the family, was reconciled to losing Monticello after the lottery law was passed.

When Jefferson died on July 4, 1826, no lottery tickets had yet been sold.

. . .

AT HIS death Jefferson owed his creditors $107,273.63. The largest amount by far was the $60,110 he owed to his grandson and executor of his estate, Jeff Randolph. Twenty thousand dollars of that amount represented a note Jefferson had co-signed for Jeff's late father-in-law, Wilson Cary Nicholas, and the balance was made up of expenses that Jeff Randolph paid while managing his grandfather's agricultural and other business ventures.

Jefferson's assets were not listed in his will. However, during the debate over the Jefferson lottery earlier that year, Monticello and its surrounding acres were valued at $71,000. His properties at Shadwell Mills and in Milton were deemed to be worth $41,500. The publicity over the lottery resulted in two other items in the estate's plus column: $10,000 contributions voted to Martha Randolph by the legislatures of South Carolina and Louisiana.

In his will, Jefferson gave his country retreat, Poplar Forest, to his grandson, Francis Eppes, the son of Jefferson's deceased daughter Maria and her husband (and cousin) John Wayles Eppes. Jefferson bequeathed Monticello and his remaining real estate in trust to his daughter, Martha. He named her son Jeff Randolph as his sole executor and also designated him as one of the estate's three trustees. The others were Alexander Garrett, the bursar at the University of Virginia, and Jefferson's grandson-in-law, Nicholas Philip Trist.

In a codicil to his will, Jefferson left his walking staff to James Madison. He gave watches to each of his grandchildren, and wanted his books to be donated to the University of Virginia—although they later were sold, instead, to raise cash. The codicil also granted freedom to five of his slaves who had learned trades, all of whom were members of the Hemings family: Joe Fossett, Burwell Culbert, and John, Madison, and Eston Hemings. Burwell Culbert (called "Burwell" by the family), Jefferson's butler and main household servant, also received $300. All five freemen were also given houses.

Finally, Jefferson directed that his farm books, account books, and letters go to Jeff Randolph. Jefferson's collection of forty thousand letters included copies of every letter he wrote—copies he made as he wrote with a device called a polygraph, which held two sheets of paper and two connected pens.

Jeff Randolph, his mother, and the trustees faced an extremely difficult task. Aside from the six-figure debt, there was the not inconsiderable problem of what to do about Monticello. Jefferson did not have enough cash to maintain the mansion properly during his retirement years. In the years leading up to his death, the house, especially the exterior, showed the strains of delayed maintenance and the continuous use by the unending parade of visitors and family members. The floors of the terrace walks had decayed and fallen in; the roof leaked badly around the skylights; the interior rooms were in need of attention.

Visitors commented on the sad state of affairs. "His house is rather old and going to decay," said Samuel Whitcomb, Jr., a bookseller who showed up to try to interest Jefferson in his wares at Monticello on May 31, 1824. "Appearances about his yard and hill are rather slovenly."

By the end of 1826, Martha Jefferson Randolph and her son decided they had only one course of action: to sell off Jefferson's lands and his household goods. They did so reluctantly. "You may suppose how unwilling we are to leave our home in a few weeks, perhaps never to return to it and how much we . . . prefer lingering here till the last moment," Mary Jefferson Randolph, Martha Randolph's twenty-two-year-old daughter, wrote to her older sister Ellen Wayles Randolph Coolidge in Boston on October 1.

Jeff Randolph placed a notice that appeared in the January 9, 1827, *Richmond Enquirer* under the headline "Executor's Sale." On January 15, the ad said, "the whole of the residue of the personal property of Thomas Jefferson" would be auctioned at Monticello. That included "130 valuable negroes, stock, crops &c., household and kitchen furniture."

The slaves were described as "believed to be the most valuable for their number ever offered at one time in the State of Virginia." The notice listed "many valuable historical and portrait paintings, busts of marble and plaster of distinguished individuals, one of marble of Thomas Jefferson by Caracci, with the pedestal and truncated columns on which it stands; a polygraph or copying instrument used by Thomas Jefferson, for the last twenty-five years" and "various other articles curious and useful to men of business and private families."

The sale began on January 15, 1827, and lasted five days. There is no complete record of who bought the items, but family letters reveal that Jefferson's grandchildren themselves purchased much of the furniture and furnishings. The rest was sold to friends, neighbors, and strangers who showed up for the sale at Monticello. Nearly all of the slaves were sold to Virginia buyers, many of them in Albemarle and the surrounding counties. According to an item in the newsmagazine *Niles' Register*, the sale brought in $47,840.

Mary Randolph wrote to Ellen on January 25 describing with great despair the siblings' feelings about the auction. "During five days that the sale lasted, you may imagine what must have been the state of our feelings, such a scene playing out actually within sight [and with people] bringing us fresh details of everything that was going on. . . ." It is better, Mary said, "to submit to any personal inconveniences, however numerous and annoying they may be, than to live in a state of society where such things as trade are of daily occurrence. . . ."

After the sale, Martha Randolph came back to Virginia from Boston with her young children and joined the rest of the family at Tufton where her father had built a house almost forty years earlier. Jeff Randolph had moved there with his wife Jane Nicholas and their children in 1817 and added a new wing. Virginia Randolph Trist and her husband Nicholas also left Monticello and joined the rest of the family, although they eventually resettled in Washington, D.C., after Nicholas accepted a clerkship at the State Department generously provided by Virginia-born secretary of state Henry Clay (1777–1852), who was aware of the family's financial difficulties.

Jefferson's art works and books were not part of the January 1827 auction. The family decided to market the paintings and other works of art in Boston, where they thought the collection would bring better prices than in Charlottesville. Martha Randolph's daughter Ellen and her husband Joseph Coolidge took charge. They held the sale at the Boston Athenaeum, the venerable independent library that had been founded in 1807 and which, the year before, had established an art gallery. The sale took place in July 1828 with disappointing results. Only one painting was sold.

In November, Jeff Randolph wrote to Joseph Coolidge to push for another sale. Despite Jeff's urging, it wasn't until five years later, on July 19, 1833, that the family arranged an auction of the paintings, this time at Harding's Gallery in Boston. Again, the results were disappointing; only a few paintings were sold and the total take was only about $450.

Jeff Randolph also had tried, without success, to resurrect the lottery and extend it to several states, including New York and Maryland. He gave up the lottery scheme and pinned his hopes on selling his grandfather's property—including Monticello—to get the estate solvent. "He hopes the property will pay all the debts and that Mama will have a comfortable support besides," Virginia said in a letter to Ellen.

Thomas Jefferson wanted his books to go to the school he founded, the University of Virginia. But, with the lottery scheme dead, Jeff Randolph decided to sell the books to raise cash to apply to the estate's debts. He sold the bulk of the collection to a Washington, D.C., bookseller in 1829. That same year Jeff Randolph sold a historically important collection of his grandfather's printed books, bound volumes, and manuscripts that dealt primarily with Virginia history to the Library of Congress. That valuable collection included early seventeenth-century Virginia colonial records, along with Jefferson's notes and commentaries on history, philosophy, and the law.

Also in 1829 Jeff Randolph—again, to raise money—edited and published four volumes of his grandfather's papers. Jeff Randolph fully realized the historical importance of the publication of Thomas Jefferson's *Memoirs*. He also had hoped that their publication would bring in cash, but he gained almost no profit from their publication.

In 1848 he sold the balance of Jefferson's public papers to the Library of Congress for $20,000. Those funds went toward paying off the estate's debt, which was not completely settled until 1878, three years after his own death.

While Jeff Randolph was scrambling to raise cash in the years after Thomas Jefferson's death, Monticello continued to suffer from neglect. "The house," Philadelphia lawyer and author Henry D. Gilpin said after a visit early in 1827, is "dark & much dilapidated with age and neglect." Things were made worse by visitors who came uninvited and helped themselves to mementos of Monticello.

It "will grieve you both very much to hear of the depredations that have been made at Monticello by the numerous parties who go to see the place," Virginia Trist wrote on March 23, 1827, in her letter from Tufton to her sister Ellen. "Mama's choicest flower roots have been carried off, one of her yellow jesmins, fig bushes (very few of which escaped the cold of last winter) grape vines and every thing and anything that they fancied."

Nicholas Trist reacted by putting a notice in the papers requesting visitors to "desist from such trespasses," she said. But it did little good. Burwell Culbert, the freed household slave who still lived on the property and maintained the house and yard, reported, she said, that the memento-seeking visitors were "worse than they were before."

Things did not get any better. Virginia Trist, in a May 1, 1827, letter from Tufton to Ellen said that "the vulgar herd that flock" to Monticello "behaved so badly that brother Jeff intends to forbid anyone's going there on Sunday." Jeff Randolph, Virginia said, also decided to "employ some respectable white man to take care of the place." Burwell Culbert, she said, "has given many proofs this winter of attachment to our family, as well as to Monticello. He has staid [*sic*] there ever since the sale, and appears to have taken pleasure in trying to keep the house clean . . . and the yard . . . in some sort of order."

That spring, Randolph family members occasionally came to Monticello to help keep things in order. "Today," Cornelia Randolph wrote to her sister Ellen from Monticello on May 18, "we have come up to have the bedding turned and house aired." One of the family's "greatest pleasures," she said, "is our occasional walk up here. The place is so lovely and in this beautiful season too, if it was not for our affection to it, it would be a pleasure to come." The house, she said, "is so cool that it is a relief from the heat of Tufton, which I fear we shall find overpowering this summer."

Burwell Culbert continued to keep the house in good condition, Cornelia said. They "found the doors and windows all open, the floors rubbed bright, and the old remaining chairs and marble tables (which mostly belong to brother Jeff. and of course have not been removed) were all set in order." The whole place, she said, "seemed to welcome us. . . . I sat in the hall a long time enjoying it . . . with a mixture of pleasure and pain which I always feel here now."

Along with keeping the inside clean, Culbert also tended to the grounds. "He has even been at the trouble of digging up the young poplars which were springing up everywhere and would soon have made a wilderness of the yard and of pruning the trees," Cornelia said. "He seems to take pleasure in keeping things as they used to be. He and all the servants have so much feeling and affection for us and I often send their lonesome message to mama and yourself."

Cornelia said that her brother Jeff had plans to turn Monticello into a "grass farm." Doing that, she said, "will cover our unsightly red soil with beautiful green which will be kept in order and, at the same time, the stock upon it will be a great source of profit."

In July, the family turned the house over to Dr. Robley Dunglison, the British-born physician who had come to Charlottesville to join the original faculty at the University of Virginia two years earlier. Dunglison, the University's first anatomy and medical professor, also was Thomas Jefferson's physician. He and his wife Hariette brought their two-year-old daughter to Monticello for "the benefit of change of air," as Mary Randolph put it in a July 29 letter to Ellen from Tufton.

"Mrs. Dunglison arrived Wednesday evening and the next day we put her in possession of all the rooms prepared for her accommodation," Mary wrote. That included, she said, "the public rooms, the two chambers opposite the dining room, with all the appurtenances, closets, cupboards, etc., also the little closet at the foot of our staircase and our old 'washroom' . . ."

Cornelia Randolph stayed at Monticello while the Dunglisons were there to help nurse Willis, an elderly family slave. Willis, Mary Randolph said, "had been declining so visibly and so rapidly for the last week that it was a very great relief to our uneasiness about him to have such an opportunity of placing him under Dr. Dunglison's superintendence. . . ."

The Dunglisons remained at Monticello until early in September 1827. Around that time Jeff Randolph and his wife Jane and their children moved from Tufton (which he subsequently sold) to a new house he had built on Edgehill Plantation six miles from Monticello.

Jeff Randolph's father, Col. Thomas Mann Randolph, Jr., had inherited Edgehill from his grandfather, William Randolph of Tuckahoe (1683–1729), who was a contemporary of Peter Jefferson. Jeff Randolph had bought Edgehill from his father in January 1826.

After Jeff Randolph moved with his wife and children to Edgehill, Mary, Cornelia, and Nicholas and Virginia Trist moved back to Monticello. The plan was for their mother Martha and the two younger children to join them there in May and set up housekeeping on the first floor.

Mary Randolph described the arrangement to Ellen in an August 10, 1828, letter from Monticello. The greenhouse, she said, "serves as a very pleasant little sitting room for us, during a part of the day (when the sun was not shining upon the windows) and is at all times a favorite play place for the children." The adjacent library or book room—"once filled with my dear grandfather's books"—was turned into a "delightful sleeping room, large enough to hold two beds and furniture enough to accommodate those persons with ease and comfort."

The adjoining sitting room also became a bedroom, in "which two more can be comfortably lodged." Those first-floor rooms, Mary said, "are laid off in a manner to suit our circumstances precisely and are besides very pleasant in themselves."

In March 1828, Thomas Mann Randolph—who was in failing health and who had been estranged from his family (especially from Jeff, his eldest son) for many years—announced that he wanted to move to Monticello. He had been living nearby in a small, five-room house at Milton. Writing in the third person, Colonel Randolph wrote to Nicholas Trist on March 10 asking for permission to move. "Mr. Randolph begs to be informed by Mr. Trist whether he can be allowed to occupy again the North Pavilion at Monticello," Randolph wrote, "as Mrs. Randolph has just communicated her intention of returning to Monticello in May and her expectation that he will reside there with her again in future."

The plan was, Randolph said, for him to live "in his own room at his own charge, making no part of the family and receiving nothing from [them] in any way whatever. He will not come on any other terms. . . . He wants only a place for his horse; the cellar under the house; one of the carriage houses for his fuel, which he will procure himself and a small spot for a garden, to be enclosed by him." Colonel Randolph asked Nicholas Trist to get back to him the next day because "his funds are getting too low for any tavern." Nicholas Trist wrote back the same day to accept.

Colonel Randolph soon took up occupancy in Monticello's north pavilion. The family members acceded to his wishes to live separately, though they tried to convince him to join the family group in the main section of the house. "We are doing everything in our power to contribute to his comfort," Virginia Trist wrote from Monticello to Ellen on March 19, "but as he expressly desired to live in solitude . . . Mary and myself never break in upon it, except for a few moments in the morning to ask how he is. . . ."

Living at Monticello was proving to be difficult for the family. Financial problems, Virginia said, probably would force them to move. Because "Nicholas cannot continue here without getting in debt," she said, he "now speaks frequently of the probability of his having to go where he can find employment that will suit him. Washington he sometimes talks of and sometimes of the south." Not long after those words were written, Nicholas Trist left for Washington and the State Department job that had been arranged for him by President John Quincy Adams.

Thomas Mann Randolph died on June 20, 1828, having reconciled with the family near the end of his life. "He had made friends with your brother [Jefferson], who sat up with him and nursed him to the last moment," Martha Jefferson wrote from Monticello on June 30, to her son George, who was in Boston with his sister Ellen.

While the Randolphs lived at Monticello the house and grounds did not receive much attention. In a July 6, 1828, letter to Ellen from Monticello Cornelia Randolph said the property was "lovely" and the house "never so beautiful." But she also described "wild things growing up in the yard," the "negro cabins lyeing [*sic*] in little heaps of ruin everywhere" and "the thickening shade of the unpruned trees closing round the house."

Cornelia also spoke of rumors that a potential purchaser wanted to turn Monticello into a boarding house. "To me this seems like profaning a temple," she said, "and I had rather the weeds and wild animals which are fast taking possession of the grounds should grow and live in the house itself. . . . I would see the house itself in ruins before I would see it turned into a tavern."

.   .   .

Soon after Colonel Randolph's death, Jeff Randolph and his mother decided to put Monticello on the market, along with other lands they had inherited in Bedford and Campbell counties. Monticello "is to be sold this fall with the remaining property of the family," Martha Randolph said in a June 30, 1828, letter to her son George. She had not decided where she would go after the sale. "That will depend on the circumstances," she said, holding out the possibility she would move to "some . . . northern town where my little income will best support my large family and where I shall be content."

The Randolphs placed a notice in the *Richmond Enquirer* on July 22 headlined "Valuable Lands For Sale." The hope was to sell Monticello by September 29—if not, an auction would be held that day on the premises.

"The whole of this property will be divided to suit purchasers," the ad said. "The sale being made for the payment of testator's debts, the desire to sell is sincere. The terms will be accommodating, and the prices anticipated low. Mrs. Randolph, of Monticello, will join in the conveyance, and will make the titles perfect."

There was no sale before September 29. Nor was there an auction on that date. One reason was that land prices in Virginia were low. Another was that Charlottesville, in rural central Virginia, was not exactly a desirable location. The few wealthy people in the area who could afford the $15,000 to $20,000 the family hoped to get for Monticello had their own estates and had little use for another, even if it had belonged to Thomas Jefferson. And Jefferson's architectural eccentricities—including the extremely narrow staircases and lack of distinct bedchambers— did little to make the property more desirable. In short, there was little prospect of selling the "dark and dilapidated" mansion.

With the auction postponed, Jeff Randolph set about selling the other parcels of Jefferson's land. He did so late in the year for what he called "low prices." In November 1828 Jeff Randolph received an offer from General John Hartwell Cocke, a longtime friend and neighbor of his grandfather's, to rent Monticello for $200 a year and use it for what he called a "gymnasium," a boys' prep school. Cocke, who helped Jefferson found the University of Virginia, envisioned the gymnasium as a feeder school for the all-male university.

An alternative plan was for six partners—including Cocke and Jeff Randolph—to purchase Monticello from the estate for $6,000 and set up a school on the premises to be run by a Professor Patten of the university. In the end, both plans came to naught.

During the first week of January 1829 Martha Randolph, her unmarried children, and Virginia Trist moved to Edgehill to live with Jeff Randolph and his family. Things continued to go downhill at Monticello in their absence. A British traveler who visited early in 1830 and toured the mansion found an empty house that he reported was "offered for sale for $12,000."

Another visitor, Anne Royall, a travel writer, came to Monticello on a snowy day in February 1830. She and her party walked into the unlocked mansion and discovered an unlikely group of people in residence—the "respectable" white people Jeff Randolph had spoken of the previous year.

"We found a great coarse Irish woman, sitting by a tolerable fire in a neat room," she reported. "This woman with her husband (then absent), were put there to take care of the house: besides herself, there was a small child and a stout coarse girl."

The Irish woman eagerly offered to give a tour of the house for a fee of fifty cents. "This I was told was contrary to the orders of the proprietors, who left directions that no stranger should pay for viewing the rooms," Mrs. Royall said.

She reported that the marble bust of Jefferson by the Italian sculptor Giuseppe Ceracchi (referred to as "Caracci" in Jeff Randolph's 1827 sale notice) was still in the house. But she found the rooms empty of furniture. In the attic, she reported, was "Mrs. Jefferson's spinnet partly broken," standing "amongst heaps of slain coffee-urns, chinaware, glasses, globes, chairs and bedsteads."

Word of the pending sale prompted an old family friend, the Virginia-born Mississippi Senator George Poindexter, to try to get the federal government to come to the aid of Martha Randolph and her family. When he learned of the Randolphs' financial plight soon after coming to the Senate, Poindexter introduced a bill in that body on February 9,

1831, to grant 50,000 acres of land in Virginia to Martha Randolph. The idea was that she would sell part of the land and live off the proceeds.

"I have brought before this honorable body a proposition calculated to animate the patriotic feelings of every American citizen," Poindexter said on February 10 on the Senate floor. The measure, he said, was designed to prevent "the only surviving child of Thomas Jefferson [from living] in poverty in her native country while every page of its history points to the glory which has been shed over it by the acts of her illustrious father."

Martha Randolph held out hope that the Poindexter bill would solve her family's financial problems. "If we succeed, my plan is to divide [the 50,000 acres] in 12 shares, retaining 2 for myself and one a piece for each of my children," Martha said in a June 21, 1831, letter from Edgehill to Ellen in Boston. That arrangement, Martha said, would allow her to keep Monticello until she found someone willing to purchase it for the $10,000 asking price.

Martha said that Jeff Randolph wanted her and his younger siblings to return to Monticello, and suggested turning it into a "grazing farm" under his supervision. "But all these are bright visions like any other waking dream," Martha said, dismissing the notion. Monticello she said, was being kept "clean" by the current caretakers, "but the grounds are shockingly out of order and the shrubs and flowers very much pillaged. . . ." She told Ellen that she had given up any idea of returning to Monticello, which she described as "a very expensive and comfortless winter residence."

Eight days later, on June 29, 1831, Cornelia wrote to Ellen from Edgehill, saying that the family was hoping that Senator Poindexter's bill would, indeed, allow them to return to Monticello. "We had been dreaming lately," she said, "almost hoping to return there to live." The family, she said, was "told by several persons that the measure was looked on favorably in Congress (the Virginia delegation always excepted)." Senator Poindexter, she said, had visited the family, explained to her mother and brother what his bill would do, and said that if Congress passed the measure, "it will enable us to live at Monticello if it is not sold."

Cornelia also predicted that Virginia's senators would oppose the measure, contending it was unconstitutional for the government to grant land to individuals. But, she said, the real reason for the opposition was "a feeling of hostility towards everything of Thomas Jefferson's in this state; it is said that in Richmond his principles are considered as having gone out of fashion. . . ."

She said that if Monticello were sold, "I shall wish never to set foot in [Virginia] again, indeed Moma has suffered so much at the prospect of losing Monticello that I wish we had not returned this summer. She had a fever for several days . . . and is by no means well now; it is cruel to think that at her age she should be driven away in exile and from a home . . . so sacred to her."

Cornelia went on to bemoan her family's fiscal ills. The Randolphs, she said, have been "people of consideration in the world and now are poor and neglected." The family was coming to grips with the prospect of selling Monticello, she said, "but it is harder to learn to consider dear Monticello the property of strangers."

Poindexter's bill didn't come up for a vote until June 27. It was defeated by a 23–15 vote. Both Virginia senators—John Tyler and Littleton Waller Tazewell—voted against it.

.   .   .

In mid-July of 1831 a serious potential purchaser of Monticello finally came to Jeff Randolph and the two entered into negotiations. Randolph had given up any idea of getting as much as the $20,000 he had envisioned as the selling price for Monticello after his grandfather died. By the start of 1831, with no buyer in sight and Jefferson's debts still largely unpaid, he dropped his asking price to $12,000. By summer he was hoping to get $10,000.

In mid-August he reached an agreement to sell Monticello and 522 surrounding acres to twenty-four-year-old James Turner Barclay for a bargain basement price of $7,000. The deal also included Barclay deeding to Jeff Randolph for $4,000 Barclay's house in Charlottesville at the northeast corner of Market and Seventh streets. He had purchased it the year before from the Reverend F. W. Hatch. The Jefferson family retained the ownership of the family graveyard containing Jefferson's tomb.

The deed of sale was recorded by the Albemarle County clerk of the court in Charlottesville on November 1, 1831. The deed of sale of the Barclay house in Charlottesville was entered on December 3, 1832.

While the family had known since well before Jefferson's death that Monticello likely would be sold, the news of its imminent sale in the summer of 1831 was something of a shock. "We are none of us in very good spirits just now owing to the probability there is of Monticello being sold," Cornelia Randolph wrote to Ellen on June 29, 1831. It is "a blow to us," Cornelia said, "particularly as we had been dreaming lately, almost hoping, to return there to live."

Martha Randolph agonized over the pending sale in a July 5 letter to Virginia Trist. "There is some prospect of selling Monticello, but I do not wish the thing spoke of yet," she said to her daughter. "I thought I had made my mind up upon that subject and I find when it comes to the point, that all my [sorrows] are renewed and that it will be a bitter, bitter heartache to me its going out of the family."

Six weeks later Martha seemed more resigned to Monticello's fate, although she said in an August 15 letter from Edgehill to Ellen that during the negotiations with Barclay "which continued some weeks," she "was in a state of great agitation." Monticello, she said, "is at last sold and, bitter as the pang was, it is over. . . . You will say it is a dreadful sacrifice, but the debts are letting the place go to ruin, and no other offer."

Martha Randolph seemed to harbor no ill feelings about Barclay's bargaining over the price. "I believe he goes as much as he can afford," she wrote in the letter to Ellen, "for, after all, it will be worth little to him." The "evil of visitors has increased to such a degree as to be a tremendous drawback on it as a residence." Barclay, she said, "has shown much kind feeling to the family and says that if at any future day they can repurchase it, he should feel himself bound to give it up."

With Barclay agreeing to buy Monticello, all the fanciful plans to keep it in the family became moot. "But now even if we have the means of purchasing, Dr. Barclay will hardly desire to part with the place," Cornelia wrote on August 28, 1831, from Edgehill to Ellen in Boston. "He is full of schemes; they tell us he intends to cultivate the grape and to rear silk worms and has some plan in his head for making a fortune which I do not know; they say he is a schemer and perhaps may get tired after a time. . . . I am doubtful of Dr. Barclay's taste and have some fear that he may disfigure that beautiful and sacred spot by some of that gingerbread work which grandpapa used to hold in much contempt."

Cornelia went on to express her deep unhappiness with the sale. "I do not think I should feel at home or happy anywhere but at Monticello," she said. "I miss the very emotion excited by that beautiful scenery. I feel compressed in a small house where there is no place to retire and be alone a moment in the day. I want those familiar [things] which alone seem to be home and which seem as if grandpapa was still there. . . ."

James T. Barclay was a learned, if eccentric, many-faceted man whose four and a half years as the owner of Jefferson's mansion have not been positively portrayed. He has been characterized as a Jefferson-hating eccentric who bargained ruthlessly with the land-rich, cash-poor Randolphs. At Monticello he set up what has been described as a crackpot scheme to grow silkworms. To that end, it is said, he cut down Jefferson's carefully cultivated trees. Barclay also let the house go to ruin, then went bankrupt and sold Monticello after being struck with fundamentalist Christian missionary fever and spiriting his family off to the Holy Land.

Merrill Peterson, for example, characterized Barclay as "a Charlottesville druggist who had ideas of silk worm culture on the mountain." Barclay, Peterson reported, "had no interest in the mansion itself, treated it shabbily, and reportedly vowed in vengeance on Jefferson's infidelity to leave not a stone . . . upon a stone."

In a popular 1925 biography of Jefferson, Paul Wilstach described Barclay as a recent resident of Charlottesville who "had a small drug business and soon acquired the title of Doctor." It would be "pleasant," Wilstach said, "to record that Barclay was an admirer of Jefferson; that he appreciated the beauties of 'the first dwelling-house architecturally in America,' that he preserved the place and maintained its tradition. The contrary of all this was the unfortunate fact."

Uriah Levy's biographers, Donovan Fitzpatrick and Saul Saphire, were particularly harsh on Barclay. He "had no interest in preserving Monticello as a shrine to Thomas Jefferson," they said. Barclay "wanted the property for a fanciful experiment—a grandiose plan to grow mulberry trees and start a silkworm business. He dug up the flower gardens and cut down most of the fine trees on the lawn—the poplar, linden, and copper beeches on which Jefferson had expended so much money and care—and replaced them with mulberry trees. So began the despoliation of the most beautiful house in America."

Another Uriah Levy biographer, Samuel Sobel, called Barclay "a bitter opponent of the late President in politics. Instead he was motivated by the dream of developing a silkworm culture." After that failed, Sobel said, Barclay "vindictively . . . proceeded to cut down other trees Jefferson had planted with such care."

The Barclay family has a much different version of James Turner Barclay's life and times at Monticello. Accounts of his life written by one of his grandsons, Julian Thomas Barclay, in 1904 and by Decima Campbell Barclay, a daughter-in-law, around 1900 based on the reminiscences of his widow portray him in a completely different light. The family claims he was an ardent admirer of Jefferson who took great care of Monticello.

"Dr. Barclay never cut down a tree at Monticello that Mr. Jefferson had planted, or that was rare, or of any value whatever," Decima Campbell Barclay's account says. "He himself planted many trees on the 'little mountain' which he loved, as he had always loved and admired the memory of its former owner; and it was his greatest pleasure to embellish and beautify the grounds. . . ."

James Turner Barclay was born May 22, 1807, at Hanover Court House, Virginia. His grandfather Thomas Barclay (1728–1793) came to this country from Ireland. He was an avid supporter of the Revolution and was appointed the first American consul to France by George Washington. Thomas Barclay, family lore has it, was "an intimate and cherished friend of Washington and Jefferson."

James Barclay's father Robert Barclay (1779–1809) died when his oldest son was eleven. His mother, Sarah Coleman Turner Barclay, subsequently married John Harris, described as "a wealthy tobacco planter of Albemarle County."

Harris saw to James Barclay's education at the University of Virginia and at the University of Pennsylvania, where Barclay was "graduated in medicine," Julian Barclay said, in 1829. He then moved to Charlottesville where he opened a drug store and married Julia Ann Stowers of Staunton, Virginia, on June 10, 1830. He was twenty-three years old. She was seventeen, the daughter of a wealthy family headed by her father, Captain Colson Stowers. Cornelia Randolph referred to Julia Ann Stowers as "an heiress."

Decima Barclay characterized her mother-in-law as "a beautiful housekeeper" who employed one maid at Monticello whose only duty was to "attend to the floors of the house, which were so tracked over daily by visitors, that it required a great deal of 'dry rubbing' to keep them in nice condition." Jeff Randolph, the account says, was "a frequent visitor" who "often complimented Mrs. Barclay on her management of the household."

"You keep the floors in a far more beautiful condition than they were ever kept in my grandfather's lifetime," Jeff Randolph supposedly said to Mrs. Barclay.

James Barclay, his daughter-in-law said, "kept gardeners constantly employed in pruning trees and shrubs, cultivating flowers, renewing the serpentine walks and improving the premises in every way in his power." He built new terraces, she said, and bought special tools to repair the great clock, which had been broken for "many years."

Julian Barclay's account mentions nothing about silkworms, hatred of Jefferson, cutting down trees, or bankruptcy. Julian Barclay says that James Barclay sold Monticello not because it was bleeding him dry, but because he "was persuaded by his mother and his wife's parents to dispose" of it.

Decima Barclay's account says that Barclay's parents begged him to leave Monticello because of the constant stream of visitors—family, friends, and strangers. Barclay insisted on staying in the house where his two sons, Robert Gutzloff and John Judson, were born, and which he loved so much. He is said to have turned down a $20,000 offer for it from "a Mr. Brown of Philadelphia."

A Barclay descendant, his great-granddaughter, Mary Barclay Hancock Carroll of Portsmouth, Virginia, told a newspaper reporter in 1978 that the unending stream of visitors to Jefferson's mountain forced the family out. "There was never a day without visitors, friends and relatives who wanted to be shown around the house and grounds," Mrs. Carroll said, citing the family history.

There is irrefutable evidence that Barclay did try to grow silkworms at Monticello. "I have often heard one of my aunts, Mrs. M.W. Gilmer, who visited Mr. Barclay frequently at Monticello whilst a little girl, say that she remembered seeing the silkworms in the glass-covered conservatory which opens out of what was Mr. Jefferson's library," Judge R. T. W. Duke, Jr., of Charlottesville wrote in 1913.

Barclay himself wrote a report about his silkworm experiences in a long, detailed letter to the editor that appeared in the August 3, 1832, issue of *American Farmer* magazine. Datelined "Monticello, July 10th, 1832," Barclay's letter spoke about his "experiments in that interesting branch of industry." He called silkworm production "one of the most lucrative as well as agreeable pursuits we can engage in" and said he had "encountered no difficulty in the business." Even sympathetic family members, however, have written that Barclay's silkworm business failed.

There is little question that the Barclays were overwhelmed with visitors during their short tenure at Monticello. The number of visitors, as Martha Randolph said in 1831, was increasing greatly when Barclay bought the place. Decima's father, Alexander Campbell (1788–1866), the founder of the Disciples of Christ who visited the Barclays at Monticello, characterized the place as "too much visited to be a private residence for any Christian man."

Whatever the reason—and it likely had to do with the visitor situation, the unsuccessful silkworm operation, and the cost of maintaining the house and grounds—the Barclays left Monticello sometime after agreeing to sell it to Uriah Levy in April 1834. Soon after, James Turner Barclay began a new life as a missionary.

James and Julia Barclay were Presbyterians, but converted to Campbell's Disciples of Christ. In 1840 Barclay packed his wife and three young children off to do missionary work in Palestine. After he returned, Barclay wrote *City of the Great King; Jerusalem: As It Was, As It Is, and As It Is To Be*, a 627-page history of Jerusalem which was published in 1858. The engraving on the first page shows a stern, solid looking man with a pronounced widow's peak and an Abraham Lincoln beard. In 1858, he took his family to Jerusalem for a second round of missionary work, returning to the United States in 1865 to teach natural sciences at Bethany College in West Virginia, the Disciples of Christ School. In 1868, Barclay resigned and moved to Alabama where he spent the rest of his life preaching. He died at age sixty-seven in 1874.

. . .

CONTRARY to the rosy picture painted by the Barclay family, Monticello was worn out during James Barclay's ownership. "The late residence of Mr. Jefferson has lost all its interest, save what exists in memory, and that it is the sacred deposit of his remains," William T. Barry, then postmaster general of the United States, wrote after an August 1832 visit. "All is dilapidation and ruin, and I fear the present owner, Dr. Barclay, is not able, if he were inclined, to restore it to its former condition."

John Latrobe—a prominent Baltimore lawyer, philanthropist, and a founder of the Maryland Historical Society—described a similarly dispiriting scene after visiting Monticello that same month.

"The first thing that strikes you is the utter ruin and desolation of everything," Latrobe wrote after the visit. James Barclay was not at home when Latrobe visited, and his only view of the house was through some open windows. "The internal arrangement, so far as I could judge of it by the peeps I made into peepable places," he wrote, "is whimsical and, according to present notions of country houses, uncomfortable, being cut up into small apartments."

Outside the house, on the terrace overlooking Charlottesville, Latrobe spotted a discarded, dismembered column pedestal, its metal rod protruding from the center. Then, on the ground nearby, he saw the column's capital, "somewhat mutilated, which had been thrown or fallen down from the pedestal." He immediately recognized the design, one in which "the place usually occupied by Acanthus leaves of the Corinthian columns is filled by ears of corn, grouped together." It was a design that his illustrious father, the architect Benjamin H. Latrobe (1764–1820), had invented and used in the U.S. Capitol building.

"I moved the stone from the wreck of the garden chair on which it had fallen," John Latrobe said, "and placed it upright."

By the fall of 1833 when Barclay put Monticello on the market, Martha Randolph had changed her tune about her feelings toward him. "The garden is ploughed up to the door and planted in corn. Those glorious oaks and chestnut oak in the grove are cut down. The place I am told is so totally changed that it is distressing to see it," she wrote in a September 15 letter from Edgehill to Ellen. "The whole will . . . be one mass of ruins so rapid has the work of destruction been."

Barclay "asked $10,000 for the house and 230 acres of the land when he only gave $7,000 for it and 500," she wrote to Ellen on October 27. "He has sold all the land, cut down the grove and ploughed up the yard to the very edge of the lawn and planted it in corn. The terrace is a complete wreck. I suppose it would take between two and three thousand dollars to make it comfortable; to enclose the land and other repairs."

Later in the letter, Martha Randolph referred to James Turner Barclay as a "mad man."

. . .

BOTH the manner in which [Uriah] Levy came to own Monticello and his reasons for buying it are shrouded in mystery," the noted architectural historian Charles B. Hosmer, Jr. said. Indeed, exactly how Uriah Levy came to purchase Monticello has been the subject of speculation, some of it overtly anti-Semitic, for more than a hundred years.

The most commonly repeated tale is that in 1834 a group of patriotic, charitable, presumably white Anglo-Saxon Protestant Americans raised money to buy Monticello from James T. Barclay and present it to the aging Martha Jefferson Randolph. These benevolent people—most often unidentified—acted, it is said, because Martha was suffering financially, and they wanted to help return Jefferson's oldest daughter to her father's home.

One of the earliest published versions of this account appeared in *The Hartford Courant* in 1897 and was retold by Amos J. Cummings in the August 24, 1897, New York *Sun*. Five years later, Cummings republished his article, titled "A National Humiliation: A Story of Monticello," in a pamphlet.

Cummings led a varied and interesting life. He fought with the Union Army in the Civil War, became a successful newspaper editor and writer with the New York *Tribune* under the famed Horace Greeley, and later with the *Sun*. He also served in the House of Representatives for one term, from 1887 to 1889, as a Tammany Hall Democrat. While serving in Congress, Cummings paid a visit to Charlottesville and Monticello. "A National Humiliation" was his report on the trip.

Merrill Peterson, the Jefferson historian and scholar, calls the article "sprightly, amusing, and here and there fanciful." It may be sprightly written in parts and somewhat amusing in others. But "A National Humiliation" amounts to little more than a racist, thinly veiled anti-Semitic attack on Jefferson M. Levy, who then owned Monticello, and his uncle Uriah Levy, who purchased it in 1834.

In the article Cummings refers to Willis Sheldon, the gatekeeper at Monticello as "an aged darkey." The word "darkey" was commonly used by whites in the late nineteenth century. Nevertheless, using the word suggests patronizing condescension at best and racist thinking at worst.

Cummings calls Uriah Levy "Judah Levy," and misidentifies him as the father of Jefferson Levy. Was this misnomer a mistake or a thinly veiled anti-Semitic slur? Cummings writes that he arrived at Monticello believing that Thomas Jefferson "owned the place," only to learn from Willis Sheldon that the owner was Jefferson Levy. Thomas Jefferson, of course, had been dead for more than a half century. Cummings goes on to accuse Levy of selfishly and unpatriotically charging admission to Monticello's grounds, and expresses outrage that visitors were not allowed into the privately owned house. He intimates that Jefferson Levy bought Jefferson's house only to turn a profit.

"Monticello is now owned by a Levy, who charges patriotic Americans, Democrat and Republican, twenty-five cents admission to the grounds alone, and refuses admission to the house at any price during his absence," Cummings says. He reminds his readers that Jefferson Levy purchased Monticello for $10,000, but "is said to value Monticello at $100,000. Possibly he imagines that he can eventually sell it to either the State or the Federal Government for this sum."

The attack on Uriah Levy begins with a summary of the article that appeared in the *Hartford Courant*. "American hearts have recently been harrowed," Cummings writes, "by a story of [Monticello's] purchase by Judah Levy, late Commodore in the United States navy." The story, he says, "asserts that efforts were made to hold the estate after Jefferson's death for his favorite daughter, Martha Randolph. About $3,000 was required.

"The money was raised by patriotic Philadelphians, and entrusted to a young Virginian, a relative of Martha Randolph. He got drunk on the way to Monticello, and arrived a day too late. It is more than intimated that Captain Levy, who was a passenger in the same stage, took advantage of his drunkenness and bought the place. The appalled Virginian besought him to be merciful after his purchase, and asked him what he would take for the homestead.

"His reply was: 'Mein frien' you are a glever feller, but you talk too much. I will take a huntret tousand tollars.' It was a story that, if true ought to bring a blush of shame to every American face."

The story, of course, is not true. But the impression Cummings leaves with the reader is that it is. The made-up dialogue in which a Shylock-like Uriah Levy—a fifth generation American—speaks in some sort of Yiddish-German accent cannot be interpreted as anything but anti-Semitic. The same can be said about the article's title. For what reason other than his religion is the fact that Jefferson Levy—the "son" of "Judah"—owns Monticello a "humiliation?"

Maud Littleton repeats the story, with a few variations, in "Monticello," a fifty-two-page booklet she wrote, published, and distributed nationwide in 1914 as part of her campaign to have the government condemn and purchase Monticello from Jefferson Levy. Unidentified friends of a "heartbroken and crushed" Martha Jefferson Randolph "asked aid to purchase Monticello to give back to her," Mrs. Littleton wrote. "About $3,000, they said, would be required to make the purchase."

A group of "patriotic Philadelphians," she said, "gave the money and entrusted it to a young Virginian to take to Charlottesville. Travelling, as a passenger, in the same stage-coach with him was Captain Uriah P. Levy of New York, who had served part of his life in the United States Navy. His career there was full of ups and downs. On the way to Monticello, the papers tell, the young Virginian became intoxicated, and arrived a day too late, for when Captain Levy, a stranger in the neighborhood, arrived in Charlottesville, he made private proposals to Barclay for the purchase of Monticello."

Around the same time, the widely read advice columnist Dorothy Dix wrote an article in *Good Housekeeping Magazine,* in which she attacked Jefferson Levy's ownership of Monticello, saying Jefferson's home had passed into "alien hands." She repeated the stagecoach story, except this time the man in question was identified as "a young relative of the Jeffersons."

Jefferson Levy spoke out strongly against the Cummings article, calling it "a scurrilous attack upon Commodore Levy." He also said that Amos Cummings "apologized to me for it. He regretted it very much," and said that the editor of the *Hartford Courant* also "apologized in an open editorial."

Apologies or not, the story did not die. An August 14, 1921, *Richmond Times-Dispatch* editorial that called for the government to buy Monticello, for example, repeated the tale. The same story, minus the overimbibing, was also included in Paul Wilstach's 1925 book *Jefferson and Monticello.*

Uncharitable versions of Uriah's Levy's purchase of Monticello continued into the 1950s. William H. Gaines, Jr., in the Spring 1952 issue of *Virginia Cavalcade* magazine, a publication of the Virginia State Library, portrayed Uriah Levy's ownership of Monticello decidedly negatively, including the way Levy allegedly gained possession.

Judge R. T. W. Duke, Jr., a Charlottesville lawyer who represented Jefferson Levy, called these stories "a tissue of fable" and "simply absurd." "No one had proposed to buy the property for Mrs. Randolph that anybody ever heard of in this section," Judge Duke said in a 1913 letter to Jefferson Levy, "and had Commodore Levy obtained the property in the way it is charged he did, it can be very well imagined that he would have met with scorn and contempt from every member of the Randolph family, but the contrary was the case. Both he and his sister [Amelia, who often visited Monticello] and the members of the Randolph family were on pleasant terms and exchanged frequent visits."

Judge Duke was not exactly an unbiased observer. However, as we will see, several members of the Randolph family did, indeed, have good relations with Uriah Levy during the period of his ownership of Monticello (1834–1862). On the other hand, there is evidence that there was at least one attempt—unsolicited and unwelcomed by Martha Randolph—to raise funds in 1833-34 to purchase Monticello and return it to her.

The offer was conveyed by a man identified by Martha Randolph and Ellen Coolidge only as "Mr. Hart," who showed up unannounced at Edgehill in mid-October 1833 with a fantastic story. He told Martha Randolph that he had been commissioned by a group of men in New York to purchase Monticello and turn it over to her—along with a yearly income sufficient for her to afford to live there. He later journeyed to Boston to deliver the same message to Ellen. Neither Martha nor Ellen knew him, and both soon came to distrust him and his offer.

"That man Hart was here," Martha said in an October 23, 1833, letter from Edgehill to her daughter Virginia Trist in Washington, D.C. He "told me that people said it was a great shame that Monticello should go out of the family, that I ought to have it, and that he was commissioned by some body or bodies in New York to make the purchase for me."

Hart told Martha that he was prepared to offer the Randolphs as much as $6,000 a year to, as Martha said, "keep up the place genteelly or decently, I forget which." He was "such a wild talker," Martha said, "that we paid no attention to what he said, except to dissuade him from taking any step in the business. . . . I told him I was much obliged to them, but it would be a source of trouble and distress to me [and] I could not afford to live there and keep it in repair." Even with the stipend, she said, she would not be able to maintain the place, and would "rather see it in the possession of someone [who] would keep it in order."

But Mr. Hart was persistent. "One and a half days," Martha said, "were spent in listening to his wandering babble, conversation it could not be called."

Four days later, on October 27, 1833, Martha wrote to Ellen in Boston, reiterating the Mr. Hart story, and adding that Hart "was such a wild talker that if anything of the kind had ever been contemplated, I hardly think he would have been the person selected for such a negotiation." Martha suspected that Hart had made up the entire story—including the line he told her that federal district court judge Philip P. Barbour of Virginia had said of his mission: "We Virginians talk, but you New Yorkers act."

Ellen Coolidge also mentions the otherwise unidentified "Mr. Hart" in a letter to her sister Virginia of April 15, 1834. She refers to Mr. Hart as "that crazy creature" who "has been lately in Boston tormenting the natives to subscribe for the purchase" of Monticello. Hart, she said, "called to see me and his mind was so evidently wandering that I was glad to have him out of the house and dissuaded him all I could from going around among persons who, besides having no friendly feelings for the name of Jefferson, were about that time almost crazed by their own pecuniary troubles."

Ellen Coolidge doesn't say so, but Mr. Hart was too late with his dubious scheme. Uriah Levy already had purchased Monticello from Barclay on April 1st. There is no further mention of Mr. Hart in the correspondence between mother and daughter. In a long letter to Ellen in Boston, dated June 20, 1834, in which Martha Jefferson writes, "I have told you every thing of any consequence for the present," there is no mention of Mr. Hart, Monticello, or of Uriah Levy.

Some sort of effort was made to raise funds for Martha Randolph to return to Monticello. But—as in the case of the lottery, and Jeff Randolph's efforts to raise funds to pay off his grandfather's debts—this financial endeavor failed. It is also apparent that tales were concocted to provide some explanation—other than financial failures on the part of the Randolphs and their friends—as to why a rich, Jewish New York bachelor came to own the home of Thomas Jefferson.

. . .

"IT IS stated that Monticello, the late residence of Mr. Jefferson, has been purchased by Lieut. Levy of the navy of the United States," *Niles' Register* of April 19, 1834, reported, "and that he intends to commence immediately such improvements and repairs, as will fully restore the building, &c. to their original condition after which it will be accessible to visitors once a week."

That one-sentence announcement in a national newsweekly magazine has been the only evidence cited by historians that Uriah Levy agreed with James Barclay to purchase Jefferson's architectural masterpiece in the spring of 1834. The deal was not cemented until more than two years later, on May 21, 1836. On that day a deed, in which Barclay conveyed Monticello and 218 acres surrounding it to Levy for $2,700, was recorded in the Albemarle County Court Clerk's office. The existence of copies of the deed have led some secondary sources erroneously to say that Levy contracted to buy Monticello two years later than he did.

In their 1963 biography of Levy, for example, Donovan Fitzpatrick and Saul Saphire create a scene, without citing any sources, in which Uriah Levy, a fervent admirer of Jefferson, makes a pilgrimage to Monticello for the first time "in the spring of 1836." After a journey "on horseback and stage" to Charlottesville, the biographers say, Levy spent the night in town.

The next morning he "hired a buckboard and drove" to Monticello, where he first saw Jefferson's grave, then "walked up the hill, and had his first view of the mansion from the lawn at the west front." Levy returned to Charlottesville that afternoon, the story goes, where he discovered Jefferson's home was for sale, and "Lieutenant Uriah Levy decided to buy Monticello himself."

That version of how Uriah Levy came to purchase Monticello is, at the very least, fanciful, although no primary sources have come to light that provide details of exactly when Uriah Levy first laid eyes on Monticello. We do know when he and Barclay agreed to a sale, and it was more than two years before the deed was recorded.

The evidence—presented here for the first time—that Uriah P. Levy and James T. Barclay signed their first contract for Monticello on April 1, 1834, comes from the records of the Albemarle County Circuit Superior Court, which are now are held at the state's Library of Virginia in Richmond. The reason the sale to Levy did not take place for two years after the contract was signed was a disagreement between the two parties about acreage and contents of the house.

Another reason the case took so long to resolve was that the courts in those days were in session only twice a year. The Albemarle County Circuit Superior Court met only in the months of April and October. Ultimately the parties sued each other and the two lawsuits were not settled until a jury reached a verdict on May 18, 1836. Two days later the deed was signed, and on May 21 it was filed with the clerk of the court.

Until now, the only detailed information about the lawsuits had been the testimony of two people who heard or read about the story second hand: Uriah's nephew Jefferson M. Levy, and Maud Littleton, the woman who spearheaded the effort to take Monticello from Jefferson M. Levy. "If I remember it right," Jefferson M. Levy wrote in 1902, "there was a legal controversy between Barclay and Commodore Levy as to the number of acres in the property." The deed, he said, "was held in abeyance until the question of the acreage was settled. Therefore, the deed was not delivered until one or two years after the actual purchase and possession."

Ten years after Jefferson Levy wrote those words, Mrs. Littleton gave her version of the same events testifying under oath on July 9, 1912, at a U.S. Senate Library Committee hearing that was held to consider public ownership of Monticello. Mrs. Littleton laid out the Levy-Barclay chronology based on research she said she had conducted in Charlottesville.

In the spring of 1834, Uriah Levy "went to Virginia to purchase Monticello, then in possession of James T. Barclay, who desired to sell it," she said. "After his purchase, there arose a dispute between him and

Barclay about the acreage, which was valued at $5 per acre, and about certain effects in the house. That is, valuable mirrors and an extraordinary clock, which had been reserved, and which Uriah Levy had manifested a desire to obtain. These disputes kept Monticello in the courts till the spring of 1836."

Although the deed book lists the selling price as $2,700, Mrs. Littleton said, "two hundred dollars was subtracted from that amount on account of the dispute about acreage, clocks, mirrors, etc., with the result that Uriah Levy paid $2,500 for Monticello and 218 acres of land."

Mrs. Littleton essentially was correct, although she left out the pertinent detail that Levy signed the contract to purchase Monticello on April 1, 1834.

Levy, the court documents show, had seen Barclay's advertisement in the fall of 1833 either in the *Richmond Compiler* or in *Atkinson's Saturday Evening Post*. Under the headline "Monticello for Sale," the ad read:

This celebrated seat, the former residence of Mr. Jefferson, is offered for sale. It is perhaps too well known to require any description, but it may be well to mention that its value has been much enhanced within the last few years by the addition of a perennial well of excellent water, in this kitchen yard, in which a new pump of the best construction has just been placed, besides many other improvements.

It may be proper also to state (in contradiction to an unfounded report) that the building, with the exception of the Terraces, which require reflooring, is in excellent preservation: being constructed of stone and brick, protected by a coating of tin, lead, zinc, iron or copper, wherever exposed to the action of the weather, it is rendered not only fire proof, but one of the most permanent buildings in Virginia.

Between two and three hundred acres of land are attached to the house, about half of which is in woods, and the remainder under cultivation. The land is generally of the best quality, well watered and susceptible of the highest degree of improvement. It is abundantly supplied with every species of Mulberry, and is perhaps one of the most eligible situations in the world for the lucrative pursuit of the culture of Silk.

If not disposed of in a short time, it will be leased out for several years.

Terms and conditions as usual with landed estates.

J. T. Barclay

In response to the ad, Uriah Levy traveled to Charlottesville to what he thought would be an auction of the property. "Lieut. Levy left here a week since to go to Albemarle, as I understand, to purchase Monticello," Jeff Randolph said in an April 4, 1834, letter from Washington to his sister Virginia Trist in Charlottesville. "Have you heard anything of him?"

When Uriah Levy arrived in Charlottesville he discovered that there was no auction. So he took it upon himself to seek out James Barclay and make an offer for Jefferson's mansion.

"In the spring of the present year," Uriah Levy said in the third person in an affidavit filed October 6, 1834, he "was called to this county by a desire to purchase a tract of land, lying therein, called [and] known by the name of Monticello, then in the possession of a certain James T. Barclay who had advertised it in the Newspapers for public sale about that time."

Uriah Levy "attended on the day and at the place of the sale," he said, "when there being no sale, then, affected by public auction under the terms of the aforesaid advertisement, he felt himself at liberty to make private proposals for the purchase thereof, which he accordingly did."

The parties agreed on a contract of $2,700—which Barclay termed "very reduced and inadequate"—for which Uriah Levy would receive Monticello and its "appurtenances" and 230 acres of land, and Barclay would keep the valuable pier mirrors and the giant seven-day clock in the entrance hall. Uriah Levy retained a Charlottesville lawyer, Isaac Raphael, to represent him in the transaction.

The question of the exact amount of the acreage was brought up either later that day or the following day by an unidentified "by-stander." Levy then went to the clerk of the court and discovered how much land

Barclay had sold of the original 522 acres he had purchased from the Randolphs. Levy calculated that all that Barclay had left was about 180 acres.

Levy and Raphael, who drew up the original April 1 contract, then paid a visit to Barclay. The following conversation ensued, according to Raphael's deposition taken eighteen months later, on October 6, 1835:

"Lieutenant Levy remarked, 'Well, Doctor, it seems the land falls short of your estimate considerably.'

"'Yes,' says Dr. Barclay, 'I regret very much to find that it does so. It was by no means intentional on my part to make any improper or incorrect statement and I am willing to deduct according to our contract for the deficiency.'"

Levy replied that the "diminished quantity of land rendered the balance less valuable," Raphael said, and asked Barclay to annul the initial contract. The parties agreed and wrote a new one in which Barclay dropped the price to $2,500 and, according to Raphael and Levy, threw in the mirrors and clock.

A few days later, probably on April 5, the parties met to close the transaction. Raphael gave Barclay $2,500 in New York bank drafts from Levy. At that time Raphael drew up a "paper," he said, "in which it was stipulated that if, upon a survey which was to be made of the land, there should appear to be a greater quantity than was supposed," Levy would pay Barclay $5 per acre over and above the $2,500. The amount of the acreage then was then deemed to be 181 1/4 acres.

A survey was undertaken by a Colonel Woods who, Barclay said, came up with a figure of 206 acres. Barclay then took the position that Levy was "bound to pay for all over 182 [acres] at the rate of $5 per acre." He also claimed that Levy "kept the mirrors and clock aforesaid and refuses to pay either for them or the excess of land."

So Barclay refused to take the final step of recording the deed until Levy paid him the extra money. Levy said Barclay was acting "in flagrant disregard" of their second contract and was "unjustly content to use [Levy's] money" while refusing "to perfect [Levy's] title to the tract of land, thus fairly purchased."

That's when Uriah Levy sued James T. Barclay. His goal was to close

the matter and take title to Monticello. In the interim, it was determined that the Woods survey was inaccurate. A new survey was ordered
by the court on October 14, 1835. Undertaken by A. Broadhead, the
new survey found the tract of land at Monticello to be 218 acres. It was
completed May 3, 1836.

During the legal wrangling, Barclay said Levy was obstinate and dis-
honest. In a deposition on January 12, 1835, Barclay accused Levy of
"grossly misrepresenting the evidence" in the case. Barclay said he "has
always been anxious to close this transaction with plaintiff [Levy] and
has manifested this anxiety by repeated offers, even to sacrifice a great
deal, to attain his end. But the plaintiff having acquired possession of
the real personal property, has been content to enjoy it, and now ha-
rasses this respondent with this suit." So Barclay countersued "for the
articles of property sold to him."

Uriah Levy, for his part, accused Barclay of being less than truthful.
Barclay "has fraudulently contrived to jeopardize [my] rights in the
premises," Levy said in his October 6, 1834, deposition. Barclay's "act-
ings, doings and pretences," Levy said, "are contrary to equity and good
conscience."

It appears that Levy obtained a judgment by default, but that a jury
set that judgment aside on May 18, 1836. The jury ordered Levy to pay
Barclay $284, with interest going back to August 3, 1834, presumably
the date when Uriah Levy won his writ of inquiry.

That same day, Wednesday, May 18, 1836, Judge Lucas P. Thompson
of the Albemarle County Circuit Court of Law and Chancery ruled in
Levy's suit against Barclay. He found that Barclay was entitled to "com-
pensations of the plaintiff for 36 3/4 acres of land—the difference between 181 1/4 and 218 acres at $5 per acre, making the sum of $183.75."
Thompson ordered Barclay to convey a deed to Levy after Levy paid
the $183.75, plus interest from April 5, 1834, plus "the costs of this
suit."

Levy paid up. Two days later the deed was recorded.

· · ·

BASED on the depositions and on Jefferson Levy's 1902 statements on
the matter, it appears that the Barclays left Monticello almost immedi-

ately after agreeing to sell it to Uriah Levy and that he took possession of Jefferson's mansion early in April 1834. Despite the legal disagreement, Jefferson Levy wrote, the court had given possession of Monticello to Uriah Levy "on payment of the purchase price" in the spring of 1834.

There also is evidence that Uriah Levy was at Monticello overseeing repairs to the mansion in the winter of 1834–35—and that the forty-two-year-old bachelor was considering marrying one of Jefferson's three unattached Randolph granddaughters, Cornelia, thirty-four; Mary, thirty-one; or Septimia, twenty-two. Levy spoke about his marital dreams in January and February 1835 to the Randolph women's sister Virginia Randolph Trist in Washington, D.C., where she was living while her husband Nicholas was serving as U.S. counsel in Havana, Cuba.

"Captain Levi is hear [sic] 'raving for a wife,'" Virginia Trist wrote to her husband January 2, 1835. "He has thrown out hints about becoming a 'complete Jeffersonian' and yesterday evening he spent with us and prevented my writing to you."

Virginia Trist elaborated on Uriah Levy's marital plans in a February 3 letter to her husband. "Capt. Levi has been here," she said. "He has talked in a way to make [me] think that he wishes a grand-daughter of Mr. Jefferson to go and share the comforts of his charming home with him." Levy, she said, "also said to Cornelia that in France he was told that to make him a complete Jeffersonian he should marry a descendant of Thomas Jefferson."

Cornelia and her sister Mary, Virginia said, "had no suspicions of mal-intention towards" Levy's motives. "I think the Captain is willing to leave it to be decided in a family council which of the three is to be Mrs. Levi. However he has only given very broad hints as to his designs and perhaps . . . may change his mind."

Uriah Levy did change his mind—if he had ever seriously considered a Randolph marriage—and no Levy-Randolph marriage materialized.

As for his new home in Virginia, Uriah Levy did not intend to live at Monticello, his residence being in New York City. The first member of the Levy family to live in Monticello was his mother, Rachel. However, it is not clear when Uriah moved her to Monticello, although it most likely was in the late spring or early summer of 1836, if Jonas Levy's unpublished memoir can believed.

Jonas Levy, Uriah's younger brother, wrote that their mother was living with his older sister Amelia at 498 West Houstan (Houston) Street in New York City on November 1, 1835, when Jonas paid her an unexpected visit after returning from a long sea voyage. A "short time" later, perhaps as early as December 1835 or January 1836, Jonas Levy went to Monticello to visit his brother who, Jonas said, "was then superintending his slaves and other workmen that he had there to work." Jonas stayed at Monticello "for several weeks," before returning home to spend time with his mother in New York City.

Back in Virginia, Monticello was now in the hands of Uriah Phillips Levy, one of the most colorful, controversial officers in the history of the United States Navy. He was a fifth generation American, the descendant of a noteworthy, accomplished family that arrived in the American colonies in 1733. When Uriah Levy took possession of Monticello, a new chapter in the life of Jefferson's beloved mansion had begun.

CHAPTER TWO

The Commodore's House

We Levys were the first Jews to land in the New World.
JEFFERSON MONROE LEVY, MAY 9, 1923

The man who bought Thomas Jefferson's Monticello in 1834 was born in Philadelphia on April 22, 1792, the third of fourteen children—ten of whom survived childhood—of Michael Levy and Rachel Phillips Levy. Very little is known about Michael Levy's family history, other than that records indicate he came to the United States from Germany as a young man. There is no evidence to support the 1923 claim by Uriah's nephew Jefferson M. Levy that his forbears were "the first Jews to land in the New World."

There is, however, a detailed, well-documented history of Rachel Phillips's family, one of the most illustrious Jewish families in the eighteenth and nineteenth centuries in the United States.

The first member of that family to come to these shores was Uriah Levy's great-great-grandfather, Samuel Nunes Ribiero, a prominent, well-to-do Portuguese physician who was born in 1668. Dr. Samuel Nunez, as he came to be known in the United States, also is referred to in eighteenth-century documents as Diogo Nunes Riberio, Samuel Riberio Nunez, Samuel Nunis, and Samuel Nunez Riberio. He was one of the most accomplished and well-known founders of the colony of Georgia.

The eventful story of how Dr. Nunez (pronounced "noon-ish" in Portuguese) and his family escaped from the Inquisition in Portugal and wound up in Savannah in 1733 was written by one of his great-great-grandsons, Mordecai Manuel Noah, and published in the mid-nineteenth century. According to this version, Dr. Nunez was a graduate of the University of Madrid who specialized in infectious diseases.

In a different version of his life story, told by another descendant, Dr. Marcos Fernan Nunez of Savannah, in the 1950s, Dr. Samuel Nunez was born in Spain and was Catholic. He served in the Spanish Navy, sailing to the West Indies, Cuba, and even to Florida. He married a young, wealthy Sephardic Jewish Spanish woman, Gracia de Siquera.

In Mordecai Noah's version, Dr. Nunez lived as a crypto-Jew, or *marrano*, in order to hide from the Inquisition the fact that he was Jewish. Sometime in the early 1720s Dr. and Mrs. Nunez and their family were caught holding a Passover Seder in their palatial house on the banks of the Tagus River in Lisbon and were thrown in jail and tortured.

They were saved from execution by the Grand Inquisitor, who happened to have been a patient of Dr. Nunez. The family was released from prison so that Dr. Nunez could treat the Inquisitor's bladder problem. One condition of the release was that two Inquisition enforcers would live with the family to make sure they did not relapse into the banned practice of Judaism.

In 1726, Dr. Nunez, his mother, wife, and their two sons and a daughter made a daring escape under the noses of their Inquisitorial overseers. The story goes that Dr. Nunez threw a grand party one evening. Among the guests was an English sea captain who invited all the revelers aboard his brigantine anchored in the Tagus. As soon as the family, with their Inquisitors, came on board, the captain weighed anchor and set sail for England. As planned, the family arrived in London with a fortune in diamonds, gold, silver, and jewels secreted in their clothing. The history does not record what happened to the Inquisition spies.

When the Nunez family arrived in London they found a colony of some six thousand fellow Jewish escapees from the Spanish and Portuguese Inquisition. Soon after arriving, on August 8, 1726, Dr. Nunez remarried his wife, Gracia (known as Rebecca) in a London synagogue. Evidence also indicates that the family fully converted to Judaism in London and that Dr. Nunez and his two sons, as part of the conversion, underwent the rite of ritual circumcision.

Rebecca Nunez bore a son on January 12, 1727. The child died in infancy. Although the records are not clear, it appears that Rebecca Nunez also died in London before the family sailed to America in the summer of 1733.

A group of wealthy London Jews underwrote the transportation costs for impoverished Londoners who joined James Oglethorpe in founding the colony of Georgia under his 1732 royal charter. Those same wealthy Jews also paid for the passage of a chartered ship that sailed from London in the summer of 1733 with forty-two Sephardic Jews aboard. That group included the Nunez family.

After a rough voyage, the ship, the *William and Sarah*, arrived in Savannah on July 11, 1733, six months after Oglethorpe had landed at Yamacraw Bluff to start the colony named after his patron, King George II. At the time there were fewer than a thousand Jews living in the British colonies.

Dr. Nunez, the only Jewish colonist who brought a servant with him to the New World, soon made a name for himself in Savannah. The first and only medical doctor in Georgia, he was almost immediately pressed into service to stem an outbreak of what the family history calls "bloody flux" among Savannah's original 114 settlers. Employing a combination of medicinal drugs, including laudanum, and various folk remedies using tree barks and roots, he stemmed the epidemic. His heroic act received an official commendation from Governor Oglethorpe, who spoke of his pleasure "with the Behaviour of the Jewish Physician and the Service he has given to the Sick." Oglethorpe rewarded Dr. Nunez with six farms.

Dr. Nunez later opened the first pharmacy in Georgia, where he specialized in making medicines out of imported and native-grown herbs. He was a close friend of the founder of the Methodist Church, John Wesley. He also helped found the Mikveh Israel Synagogue in Savannah in July 1735, which to this day uses the Torah that was brought to Savannah by the Jews on the *William and Sarah* in 1733. The town of Nunez in Emanuel County eighty-five miles northwest of Savannah is named for his great-great-grandson, Dr. Philip Nunez, a colonel in the Confederate Army who was killed at the Civil War Battle of Petersburg.

In August of 1740, fearful of growing Spanish influence in nearby Florida, Dr. Samuel Nunez moved his family north to Charleston, South Carolina. It appears that he later returned to Savannah. Among his descendants are several physicians, including Dr. Marcos F. Nunez, who retired in Savannah in the 1950s after a long career.

Not long after the Nunez family arrived in Savannah, nineteen-year-old Maria Caetana Nunez (known as Zipporah), the oldest daughter, married David Mendes Machado, another Sephardic Jew who had sailed from London with the first group of Jews who came to Georgia. David Machado, who was thirty-eight, was a member of another well-to-do Portuguese *marrano* family. He was a theologian and a scholar who was an expert in Hebrew and Jewish traditions, even though he had been forced to live as a Catholic in Portugal.

Less than a year after the wedding, David and Zipporah Machado moved to New York City. They came north after David Machado was appointed hazzan at Congregation Shearith Israel, the Spanish and Portuguese Synagogue, the first Jewish congregation established in North America. Shearith Israel was founded in 1654 by the first Jews who had come to Nieuw Amsterdam, as New York City was then known, from Recife in Brazil. Until 1825, it was the only Jewish congregation in the city.

As hazzan, the Reverend Machado, as he was known, had many duties, including granting licenses to inspect and kill cattle under Jewish dietary laws. He also conducted religious services and was responsible for reciting certain prayers.

David and Zipporah had two children. The oldest was Rebecca, who was born November 21, 1746. David Machado died at age fifty-three the following year, and Zipporah remarried Israel Jacobs of Pennsylvania. Zipporah died in Philadelphia in 1799. "She was a woman of many accomplishments," a family member later wrote, "conversant with several languages, and until her death maintained a lofty dignity, and was known in her earlier years as a great beauty."

Eleven days before her sixteenth birthday, on November 10, 1762, Rebecca Machado married Jonas Phillips at Hickory Town in Montgomery County just outside Philadelphia. Jonas Phillips, Uriah Phillips

Levy's beloved grandfather, was a remarkable man. He was best known for his Revolutionary War patriotism and his dedication to securing full religious freedom for Jews in the new nation he fought to create.

He was born in 1735 in Busek, a village in Prussia and named Jonah. His father was known as Aaron Phaibush, a rough translation of the Hebrew name, Aaron Uri. Jonah Phaibush anglicized his name to Jonas Phillips when he came to Charleston (then called "Charles Town"), South Carolina, in November 1756 on the ship *Charming Nancy* from London. He was twenty-one years old and made the arduous sea journey to the American colonies to seek his fortune. A few years later he moved to Albany, New York, where he became a Freemason and opened a store in which he sold food and spirits.

Jonas Phillips left Albany in 1761, married Rebecca Machado a year later, and settled in New York City where he again owned and operated a retail store. He also was an auctioneer and served the Jewish community as a shohet (ritual slaughterer) and bodek (meat examiner). Jonas became a naturalized citizen in April 1771. Around 1774 he moved his growing family to Philadelphia where he opened another store at the upper end of Third Street.

Jonas Phillips was swept up in the revolutionary fervor in New York and Philadelphia in the 1770s. He spoke out publicly on British abuses of colonists' rights and signed a letter that was published in the *New York Gazette* on January 23, 1770, supporting the strongly anti-British Non-Importation Resolutions of 1765. He also participated in running the British blockade of Philadelphia. On October 31, 1778, at age forty-three, Jonas Phillips joined the Philadelphia militia as a private in Captain John Linton's Company of Colonel William Bradford's Battalion. As a result, all of his descendants qualify to be members of the Sons and Daughters of the American Revolution.

His most famous public religious act was the letter he wrote to the Constitutional Convention in September 1787. Identifying himself as "one of the people called Jews of the City of Philadelphia," he called on the body to provide "all men" in the Constitution "the natural and unalienable Right to worship almighty God according to their own Conscience and understanding."

He also was instrumental in raising funds to purchase a new building for the Mikveh Israel Synagogue in Philadelphia in 1782. Jonas Phillips later was elected the president of that Spanish and Portuguese congregation, which had been established in 1740. As the head of the congregation, he invited George Washington to attend the dedication ceremonies of its new building.

Jonas Phillips died in Philadelphia on January 29, 1803. He and Rebecca Phillips had twenty-one children. Several died as infants, including Sarah Phillips, who was born May 23, 1769. Her twin sister, Rachel Phillips, married Michael Levy in Philadelphia in June 1787 when she was eighteen. A description of their wedding—thought to be the first recorded of a Jewish wedding ceremony in the New World—was written in a June 27, 1787, letter to his wife by Dr. Benjamin Rush (1745–1813), the noted physician and patriot.

Family tradition holds that George Washington, who was then president of the Constitutional Convention in Philadelphia, attended the wedding. Other family lore holds that Washington had danced at the wedding of Jonas Phillips and Rebecca Machado in 1762.

Uriah Levy never claimed—at least in any letter or other document that survives—that he was descended from the first Jews who came to America. But his nephew, Jefferson M. Levy, was prone to pronouncing that he and Uriah Levy were descendants of Asser Levy, a leader of the twenty-three original Sephardic Jews who came to New York City in 1654.

Asser Levy successfully fought for civil rights for himself and the other Jewish settlers in the Dutch-owned city governed by Peter Stuyvesant. He eventually won the right to serve in the militia and became a licensed butcher. Asser Levy also has the distinction of being the first Jew to own a house in North America.

"The Levys I belong to came to New York from Spain by way of Holland," Jefferson Levy told a newspaper reporter in May 1923. "The first, Asa Levy, had a son and a grandson of the same name. Then came Benjamin, my great-grandfather, who lived in Philadelphia and was a signer of the Non-Importation Act" and "was one of five men authorized by Congress to sign the Colonial money. His son Michael, who was my grandfather, was in the Revolutionary Army."

In 1910, Jefferson Levy was quoted in the New York *Evening Telegram* saying that his family had been in the United States since 1660. In 1912, he told the New York *Herald:* "Our family has been in this country since 1668." The 1883 obituary of his father, Jonas Phillips Levy, in *The New York Times* said his "ancestors emigrated to New York City from England in 1650." The 1921 *New York Times* obituary of Jefferson Levy's brother, Louis Napoleon Levy, said the family "was descended from Asa Levy, who came to this country from England in 1654. His family numbers among its members Benjamin Levy, one of the signers of the Colonial currency."

The fact is that there is no record of Asser (a.k.a. "Asa") Levy having had any children. And Benjamin Levy (1726–1822), the Philadelphia Jewish Revolutionary War patriot whose signature is on the colonial two-dollar bill (he was one of twenty-eight signers; not five as Jefferson Levy said) and who was one of the signers of the original 1765 Non-Importation Resolutions, was not the father of Michael Levy. Genealogy records show that Benjamin Levy had five children—Nathan, Abigail, Hetty, Jacob, and Robert—none of whom was named Michael.

As for Michael Levy—Uriah's father and Jefferson M.'s grandfather—he was born in 1755, most likely in Germany, according to the authoritative genealogy of early American Jewish families compiled by Malcolm Stern. Michael Levy's father Isaac, it appears, took his family from Prussia to England. The fact that Michael Levy is listed as a charter member of the German Hebrew Congregation Rodeph Shalom in Philadelphia, which was organized by Jewish immigrants from Germany around 1780, is further evidence that he was born in Germany and was not a son of Benjamin Levy of Philadelphia.

In an unpublished family memoir, Jonas Levy (Jefferson Levy's father) says that his father, Michael, "came to this country from old England when about ten years of age, and was brought up to the Mercantile business which he continued until his death in high repute." Advertisements in the September 30, 1785, *Maryland Gazette* and the

Pennsylvania Journal of November 1, 1780, lend credence to Jonas's statement.

The ads said that Michael and Isaac Levy, who most likely were brothers, were "CLOCK and WATCHMAKERS, Late from London" who were offering for sale "a large assortment of the most elegant and fashionable CLOCKS and WATCHES." It appears, then, that German-born Michael Levy had a watch and clock shop in Philadelphia, where he met and married Rachel Levy in 1787. He died in 1812.

Michael Levy and Rachel Phillips Levy had fourteen children, three girls and eleven boys. The fourth child, Uriah Phillips Levy, was born in Philadelphia on April 22, 1792. He would become a naval hero of the War of 1812, a very rich man through real estate deals in New York City, the first Jewish U.S. Navy Commodore, and the purchaser in 1834 of Thomas Jefferson's Monticello.

Uriah Levy, though, wasn't the only grandson of Jonas Phillips who had a connection to Thomas Jefferson. A second cousin, Mordecai Manuel Noah (1785–1851), a well-known diplomat and journalist, was the recipient of a famous letter from Jefferson in which he expressed his views on freedom of religion and Judaism.

In 1818, Mordecai Noah had given a speech at Shearith Israel in New York, a copy of which made its way to Monticello. Jefferson wrote to Noah on May 28, 1818, saying he had read the speech "with pleasure and instruction, having learnt from it some valuable facts about Jewish history which I did not know before. Your sect by its sufferings has furnished a remarkable proof of the universal spirit of religious intolerance, inherent in every sect, disclaimed by all while feeble, and practised by all when in power. Our laws have applied the only antidote to this vice, protecting our religious as they do our civil rights by putting all on an equal footing, but more remains to be done."

That letter was sold October 29, 1986, at Sotheby's in New York for $396,000—at the time the highest price ever paid at auction for any letter or presidential document.

· · ·

URIAH P. LEVY was an intelligent, ambitious, tempestuous, bold, extravagant, physically powerful man who was a success in virtually every endeavor he undertook. Even if he had not purchased Monticello and restored it to physical health he would have made his mark both in the history of the United States Navy and in the annals of Jewish-American history.

He is best known for his fight for the abolition of flogging in the Navy, for his courageous service in the War of 1812, and for overcoming more than his share of anti-Semitism to attain the Navy's highest rank. He has won a place of honor in Jewish-American history for resisting and defeating a vicious anti-Semitic climate in the Navy and for his continuous strong defense of his faith throughout his life.

"My parents were Israelites," Uriah Levy said in 1857. "I was forced to encounter a large share of the prejudice and hostility by which, for so many ages, the Jew has been persecuted."

Levy also was quick to take offense, often acted on impulse, and had an exalted opinion of himself that he was not shy about expressing. During his long, checkered Navy career Uriah Levy was court-martialed six times and killed a man in a duel. His biographers, all of whom were favorably disposed, chose titles for their books that reflected Levy's controversial, confrontational nature: "Navy Maverick," "Pugnacious Commodore," and "Intrepid Sailor."

The United States Navy considers Uriah Levy a genuine hero. A 1,240-ton destroyer escort named after him, the USS *Levy*, was commissioned in 1943 and served in the Pacific from August 1943 through the end of World War II. Its officers hosted the surrender ceremonies of the Japanese Navy in the southeastern Marshall Islands.

The first permanent Jewish Chapel built by the United States armed forces, the Commodore Levy Chapel at the Navy Station in Norfolk, Virginia, was dedicated in 1959. The Jewish Center and Chapel, to be built in 2002 at the U.S. Naval Academy in Annapolis, will be named after him. A full-length oil portrait of the Commodore is on display at the Academy's Museum.

Among Jewish Americans, Levy is a pioneering, heroic figure. Lodge No. 2392 of the Jewish fraternal organization B'nai B'rith in northern Virginia is named for him. In 1997, the National Museum of American Jewish Military History in Washington, D.C. mounted an extensive exhibit, "An American, a Sailor, and a Jew: The Life and Career of Commodore Uriah Phillips Levy, USN (1792–1862)." Jewish War Veterans, U.S.A., a national veterans service organization, honors Jewish leaders with its Commodore Uriah P. Levy National Leadership Award.

In 1988, he was inducted into the Jewish-American Hall of Fame at the Judah L. Magnes Memorial Museum in Berkeley, California, and a medal was issued in his honor. That put Levy in the company of previous honorees such as Albert Einstein, George Gershwin, Levi Strauss, Jonas Salk, and Isaac Bashevis Singer.

The details of Uriah Levy's naval career are well documented; extensive records of his naval service survive and are catalogued in the National Archives and in the Library of Congress. The same, however, cannot be said about his personal life, including his purchase and ownership of Monticello.

Uriah Phillips Levy was born and grew up in Philadelphia when that city was a thriving seaport. His grandfather Jonas Phillips was an early and important influence. Uriah loved the sea from an early age. He idolized John Paul Jones, the Revolutionary War naval hero who died three months after Uriah was born.

Uriah, his biographers say, was "good-sized for his age; lean and wiry, [with] curly dark hair, snapping black eyes, and a swarthy complexion that contrasted oddly with the faint Yankee twang in his high-pitched voice." The good-sized boy first displayed his willfulness and determination in 1802 when he ran away from home and shipped out as a cabin boy on the *New Jerusalem*, a trading ship. He was ten years old.

Uriah told the ship's captain that he intended to return home for his Bar Mitzvah, the Jewish male initiation rite held at age thirteen. He did come home, but shipped out again at fourteen as a common seaman on the schooner *Rittenhouse*. Before he turned twenty, Uriah had learned to become a sailing master and became part owner of the merchant schooner *George Washington*.

When the United States declared war on Great Britain on June 12, 1812, Levy had the opportunity to join the Navy as a midshipman—a grade between the enlisted and officer ranks. He chose, instead, the rank of sailing master. In that era, the sailing master on a Navy ship was a commissioned officer who handled all aspects of navigation, including setting the sails. During sea battles, the sailing master took charge of navigating the ship while the captain directed the fighting.

On October 21, 1812, Uriah Levy received his official U.S. Navy appointment from President James Madison and was ordered to New York. Uriah served briefly on the USS *Alert* in New York Harbor. Then, in June 1813, he joined the crew of the USS *Argus*, an eighteen-gun brig sloop commanded by William H. Allen, as an extra, or supernumerary, sailing master.

The *Argus* set sail for the English Channel and had considerable success capturing English merchant ships. In one day alone, August 11, 1813, the *Argus* captured six ships, including the *Betsey*, laden with a valuable cargo of sugar. Allen ordered Uriah Levy to sail the *Betsey* to the nearest French port, and Levy took over the captured vessel and headed east. The next day the *Argus* was attacked and captured by the HMS *Pelican*. The *Betsey* also was recaptured that day and Levy and his crew were taken prisoner.

Every secondary source that recounts this episode in Uriah Levy's life reports that he was sent to the infamous Dartmoor Prison in Devonshire. Some 1,500 American and French prisoners died at Dartmoor between 1812 and 1816 and thousands of others were brutally mistreated there. It's a compelling story of survival and part of the iconography of the life of Uriah Phillips Levy, but it is likely not true.

"Uriah Levy never set foot in Dartmoor prison, ever," says Ira Dye, a retired naval officer, naval historian, and the author of a well-received book on the *Argus*. Dye, who is writing a book on Uriah Levy's naval career, said that after the *Betsey* was captured, Levy "spent the rest of the time on parole in a little town in England called Ashburton," along with several hundred captured American and French officers.

"They gave their word that they would follow a certain set of instructions, [including] not going more than a mile in any direction, not writing letters that were subversive, having their letters home cleared, and behaving well," Dye says. In return, Levy and the other captured French and American sailors in Ashburton were permitted to "live in town. In fact, they got a couple of shillings a day from the British government for subsistence."

Uriah Levy returned to the United States in February 1815, reaching Norfolk on December 14. after the United States and Britain had signed the Treaty of Ghent ending a war that was sometimes called the Second American Revolution. He was assigned to the Philadelphia Naval Station in his hometown the next year. In 1816 he served as second sailing master on the USS *Franklin*. In June, Lt. William Potter challenged him to a duel after an altercation at the Philadelphia Patriot's Ball during which Potter called Levy "a damned Jew" and Levy responded physically.

The duel took place on June 21 across the Delaware River in New Jersey. Potter, the story goes, fired four times and missed Levy, who responded each time by purposely firing into the air. After Potter's fifth missed shot, Levy shot Potter in the chest, killing him on the spot. Uriah Levy was brought to trial after the duel, and was acquitted of murder in Philadelphia County court.

The first of Levy's six courts-martial came on July 21, 1816. It stemmed from a shouting incident—again, with anti-Semitic epithets. He was found guilty and reprimanded. On March 5, 1817, Levy received his commission as a lieutenant. The next year, he was court-martialed for striking a boatswain's mate. He was found guilty and ordered off the ship, but the conviction was overturned. On February 12, 1819, Levy was found guilty of a host of charges and dismissed from the Navy. President Monroe overturned the conviction. On June 8, 1821, Levy was charged with "provoking and reproachful words" against a shipmate, found guilty, and given a reprimand.

Uriah Levy was not court-martialed again until 1827. In the intervening six years he served on several ships and commanded a gunboat in the West Indies. During the long periods between postings he tended to personal business and in 1823 and 1824 spent time in England and France. Early in 1824 he paid a visit to one of his heroes, the Marquis de Lafayette. "They spoke at some length of Thomas Jefferson, currently busy designing the buildings for the soon-to-be-completed University of Virginia," Levy's biographers say.

On November 1, 1827, Levy was court-martialed for conduct unbecoming and found guilty on several charges. He received a reprimand and no other punishment. His last court-martial came in 1842 when he was convicted for ordering inappropriate punishment for a sailor. Levy was found guilty and dismissed from the Navy. President John Tyler mitigated the sentence to a one-year suspension and reinstated Levy.

Uriah Levy spent a good deal of time on leave after the 1827 court-martial in Philadelphia. Part of the time he was recuperating from a stomach ailment that troubled him intermittently throughout his life. After being granted six months' leave on January 21, 1828, he moved to New York City and began investing in real estate. That year he bought three rooming houses in Greenwich Village, two on Duane Street and one on Greenwich Street. Thereafter, Levy specialized in acquiring rooming houses in the Village and elsewhere in lower Manhattan. It was a propitious time to do so.

Greenwich Village was experiencing a growth spurt in the 1820s. As the streets were paved and the sidewalks flagged, the area's population increased, property values rose, and hundreds of new businesses opened. The area was "a house-and-shop stronghold," the New York City historians Edwin G. Burrows and Mike Wallace noted. "Especially after the Christopher Street pier (1828) became the main port of entry for building materials used in transforming the uptown cityscape, the area grew dense with carpenters, masons, painters, turners, stonecutters, dock builders and street pavers."

Levy amassed a not inconsiderable fortune through his New York City real estate holdings. In 1855, he was listed as one of the wealthiest men in Manhattan in the twelfth edition of Moses Y. Beach's *The Wealth and Biography of the Wealthy Citizens of the City of New York*. Beach estimated Levy to be worth $500,000. He and August Belmont (1816–1890), the German-born banker and diplomat, were the only Jews on Beach's list.

Uriah Levy was a bachelor, and with his newfound wealth he lived well. He liked traveling. He enjoyed the company of women. He came close to marriage on at least one occasion, in 1833. The woman in question was Jane Griffith Koch, the widow of the wealthy Philadelphia merchant Jacob Gerard Koch, who was living in Paris. Her letters indicate that marriage plans were afoot, but none materialized.

As we have seen, Uriah Levy at least flirted with the idea of marrying one of Thomas Jefferson's granddaughters in January of 1835. The next winter, while he was in Washington, Levy proposed marriage to Elizabeth McBlair, the daughter of Michael McBlair, a Baltimore merchant and customs official—at least according to McBlair family members. Elizabeth, the belle of that winter's social season in Washington, turned him down.

Uriah spent a good deal of time in Paris, and lived there for a year beginning in August 1828. In 1831, he sailed to London, and the next year journeyed again to Paris. There, in the City of Light, Uriah Levy took the first steps that led to his purchase of Monticello.

. . .

IN THE fall of 1832, during one of his seemingly perpetual leaves from active duty in the Navy, Uriah Levy came to Paris with a mission: to honor Thomas Jefferson, whom the patriotic, religious Levy admired particularly for his dedication to religious freedom.

"I consider Thomas Jefferson to be one of the greatest men in history—author of the Declaration of Independence and an absolute democrat," Levy wrote from Paris in November to his old friend, the Philadelphia shipbuilder John Coulter. "He serves as an inspiration to millions of Americans. He did much to mold our Republic in a form in which a man's religion does not make him ineligible for political or government life."

"As a small payment for his determined stand on the side of religious liberty," Levy said, "I am preparing to personally commission a statue of Jefferson."

Levy was familiar with the work of the noted French sculptor Pierre-Jean David d'Angers (1788–1856) and presented him with a commission to create a full-scale bronze of Jefferson. David, the son of a wood carver, was born in Angers, in the western Loire Valley. He studied drawing and sculpture in Paris and Rome. After receiving a generous pension from his hometown, he adopted the name David d'Angers and signed his work "David."

In the 1830s David—not to be confused with his near contemporary, the French neoclassicist painter Jacques-Louis David (1748–1825)—was the leading monument maker in Paris. Commissions for statues, portraits, busts, and medallions came from patrons throughout the world. Many famous and wealthy people sat for David, who was renowned for his bas-relief sculptures.

His most famous is "Nation Distributing Crowns to Genius," a series of pedimental decorations he created from 1830 to 1837 for the Pantheon—the monumental eighteenth-century edifice on Paris's Left Bank in which many of the nation's greatest figures, including Voltaire, Rousseau, Hugo, and Zola, are entombed. Much of his work is on display today in the Musée David at Angers.

In Paris in the fall of 1832, Levy paid a visit to the seventy-five-year-old Lafayette, who lent Levy a portrait of Jefferson by the American painter Thomas Sully, which David used as his model for Jefferson's face. Levy stayed in Paris until David completed the statue early in 1834.

On July 4, 1833, Levy was involved in a public incident during which he exhibited two of the traits that he was famous for: his quick temper and ardent patriotism. As Levy told the story, he was attending a banquet given by American residents of Paris. Lafayette was among the honored guests. When it came time for toasts, Levy proposed nine cheers for President Andrew Jackson and got an unsettling reaction.

"This toast in an assemblage of Americans in a foreign land instead of being cheered, was received with groans and hisses," Levy said in 1857.

Lieutenant Levy took great offense to this and to the fact that the French national toast "was drunk with three times three and one more." He promptly threw a glove at one of the Frenchmen in attendance—appropriately, a glovemaker—and challenged the man to a duel on the Champes Elysées the next morning. The man apologized and the duel did not take place. There are no other reported instances of eruptions of the famous Levy temper during his stint in Paris, which ended early in 1834 when David finished the statue.

David's Jefferson stands seven and a half feet tall and depicts him holding a quill pen in his right hand. In his left is an etched, word-for-word copy of the Declaration of Independence, complete with signatures, including the large "John Hancock." Behind him are two large books, topped with a laurel wreath. The statue was cast in bronze by Honore Gonon and Sons, and Levy shipped both the finished statue and the plaster mold used to cast it to the United States.

On February 6, he presented the painted plaster model to the City of New York, which gratefully accepted it. The city fathers gave Levy the "Freedom of the City" and a gold snuff box in appreciation. The statue was placed on the second floor of the Rotunda at City Hall. It was the only piece of art in the Rotunda, "symbolically the most important public space in the building," according to Deborah Bershad, executive director of the city's Art Commission.

The statue is inscribed: "Thomas Jefferson by David D'Angers, Presented to the City of New York by Commodore Uriah P. Levy, USN, February 6, 1834." It was moved into the ornate City Council Chamber in the 1950s where today it is the only piece of sculpture in a room filled with oil portraits and crowned by an enormous ceiling painting, "New York City Receiving the Tributes of the Nation." The oils include a large portrait of Lafayette by Samuel F. B. Morse and one of George Washington by M. M. Sweet.

A month after he gave the model to New York City, Uriah Levy was in Washington where he presented the bronze Jefferson to the United States government. He had the words "Presented by Uriah Phillips Levy of the United States Navy to his fellow citizens, 1833," etched on one side of the statue's bronze base.

"I beg leave to present, through you, to my fellow citizens of the United States, a colossal bronze statue of Thomas Jefferson," Levy said in a March 23, 1834, letter to the House of Representatives. "The statue was executed under my eye, in Paris, by the celebrated David and Honore Gonon, and much admired for its likeness to the great original, as well as the plain republican simplicity of the whole design."

Levy spoke of his "pride and satisfaction" in offering "this tribute of my regard to the people of the United States" through Congress. He was sure, he said, "such disposition will be made of it as best corresponds with the character of the illustrious author of the declaration of our independence and the profound veneration with which his memory is cherished by the American people."

In turned out that the disposition of the statue was not decided until forty years later. The Joint House-Senate Library Committee took up the matter and recommended that the statue be placed in the center of the square in the eastern front of the Capitol, the front facing the Library of Congress and Supreme Court. On March 27, Senator Asher Robbins of Rhode Island, who chaired the Library Committee, sent a letter to Uriah Levy expressing Congress's appreciation for the gesture.

"It is every way fit and proper that the statue of the author of the declaration of American independence should find a place at the Capitol," the letter said. "This would doubtlessly, sooner or later, have been ordered by the Representatives of the States and the people. You, sir, have manifested, in so doing, a devotion to the principles contained in that celebrated instrument, equally felt by all classes of your fellow citizens."

Uriah Levy was breaking new ground. In 1834 the city of Washington did not have one monumental statue on display honoring an individual. The Senate passed a resolution on May 12 accepting the statue and directing that it be placed outside the Capitol's east front. During debate on the same measure in the House on June 27, however, more than a few members opposed the action.

Rep. William Segar Archer of Virginia, for example, argued against accepting a statue from an individual American, saying that it would be more appropriate for Congress itself to procure such a statue. Archer also said that it would be inappropriate for Congress to accept a statue of Jefferson when there was as yet no statue of George Washington in the Capitol.

Rep. Charles Fenton Mercer of Virginia objected to accepting the David because, he said, it was not a good likeness of Jefferson. Amos Lane of Indiana spoke up for Uriah Levy, saying he hoped the House would not reject the statue simply because it was offered by a Navy lieutenant rather than a commander. In the end the House voted, 69–55, in favor of the resolution to accept the statue.

Even though both the House and Senate resolutions called for the statue to be displayed outside the Capitol's east front, for reasons that are unclear it was placed inside the Capitol, in the Rotunda. On February 16, 1835, a resolution was introduced in the House to remove the statue from the Rotunda "to some suitable place for its preservation, until the final disposition of it be determined by Congress." After some debate, during which Representative Mercer said that Congress should accept statuary only from "distinguished" sources, debate was cut off and no action was taken.

Sometime during the James K. Polk administration (1845–1849)—the exact date is not certain—the statue was indeed removed from the Rotunda. It was shipped up Pennsylvania Avenue to the White House where, with the permission of President Polk, it was placed on the grounds on the north side facing Lafayette Park.

Flash forward to 1874. Jonas Phillips Levy, Uriah Levy's youngest brother, spearheaded a campaign in February of that year to get the David sculpture off the White House lawn, where it was not holding up well under the elements. In a letter dated February 16, 1874—twelve years after Uriah's death—to the House Committee on Public Buildings and Grounds, Jonas asked Congress to accept the David statue officially or return it to the family. In the letter Jonas Levy was not shy about comparing his late brother favorably to Thomas Jefferson.

"I desire to honor the name of Jefferson and the memory of the would-be donor who was a meritorious officer in the service of the U.S. Navy 50 years, and at his death, the owner of Monticello, the home of Jefferson," Jonas Levy said. "I may add that quite an interest is now felt for anything which could or would affect the memory of the sage of Monticello, Va., that great man, Thomas Jefferson, and the memory of my brother, the late Commodore Uriah P. Levy, the father and author of the abolition of corporal punishment in the United States Navy."

If Congress did not accept the statue, Jonas Levy said, "I have to request as one of the heirs to the said property and its recent owner that the statue may be turned over to us, with as little delay as possible, and in as good condition as it now appears in." The family, he said, "will preserve it that it may bring to generations to come the memory of the great men of our great and glorious union."

The statue was subsequently cleaned up and moved into National Statuary Hall in the Capitol Rotunda, where it stands today, the only one in the building donated by an individual citizen to Congress. The Rotunda houses two other David pieces: a bronze bust of George Washington and a marble bust of Lafayette. The David Jefferson is considered to be one of the most valuable pieces of artwork in the Capitol.

There is a postscript of sorts to the story of the wandering David statue. In an appended section of the 1902 book, *Monticello and Its Preservation Since Jefferson's Death, 1826–1902*, published by Jonas Levy's son Jefferson M. Levy, George Alfred Townsend gives a different version of the reasons behind the 1874 move of David's statue from the White House to the Capitol Rotunda. Jonas Levy is not mentioned.

This version begins with the sculptor Henry K. Brown—best known for his 1856 "Washington on Horseback" bronze in New York City's Union Square—"strolling around the public grounds" in Washington after the Civil War. At the White House, Brown "came upon a statue of Jefferson he had never heard of. He rubbed the verdigris which encoated it and saw the name of David of Angers.

"'Here,' said Mr. Brown, 'is your best piece of sculpture at the Capitol City and by the best master of the art. Why do you banish it to a garden? Put it in your Capitol!'"

Following Brown's admonishment, the book says, "the statue [was] cleaned and placed in the Areopagus of statuary in the old Hall of Representatives, of which it is the dean, following Houdon's Washington. It puts Commodore Levy's devotion to Jefferson in the story of the Arts."

The story goes that when Uriah Levy met with Lafayette in Paris in the fall of 1832, the marquis asked the young Navy lieutenant what had happened to his old compatriot Jefferson's beloved home. Lafayette had paid two visits to Monticello during his long, triumphant tour of the United States in 1824–25. When Jefferson had learned in the fall of 1824 that Lafayette was making his first trip to America after the Revolution, he invited him to make his "head-quarters with us at Monticello."

Lafayette's first visit to Monticello, in November 1824, turned into a memorable event.

Lafayette's entourage, which included a military escort, arrived in Charlottesville on November 4, after a two-week journey from Yorktown. The town fathers declared the day a holiday. Jefferson sent a carriage drawn by four gray horses into the nearby town to bring Lafayette up to Monticello. The carriage made the short trip in a long procession, complete with a cavalry detachment. When the party arrived on the mountain, a bugle sounded and hundreds of spectators and the cavalrymen formed a semicircle in front of the house.

"Silence fell as the carriages neared the house, and the host advanced to meet his guest," Dumas Malone wrote. "It is said that they both shed tears as they embraced. This was one of the most sentimental moments and most dramatic events in the entire lifetime of [Jefferson], this highly disciplined and characteristically undramatic man."

Lafayette and his party spent ten days enjoying Jefferson's hospitality and being feted at the University of Virginia. After the Frenchman left Jefferson wrote to a friend that he had to replenish his stock of red wine. Lafayette's second visit, in August 1825, was a brief one because Jefferson was ill.

Seven years later Uriah Levy promised Lafayette that he would look into Monticello's fate when he returned to the United States. Levy, of course, did much more than that. He bought Monticello. Ever since, one question about that transaction remains unanswered: Exactly why did a forty-two-year-old U.S. Navy lieutenant from Philadelphia who had a home and a thriving real estate business in New York City buy Jefferson's architectural masterpiece in rural central Virginia?

The answer has been elusive because no letters, journals, or newspaper interviews have surfaced in which Uriah Levy addressed his reasons for buying Monticello. The closest thing to an explanation is a flowery, abstruse statement Uriah Levy gave in his October 6, 1834, affidavit in his lawsuit against James Turner Barclay. He did not buy Monticello "with any view to farming purposes," Levy said. Rather, he was attracted by "the eligibility of the particular site, and commodiousness of the buildings thereon."

Further complicating the matter are stories that grew up purporting to explain Uriah Levy's motives and motivation for buying Jefferson's house.

Jefferson M. Levy believed that his uncle bought Monticello "solely out of patriotic feeling and out of reverence for Jefferson," as he put it in a 1912 letter. On the other hand, Jefferson Levy often repeated a surely apocryphal story that Uriah Levy bought Monticello on the orders of President Andrew Jackson.

Navy Lieutenant Levy, his nephew said in 1914, "bought Monticello at the request of Andrew Jackson, who said to him: 'Lieutenant, I order you to purchase Monticello and to preserve it.' He replied to him: 'I always obey my commander's orders.'"

Jefferson Levy may have gleaned that information from an article about Monticello that appeared in the February 8, 1862, issue of *Frank Leslie's Illustrated*. The Andrew Jackson story, though colorful, is, in all likelihood, not true.

There is no evidence that Uriah Levy even met Andrew Jackson, much less that Old Hickory ordered him to purchase Monticello. "I've checked through the most detailed history of the Jacksonian era that I could find, and I can't find that there was ever any connection or meeting or anything else between Uriah Levy and Andrew Jackson," says the military historian Ira Dye.

So what motivated him?

Uriah Levy obviously admired Jefferson. But so did many others and they did not buy his house. However, Levy had the means and he had the opportunity. He also had shown his extraordinary reverence for Jefferson by commissioning the David statue and presenting it to the nation.

"I think he just went down there, found it, liked it, bought it, that was it," Ira Dye says. "Just two years before [the deed was filed] he bought this nice statue of Jefferson in France and brought it home. He clearly was an admirer of Jefferson of a major order and was not bashful about saying why."

Theodore Fred Kuper, the national director of the Thomas Jefferson Memorial Foundation from 1923 to 1935, agreed with that assessment, as does James A. Bear, Jr., the former curator of Monticello. And there is contemporary evidence that backs up the idea that Uriah Levy was motivated by his strongly held patriotic regard for Jefferson.

In 1836, Joseph Martin of Charlottesville wrote: "It is believed that the deep veneration entertained by the present owner for the character of Mr. Jefferson, and the respect he entertains even for the inanimate objects associated with his memory, will lead him to restore it, as far as possible to the condition in which he left it, and attend carefully to the preservation of every object which could be supposed to have occupied his attention, or added beauty to the residence."

The peripatetic Navy lieutenant considered Monticello his part-time country home. Nevertheless, Uriah Levy spent significant amounts of time there after the purchase was finalized in May 1836. During the first few years of his ownership Levy was on hand to oversee the slaves and hired workers who labored to resurrect the long-neglected house, which was badly in need of repair.

With his naval career on hold, it appears that Uriah Levy spent time at Monticello in the summer of 1836 and may have been in residence when Martha Jefferson Randolph, who was living at Edgehill, died in her sixty-fourth year. She was buried in the Jefferson family graveyard at Monticello.

Levy spent the winter of 1836–37 in New York. He added more city real estate to his portfolio at that time, including a four-story brick house at 107 East Ninth Street. He moved into that house, stocking it lavishly with French furniture and English tableware. He also moved his mother and his unmarried sister Amelia from Houston Street into the Ninth Street house, along with two Irish servants.

In the spring of 1837 Uriah Levy returned to Monticello and brought his sixty-eight-year-old mother Rachel with him. Even though he had been on leave from active duty since June 1828, Levy had received a promotion on March 6. He was a newly minted Navy master commandant, the equivalent to today's rank of commander.

In October 1837 Levy added significantly to his land holdings at Monticello, purchasing a 961-acre tract of land adjacent to Monticello that once belonged to former President James Monroe. That parcel was part of a 3,500-acre tract that Monroe had sold to the Bank of America in 1827 to settle outstanding debts. Levy paid the bank $1,742.04 for the 961 acres in a transaction that was filed in the Albemarle County Courthouse on October 31, 1837. On January 20, 1840, Levy purchased a tract of 142 3/4 acres of land adjacent to Monticello from John P. and Jennetta Sampson for $1,427.50.

He was back in New York in the winter of 1837–38. On April 20, in the New York City law offices of his nephew Asahel Levy, Uriah signed a document in which he named George Carr of Charlottesville his attorney to "give a general superintendence over my possessions in Albemarle County." Levy authorized Carr to "purchase such articles as may be necessary for my servants and farm" and to act as his agent in selling his farms' crops. The paper gave permission to Carr to do whatever was necessary for the "preservation and protection" of his property in the county.

George Carr, who would play a crucial role in the fate of Monticello in the years following Uriah Levy's death in 1862, was born in Albemarle County in 1800. He was educated at local schools and became a grammar school teacher in Charlottesville. Among his students was one of Jefferson's grandsons. Carr, while teaching at Samuel Minor's school, began studying the law. In 1822 he obtained his license to practice in Virginia.

In 1838, Carr took over the management of Uriah Levy's farming operations when Levy was away from Monticello. Uriah spent time that year in Washington, D.C., and in London. When he was at Monticello, his letters show, he enjoyed horseback riding and gardening. "The commodore delighted in donning an old hat and coat and equipping himself with a pair of shears and going out to prune the shrubbery," according to Uriah's wife Virginia, whom he married in 1853.

In the summer of 1838 Uriah Levy's youngest brother Jonas, the merchant marine captain, came from New York to visit him and their mother at Monticello. "I stopped with her for two months," Jonas Phillips wrote in his unpublished memoir, "having brought my sister-in-law with me for health."

On September 7, Uriah was ordered to report to Pensacola, Florida, to take over command of the USS *Vandalia*, a 783-ton sloop of war stationed off the Gulf of Mexico. By all accounts, the ship was in terrible physical condition and its crew was little more than an undisciplined mob when Uriah Levy assumed command a week later. Levy set about refurbishing the ship and reforming its crew. One way he won the men over was doing away with corporal punishment, including flogging.

Under Levy's command, the *Vandalia* made the rounds of Mexican ports in the Gulf of Mexico, showing the flag and offering protection to Americans. The political situation in Mexico was highly unstable. Unrest swept the country in the wake of the 1836 Texas Revolution, which resulted in the independence of the former Mexican territory. Throughout the country there were periodic rebellions and insurgencies and American diplomats and other citizens in Mexico often were harassed.

Levy made several stops in Mexico—at Matamoros, Tampico, and Veracruz—and several places along the Yucatan Peninsula. He made a second cruise the following summer. Levy and his men found themselves in harm's way on several occasions during their Mexican sojourns, but escaped unscathed. It was the closest Uriah Levy would get to military action there. During the 1846–48 U.S.–Mexican shooting war, he was on land awaiting orders.

While Levy was commanding the *Vandalia*, his mother died at Monticello on May 1, 1839. He apparently did not find out until six months later when he arrived at Monticello after the cruise ended and the ship put in at Norfolk. The manager of Monticello had gotten in touch with Uriah's siblings Jonas and Amelia when their mother died and they arranged to have her buried near the house.

The tombstone Uriah Levy later erected included the Hebrew month and year of his mother's death. It was inscribed: "To the memory of Rachel Phillips Levy, Born in New York, 23 of May 1769, Married 1787. Died 7, of IYAR, (May) 5591, AD (1839) at Monticello, Va."

In May of 1840, while he was on leave at Monticello, Uriah Levy was ordered to report to Pensacola to—of all things—be a witness in a court-martial (not his own) scheduled for July 15. He had to delay his departure, though, due to injuries he sustained in a riding accident. By the time he arrived in Florida the court-martial had adjourned.

His biographers describe the next seventeen years as "the long years of Uriah's discontent." The discontent included his sixth and final court-martial, which was convened April 6, 1842, in Baltimore. Levy—the man who was well known for his crusade against flogging—was convicted for meting out "cruel and scandalous" punishment while commanding the *Vandalia*. He had ordered that a miscreant cabin boy be punished by applying a "small quantity" of tar to his back, along with "a half dozen parrot's feathers" instead of the traditional whipping with a cat-o'-nine-tails.

Uriah's punishment: dismissal from the Navy. The conviction, however, was reviewed by President John Tyler who reinstated Levy in the Navy, but ordered that he be suspended without pay for twelve months. Two years later, on May 4, 1844, Tyler signed an order promoting Commander Levy to the rank of captain.

Captain Levy spent most of the next thirteen years in New York, where "he cut something of a swath in the social life" of the city. "In his early fifties, his hair and moustache were frosted almost clear through," Levy's biographers say. "Good food and excellent port had thickened his once-lean body and given him something of a paunch, but his carriage was as stiffly erect as ever, his eyes bright and alert. His civilian clothes were expensive, always in the height of fashion." An "excellent dancer, he attended parties and balls and enjoyed the company of pretty women."

Meanwhile, back at Monticello, things were quiet during these years. Carr took charge of legal and business matters in Levy's absence, and he hired men to manage day-to-day operations of the mansion and farm. Repairs had been made to the interior and exterior.

"With the exception of the terraces, the whole building is in good repair, and neatly, if not tastily furnished," the Charlottesville *Advocate* reported. Uriah Levy arrived for periodic visits and took more than passing interest in the farming operations.

As in the past, the home of Jefferson was a magnet for visitors. "We were overrun with sightseers at Monticello," Uriah's wife, Virginia Lopez Levy, said in a 1925 interview. Contemporary evidence includes the July 1839 issue of *The Collegian*, a University of Virginia student magazine, which contains the report of a visit by a group of students to "the sage's dwelling place."

The anonymous student author briefly described the interior in glowing terms. The parlor, which the writer called Monticello's "chief room," is "an octagonal apartment beautifully decorated, with rich diamond floors and lofty ceiling," he said. He also commented on Jefferson's narrow staircases. "They are dark, of steep ascent and so narrow that a fat man would find difficulty in passing along."

The writer also remarked on the "hospitable reception" the party received. "Capt. Levy, the owner of Monticello, was then absent on a cruise," he said. "His family were, however, at home; and their kind hospitality to our party will long be remembered."

The Reverend Stephen Higginson Tyng (1800–1885) of Philadelphia, in Charlottesville to attend a Reformed Episcopal Church convention, paid a visit to Monticello on May 27, 1840. The reverend was a Jefferson hater who "had no respect for him while living" because of Jefferson's strong stand against the Episcopal Church's involvement in governmental matters. Nevertheless, Tyng used "the patronage of a member of Mr. J's family" to get an invitation from Captain Levy to tour the house.

It was well known, Tyng later wrote, that Levy "has been so troubled with the frequency of visits to his dwelling that he has the reputation of being averse to receiving company to his house." But Levy was always hospitable to members of Jefferson's family, Tyng noted, "to whom it is understood the doors are always open."

Tyng found Uriah Levy at home. He described Levy as "very polite, and ready to welcome us to a view of the premises." Tyng reported that he found the entrance hall "handsome" and said that the parlor (which he called a "drawing room") had "a highly polished tesselated floor of beech and cherry wood, which is truly beautiful." Jefferson's bed, Tyng said, "remains in its position." The bed and the pier mirrors, he said, "constitutes the remnant of his furniture, which is there to be seen."

James Silk Buckingham (1786–1855), a well-known British writer and former member of Parliament who founded the literary review *The Athenaeum* in 1822, visited Monticello during a lecture tour of the United States in 1841. Buckingham, in his account of the visit, complained that he had "some difficulty" gaining entrance into the privately owned house. Monticello, he groused, "was in the occupation of a family very little disposed to encourage the visits of strangers."

The "present proprietor," he reported, was "a Captain Levy, of the United States Navy, now absent on duty in the West Indies." In fact, Master Commandant Levy most likely was en route to Pensacola when Buckingham arrived at Monticello, a self-described "stranger" wishing to inspect the house that Jefferson built. Levy, Buckingham said, "is by birth and religion a Jew, was a common sailor before the mast in the merchant service, rose to be a mate, and was admitted from the merchant service into the Navy, and is now a captain."

Levy, Buckingham continued, "is reputed to be very rich, but the present condition of Monticello would not lead the visitor to suppose that it was the property of a person either of taste or munificence." He wrote that "nothing has been done" to improve the house or Jefferson's tomb, but noted that the interior of the house was "in a better condition than we had expected." He complained about Levy's "additions," though. These included the headstone from Jefferson's grave, which Levy had taken from the graveyard and mounted on a wall in the Entrance Hall because vandals had repeatedly chipped away at the stone.

Buckingham also was displeased with Uriah Levy's artwork in the entrance hall. He complained specifically about a full-length oil portrait of Levy in uniform, a small lithograph depicting Levy as a boatswain's mate and a lithograph of Stephen Girard (1750–1831), the Philadelphia banker and philanthropist who helped underwrite the War of 1812.

The latter two, Buckingham said, "were without frame or glass and merely pinned up against the wall." Other "incongruities of evidently recent introduction," he said, were "strewed around."

He happily reported that he saw some "relics" of Jefferson's time, including "some good paintings" and "a full-length statue of Mr. Jefferson, and a good bust of Voltaire." Buckingham, however, must have been mistaken about the full-length Jefferson statue. There is no record of Uriah Levy having had one, except for the David sculptures he donated to New York City and to Congress in 1834. If Buckingham's report is accurate, Uriah Levy had reacquired Jefferson's Voltaire bust, or, more likely, a similar one. As for the unidentified "good paintings," they probably had not belonged to Jefferson.

"I don't think Uriah Levy owned [any] of Thomas Jefferson's paintings," reports Susan Stein, the curator at Monticello who traced the provenance of Jefferson's art work in her 1993 book, *The Worlds of Thomas Jefferson at Monticello*. "He did own several of the same subjects."

The winter of 1842–43 found Uriah Levy living at Monticello, enjoying his country property and paying close attention to agricultural matters. Levy reported that he was "hard at work in the field," in a December 1, 1842, letter to his friend, the New York City lawyer David Coddington, who two decades later would be one of the executors of Uriah Levy's estate. Levy invited Coddington to visit him and his sister Amelia at Monticello.

"Come and let it be very soon," he said. "The weather has been fine dry & bracing and not as you would have expected it to be." Levy then rhapsodized about his Virginia property, which he especially valued after spending "the last six months in the good Democratic City of New York." When he arrived at Monticello, Levy said, he "walked out to my favourite spot, a little elevated about the Lawn. Then I cast my Eye on fields. My Woods. My Hills. My Silver River, My Hounds. My servants. My friends and peaceful home, then there my heart swells with joy & only sighs for her alone."

He signed the letter "U. P. Levy of Monticello."

The most extensive report on Uriah Levy's Monticello during this period was an article that appeared in the July 1853 issue of *Harper's*

New Monthly Magazine by Benson J. Lossing. In it, Lossing described a visit he paid to Monticello in March of that year, "when the buds were just bursting, and the blue birds were singing their first carols in the hedges."

Lossing made the obligatory first stop at Jefferson's grave, where he found the granite monument "shamefully mutilated by thieving visitors." Uriah Levy, who had arrived at Monticello the day of Lossing's visit, showed him the interior of Jefferson's house. Lossing—who referred to the owner both as "Commodore Levy" and "Captain Levy" —said the exterior "in general appearance" was "the same as when Jefferson left it."

The only piece of artwork in the house from Jefferson's day that remained, he said, was a bust of Voltaire. In the entrance hall Lossing found a plaster model of a column capital designed by Jefferson "in which the column was to consist of a group of maize or Indian corn stalks." Also in the entrance hall was a plaster bust of Jefferson "made in the same mould in which was cast the fine, life-size bronze statue of the Patriot which now stands in front of the Executive Mansion in Washington." Nearby was a model of the *Vandalia*. On the wall was a portrait of "Madame Noel, an aunt of Captain Levy," by the famed British portraitist Sir Joshua Reynolds (1723–1792), Lossing said, along with "two or three more modern paintings," and the great clock.

Lossing described the parlor's "beautiful tessellated floor, made of inlaid satin-wood and rose-wood" as "polished like a table." Its value, he said, was two thousand dollars.

Uriah Levy tried, without success, to return to sea duty before, during, and after the U.S.–Mexican War. He also wrote articles in New York, Philadelphia, and Washington newspapers, advocating the abolition of flogging in the Navy. He pushed the message with a series of lectures and was joined in his campaign by Herman Melville, the celebrated author of *Moby Dick*. They succeeded in 1853 when the U.S. Navy banned the practice of flogging. Congress made it official with a law in 1862, the year Levy died.

Uriah Levy actively was involved in religious affairs during his "discontentment." He was a member of Shearith Israel Congregation in

New York City, the Portuguese synagogue where his great-grandfather David Machado had served as hazzan a century before. He was also a charter member and the first president of the Washington Hebrew Congregation, which was organized on April 25, 1852.

. . .

WHEN he was sixty-one years old Uriah Levy married Virginia Lopez, his niece. In doing so, he was following an ancient, if obscure, Jewish tradition that obligates the closest unmarried male relative of a recently orphaned or widowed woman in financial difficulties to marry her. Virginia Lopez, the daughter of Uriah's sister Frances (Fanny) and the late Abraham Lopez, was eighteen years old.

It is not certain exactly when and where the marriage took place. His biographers only say it happened in "the autumn of 1853." They mention neither the venue nor what type of ceremony it was. Other secondary sources say the Navy captain married his Jamaican-born niece—the youngest of the three Lopez children—at Monticello.

Abraham Lopez, sometimes referred to as Judge Lopez, had fallen on hard financial times by the time he died. Before that, however, he had prospered and provided well for his family. Virginia attended boarding school in England. She and her mother were in New York after her father's death where she met Uriah.

Levy's biographers describe Virginia Lopez as "a charmer," who had "the beauty of a Spanish senorita." She was "extremely vivacious, with dark eyes and hair and a lovely olive complexion," and was "spirited, witty, a good dancer, fluent in French and Spanish. She also possessed a good measure of conceit, and was not at all bashful in describing her conquests and flirtations."

After the wedding, the May-December couple moved with Virginia's recently widowed mother, Uriah's sister Fanny, into Uriah's new large house at 107 St. Mark's Place in New York City. In a concession to his youthful consort, Uriah Levy appears to have dyed his gray hair and moustache black.

The couple spent the summer of 1854 at Monticello, where contemporary evidence indicates that the marriage did not go over well with the local populace—many of whom "were resentful and regarded the Levys as intruders," according to Charlottesville resident Anna Barringer. Another resident, George Blatterman, described Uriah Levy and his marriage disparagingly and with anti-Semitic overtones in a handwritten memoir dating from the turn of the twentieth century.

"Capt. Uriah P. Levy, a Capt. in the U.S. Navy, purchased Monticello at a very small price," Blatterman, the foster son of a prominent University of Virginia professor, said. "He was a Jew of the Jews and very unpopular. I think he was a good naval officer. His . . . sister Amelia and his mother lived with him."

Uriah Levy's "niece came to live with them," Blatterman said. "In the course of events he married her and this being in direct violation of the constitution of Virginia added to his already great unpopularity." Blatterman said that in 1850 he "rode in company with [Uriah Levy] several miles and he complained very bitterly of the animosity of the people." Levy, Blatterman added, left Charlottesville periodically "just to escape indictment."

Blatterman was in his early eighties when he wrote those words. Some of the details, such as having Uriah speak of his marriage in 1850—three years before he married Virginia Lopez—are not correct. However, the portrait of a shunned and disliked Levy rings true. So, too, unfortunately, does the memoir's anti-Semitic tone.

Virginia Lopez Levy loved spending time at Monticello. "How I did enjoy galloping over those hills around Monticello," she said in an interview just before she died in 1925 in her ninetieth year. She also expressed patronizing and racist views when describing the slaves at Uriah Levy's Virginia farm.

"In my youth I was very anxious to become an expert equestrienne and do the stunts that a little darky boy, whom I made somewhat of a pet of, and who was always guarding me like a dog, could accomplish," she said, "so I promised him a wonderful present if he succeeded in teaching me."

In another anecdote, she said: "The darkies were very amusing. I remember one day accidentally coming across our cook, Aggy, in the drawing room. She was standing in front of a figure of a woman in bronze, evidently comparing her arm with this figure. Finally she ejaculated: 'My arm's a heap sight prettier dan dat dare black woman!'"

Virginia Lopez Levy, who married William John Ree after Uriah's death and was then known as Mrs. Ree, also reported a continuing problem with uninvited visitors. She spoke of one occasion when Uriah Levy was away that a "party of sight-seeing hilarious students who had been carousing rode up to the house." One rowdy student decided to ride his horse into the house.

"The darkies remonstrated to no avail," Mrs. Ree said, "so I took the Commodore's revolver out of a drawer where no doubt he had it for years." She threatened to shoot the boys, who laughed at her, but agreed they would leave if she put the weapon away.

"I looked at the revolver and found it swathed in bandages," she said. "I then laughed myself and we parted friends."

Two unidentified visitors, who reported on a May 20, 1856, excursion to Monticello, also made note of a continuous stream of fellow pilgrims to Jefferson's mountain. The visitors said that an unidentified overseer, probably Joel Wheeler, told them they had to pay twenty-five cents "to see the premises." That money, they said, "we presume is to compensate the overseer for the trouble and loss of time occasioned by the number of visitors to Monticello, who always desire his attention."

The visitors paid their money, and commented favorably on the landscaping. "The yard is spacious," they said, "and is ornamented by large trees of various kinds, most of which were planted by Jefferson himself." Inside, they reported that the inlaid wooden floor in the entrance hall was "highly waxed and polished." When they asked Wheeler which items in the house belonged to Jefferson, he pointed to "an alabaster lamp, a ladder and a bust of Voltaire." The ladder was one Jefferson designed to wind the Great Clock, which the visitors described as unused. "Dust and rust corrode the silent wheels," they reported.

In the previous year, 1855, Uriah Levy, along with many other naval officers, had been dropped from the Navy's active duty lists. He did not take the news well. He decided to fight his removal, basing his defense on anti-Semitism. Levy put together a vigorous case with the help of an old friend, the influential New York lawyer Benjamin Franklin Butler (1795–1858), a former U.S. attorney general.

Some have compared Levy's case to the 1894 Dreyfus Affair in France in which the Jewish French army captain Alfred Dreyfus was convicted of treason and sentenced to life imprisonment at Devils Island in a court-martial marked by overt anti-Semitism. The case became a political *cause célèbre* in France. It may be a stretch to compare the two cases, but Levy and Butler did base their case on anti-Semitism, and put together an impressive array of witnesses to testify on Levy's behalf at a Navy Court of Inquiry that was held in November 1857 in Washington. Butler and Levy brought in thirteen naval officers and government officials, including the historian and former Navy secretary George Bancroft (1800–1891) to help make his case. The month-long proceeding was heavily covered in the nation's newspapers.

Uriah Levy himself contributed significantly to his case with a passionate speech, the transcript of which runs to 115 pages.

"My case is the case of every Israelite in the Union," Levy said. "Are the thousands of Israel and the tens of thousands of Judah, in their dispersion throughout the earth, who look to America as a land bright with promise, are they now to learn, to their sorrow and dismay, that we too have sunk into the mire of religious intolerance and bigotry?"

He ended with a warning. "What is my case today, if you yield to this injustice, may tomorrow be that of the Roman Catholic or the Unitarian, the Presbyterian or the Methodist, the Episcopalian or the Baptist. There is but one safeguard: that is to be found in an honest, wholehearted, inflexible support of the wise, the just, the impartial guarantee of the Constitution."

Levy and Butler won their case. Levy was reinstated on the active duty rolls of the U.S. Navy on January 29, 1858. Less than three months later he was given command of the USS *Macedonian*. It was his first posting on a ship in two decades.

The ship Levy commanded had started life in 1810 as the HMF *Macedonian*, a British frigate. It was captured by the USS *United States* (a ship Levy had served on in 1818–1819) under famed American naval officer Stephen Decatur (1779–1820) during the War of 1812. When

Uriah Levy took over in 1858, the ship was being refitted in Boston. When he arrived in Boston to take over command, he brought his young wife along.

Levy had secured unprecedented permission to take his wife to sea with him on the voyage. Naval historian James Tertius de Kay described the scene when the odd couple arrived at Boston's Charlestown Navy Yard.

"Captain and Mrs. Levy made a striking couple as they alighted from their carriage. He was a very tall, somewhat stiff officer in his mid-sixties, with a round, stubborn face, and dark, intelligent eyes set off by a black, tightly curled handle-bar moustache." A British diplomat described Levy a year later as "a fine looking rosy old fellow" with "strong Jewish features which looked curious with cocked hat, epaulettes and eagle buttons with abundance of jewelry."

Virginia, de Kay said, "was a dainty and vivacious beauty, with large, dark eyes and a creamy complexion. She was dressed in the height of fashion and carried herself with a confidence and aplomb she had undoubtedly learned from her distinguished husband." Once on board, Virginia Levy ordered the ship's carpenter to put a mezuzah—a small, oblong prayer box containing a written prayer that is meant to bless a Jewish home and usually is placed on the upper side of a door post—on the frame of the door to the captain's quarters.

For two weeks, de Kay said, a "parade of dignitaries, artists, and men of affairs" came to the navy yard "to wish the couple a happy voyage." The parade included "governors, college presidents, lawyers and intellects of every stripe," including the poet Henry Wadsworth Longfellow.

"I had a most enjoyable stay" in Boston, Virginia said in a 1925 interview, "and met interesting people, including our own Mr. Longfellow, from whom I received an autographed copy of the 'Psalm of Life,' which I always thought was one of the most beautiful things ever written."

The *Macedonian's* mission was not exactly hazardous. The ship was ordered to the Mediterranean to protect American shipping and promote American goodwill. The mission, which began June 6 with a detour to Key West, was "less like a military cruise than a social saga,"

Levy's biographers said. The mission involved "little more than [cruising] from port to port, showing the flag and putting on a display of good manners," said de Kay. The Levys' "duties included attending an almost endless round of balls, receptions, and reviews."

The vivacious Virginia Levy made the most of the social opportunities presented to her during the tour, which lasted nearly two years. She took extended trips off the ship, spending time among the rich and famous in Key West, Gibraltar, Marseilles, Alexandria, and Cairo, and along the Italian coast. She went to parties in honor of Queen Victoria's teen-aged son Albert, the Duke of Edinburgh (1844–1900), in Alexandria and met Viscount Ferdinand Marie de Lesseps (1805–1894), the French diplomat and engineer who built the Suez and Panama Canals, in Marseilles.

In Naples, Virginia spent the Jewish holy day of Yom Kippur of 1858 with international financier Baron Lionel Nathan de Rothschild (1808–1879) who, she said, had a synagogue in his home. Virginia also spent quality time in Venice and Genoa and in Florence, where the popular American sculptor Hiram Powers (1805–1873) asked her to pose for him.

There was a particularly memorable stay in Paris, during which Virginia attended a lavish costume ball given by Emperor Louis Napoleon (1808–1873). At the ball Virginia indulged in a "violent flirtation with another masked reveler," who turned out, she says, to be "Prince Metternich."

In all likelihood the masked man she referred to was not the famed Austrian statesman who was then eighty-one years old, but his son, the diplomat Richard, Furst von Metternich, who in 1859 became Austria's ambassador to Paris. Virginia Levy said she met the younger Metternich "afterwards in different salons and had many interesting conversations with him."

While his wife was socializing, Captain Levy, aboard the *Macedonian*, continued to supervise affairs at Monticello. In a letter he wrote to George Carr on June 4, 1858, just before the ship set sail, Levy gave his Charlottesville lawyer directions for handling his "farming affairs." Levy reminded Carr that he had been given "the power to supervise Mr.

Garrison [presumably, the farm manager] and hope you will see that he is economical in his expenditure of money and materials. He has always done well in this particular and I have found a very good man whose services I wish you to retain unless you think it advisable to change.

"You know how much a Farm requires the eye of the master and how much it suffers from his absence. Mr. Garrison is an excellent man but he will need your counsel and advice and I hope you will give him the benefit of your superior knowledge." Levy told Carr that he had ordered a $110 seeding machine, "which is to be paid out of the proceeds of the sale of my wheat next fall." He also complained about a recent poor tobacco crop. The tobacco, he said, "was too light and we must try and do better."

Levy then said that he did not know if his sister Amelia and other members of his family would be at Monticello during that summer. "If none of the family go there," he said, "you will be welcome to occupy the mansion with your family for the summer and I hope you will make yourself comfortable. . . . Should you want a horse, let Mr. Garrison know that I wish you to be accommodated with one."

Monticello matters were very much on Uriah Levy's mind in a September 17, 1858, letter he wrote to Carr when the *Macedonian* was docked in Spezia, Sardinia. In this letter Levy also expansively expounded on his feelings about Thomas Jefferson. After learning from Carr about the July 4th celebration at Monticello, Levy said: "I am rejoiced that Virginians more and more appreciate the nation's birthday and honor the memory of the man who was among the first, if not the first, to call the Nation into being, who guided its infant footsteps aright and taught its infant tongue to lisp no other sentiments than those which were truly Republican."

Let "every year add to our love and veneration for Thomas Jefferson," Levy continued. "There is no fear of his being made an idol. His life, his writings, his acts and example forbid that but the most grateful emotions of our hearts can not inspire our lips to utter language which will more than express the just mede of praise we owe him. There is something appropriate in solemnizing the Nation's natal day at the tomb of Jefferson and although I was many miles from Monticello I was full of thought of what might be happening there."

As Jefferson did, Levy referred to the slaves at Monticello as "servants." He wrote that he was saddened by the death of one of them— Aggy, the cook Virginia Levy spoke about in her 1925 reminiscences. "Mr. Garrison has written to me [and] afflicts me very much by the announcement of the death of my faithful servant Aggy," he said. "I shall miss her very much for she is identified with Monticello and was much attached to me as I was to her."

Levy went on to complain about something he and Jefferson had in common: bad luck with farming operations. "Shall I ever hear that our part of Virginia has produced good crops?" Levy wrote. "The wheat has turned out badly, the tobacco crop will or has failed, the oats are all straw, we have had too much or too little rain has been the dolorous burden of the song for many years."

He told Carr that his sister reported that the gates and fences at Monticello were "in very bad condition and I will thank you if you will give a look to these things and advise and direct Mr. Garrison." He was wary of his manager's abilities and asked Carr to watch him more closely. "Impress upon him that he must be careful of stock and utensils and do not let him disburse money without consulting you. I have heretofore found Mr. Garrison faithful and attentive but he needs someone to advise and direct him. You must give him the benefit of your superior judgment and experience."

On January 7, 1860, near the end of his tour of duty, Uriah Levy was given the command of the entire American Mediterranean Squadron, a position that entitled him to the rank of Commodore, the Navy's highest at the time. When he received the news, an "exultant Levy immediately ordered the departure [from Alexandria, Egypt] for Italy," de Kay wrote, "and on February 21, 1860, in the harbor of Genoa, he watched his personal pendant hoisted to the top of the mizzenmast, to the accompaniment of a 13-gun salute from the rest of the squadron."

Uriah Levy never was officially commissioned as a commodore. That—and the fact that Levy chose to identify himself as a captain on his tombstone—led to a debate a half century later over whether or not Levy was, in fact, a commodore. A war of words over the issue flared up in January and February of 1911.

It began with a letter to the editor of the *Hebrew Standard* newspaper by the writer Isaac Markens, who in 1888 had written a book, *Hebrews in America.* Markens said he had had three mistakes about Uriah Levy in that book: that he "attained the rank of commodore," that he was "the ranking officer of the navy when he died," and that he was "the author of the anti-flogging measure." Markens said that Uriah Levy merely was one of scores of people who fought against the practice of flogging and that he "was never more than a captain."

That prompted two replies from Uriah Levy's nephew Jefferson M. Levy, who then was the owner of Monticello. Jefferson M. Levy made a case that Uriah was "the father of the [anti-flogging] movement." He also produced a February 8, 1911, letter from the assistant secretary of the Navy saying that the rank of commodore was not established officially until 1862. In 1860, the letter said, "captains in the United States Navy commanding, or having commanded squadrons were considered commodores, though not commissioned as such, and in accordance with this custom, Captain Levy was recognized as commodore and so addressed in official communications."

Uriah Levy "was definitely entitled to the honorary title of commodore. He had every right to it after 1860," the naval historian Ira Dye says. "He never had the rank of commodore because it didn't exist until after he was dead. He was never the senior officer in the Navy."

Less than three months after Levy hoisted his personal pennant in Genoa, he was ordered home. On July 14, 1860, he sailed the *Macedonian* into the navy yard at Portsmouth, New Hampshire. Two days later, he was detached from the ship and granted three months' leave. His biographers report that Uriah and Virginia Levy spent the summer of 1860 at Monticello.

After the Civil War began on April 12, 1861, with the firing on Fort Sumter, Levy asked to be included in the Union effort, but was repeatedly put off. Stories that likely are apocryphal circulated that a frustrated Levy wrangled an audience with President Lincoln at the White

House during which he pleaded to take part in the naval war against the South. These stories also have Levy patriotically offering, as one chronicler put it, to "place his entire fortune at [Lincoln's] disposal."

Although there is evidence that Uriah Levy did meet Lincoln once, at a White House reception, no "specific direct evidence" has arisen showing "that he offered his fortune to Lincoln for the war effort," Ira Dye says. "Nor have I seen any letters in Navy files, where they should be, in which Uriah Levy asked for an active assignment at sea in the Civil War." Normally, Dye says, "you would ask the Secretary of the Navy."

Uriah Levy did not get a wartime assignment until November 1861. He was ordered to—of all things—take charge of the Navy's Court-Martial Board in Washington. The Levys came to Washington in November 1861, took up temporary residence in a hotel, and he went to work.

In March, Uriah Levy took a leave of absence from the job because of illness. He returned to New York City where on March 22, 1862, he died of pneumonia in his house at 107 St. Mark's Place.

His demise nearly led to the death of Monticello.

CHAPTER THREE

Saving Monticello

Monticello "has been confiscated, with all its lands, negroes, cattle, farming utensils, furniture, paintings, wines, etc. . . ."
FRANK LESLIE'S ILLUSTRATED NEWSPAPER, FEBRUARY 8, 1862

U riah Levy's family followed Jewish tradition and buried him as soon as possible after he died. His funeral, which was held in New York on March 26, was described in detail in the *New York Herald* and *New York Times*. It was a Jewish funeral—with patriotic flourishes. Rabbi Lyons of Shearith Israel presided. Three companies of U.S. Marines, a detachment of eighty sailors from the USS *North Carolina*, and the Navy's brass band escorted the body from Levy's St. Marks Place house to the cemetery in Brooklyn.

Uriah Levy was buried in a plain rosewood coffin. "On the lid of the coffin," according to the *Herald*, "were placed the sword, hat and coat of deceased, while a solitary candle burned at the head and feet of the same. The parlor where the body reposed, and the bedchambers leading thereto were crowded with sympathizing friends and naval officers. A large full-length portrait of the Commodore hung upon one of the walls, around which were grouped persons who evidently had gazed upon the original while the warm lifeblood still bounded through his manly frame."

"Arriving at the cemetery," the *Times* reported, "the deceased was placed in the receiving-house, when the mourners, in accordance with Jewish custom, made the circuit of it seven times, chanting verses illustrative of the mercy of God and the mortality of man. Finally the body was lowered into the grave when the nearest relatives offered a prayer, threw dust upon the coffin and the obsequies were finished."

Uriah Levy had no children. In his complicated will, he left Monticello to the country he venerated to be used as a farm school for the orphans of Navy warrant officers. But Monticello and all of his adjacent Virginia land were seized by the Confederacy under the sequestration terms of the Alien Enemies Act, which had been passed by the Confederate Congress and approved by Confederate President Jefferson Davis on August 8, 1861.

That act called for the removal of all residents of northern states from the Confederacy. It also authorized the Confederate States to take possession and ownership of property in the South owned by ousted Northerners. According to an article in the *Richmond Examiner*, proceedings had begun on October 10, 1861, to "sequestrate 'Monticello' as the property of an alien enemy, the present owner, Levy, being abroad being in charge of a United States ship of war."

Levy, in actuality, was in Washington preparing to take over the Navy's Court-Martial board. The *Richmond Examiner* article went on to point out that the "people of Charlottesville called the late owner of Monticello 'Commodore Levee.' He is a first Captain in the United States Navy, and of Jewish parentage."

Monticello "has been confiscated," *Frank Leslie's Illustrated Newspaper* of New York City reported four months later, "with all its lands, negroes, cattle, farming utensils, furniture, paintings, wines, etc., together with two other farms belonging to the same owner, and valued at from $70,000 to $80,000." The newspaper went on to expound on Uriah Levy's patriotism and military service, and concluded: "Certainly no officer in the army or navy has been so victimized by the rebels."

Monticello was not sold by the Confederate government until November of 1864. In the interim, it remained under the day-to-day control of Joel Wheeler, Uriah Levy's overseer, and George Carr, his Charlottesville lawyer. Visitors reported that Wheeler and his family had taken up residence in the house.

The Commonwealth of Virginia was the main battleground of the Civil War, but no fighting of consequence took place near Monticello.

Charlottesville, however, played an important support role for the Confederate Army, and there was a military hospital in the city. Large shipments of supplies came through town via the railroad, and several Charlottesville businesses provided clothing, supplies, and weapons for the Army.

Some Confederate and Union troops stopped to see Monticello during the war. Confederate soldiers recuperating from their wounds in Charlottesville hospitals journeyed up the mountain and had picnics. Many wartime visitors—soldiers and civilians—left their marks on the mansion, literally, by writing their names on walls of the upstairs dome room and by helping themselves to souvenir pieces of the house and of Jefferson's tombstone.

By the summer of 1864, with the Wheeler family living in the house, Monticello was showing the effects of neglect and of the ravages of the "relick" hunters. "The place was once very pretty, but it has gone to ruin now," wrote Sarah Strickler, an Albemarle Female Institute student who visited in August. She said there were a "thousand names" scrawled on the walls of the dome room and that Jefferson's graveyard suffered "from the same want of attention that the house and grounds do." Others reported that the house's furniture had been broken or destroyed and that Jefferson's graveyard was badly defaced.

The Confederate States of America got serious about selling Monticello in the fall of 1864, a time when the South's treasury was in dire need of cash to carry on the war effort. When Carr and Wheeler tried to stop the sale, the Confederate government sued them. The suit was heard in the District Court of the Confederate States of America for the Eastern District of Virginia in Richmond on September 27, and the CSA prevailed.

Soon thereafter, an advertisement for a receiver's sale of Monticello ran in the *Richmond Enquirer.* The sale would take place at Monticello, "a large and commodious Brick Dwelling House," the ad said, "late the property of Captain U.P. Levy, deceased, an alien enemy." Lieutenant Col. Benjamin Franklin Ficklin of the Fiftieth Virginia Regiment purchased Monticello for $80,500 at the auction, which was held on site on November 17.

The New York Times account of that day's events reported that "a large number of people" were present. In the crowd was Uriah Levy's youngest brother, Jonas Phillips Levy, who then was living in Wilmington, North Carolina. How Jonas Levy—a born and bred northerner who had fought with distinction as the commander of the USS *America* during the Mexican War—came to live in the South and to show up at Monticello on November 17, 1864, is a strange and intriguing tale.

In his unpublished memoir, Jonas Levy makes only the barest mention of his adventures during the Civil War, and he never explains why he went over to the Southern cause. He writes that he was in Washington with his wife and four young children in 1861, then went to Baltimore where he remained "until the breaking out of the revolution with the South." He left Baltimore, he said, when "U.S. troops took possession of Fort McHenry" with "the intention of going to Mexico. Got as far as Wilmington, N.C. until 1865, when the War ended and I returned to the City of New York in November 1866."

Levy skips over the reasons why he essentially abandoned his wife and children in Washington, where he had been living since 1854 and had been operating a "shipping store." He also was active in religious affairs in the city, and was a founder, with his brother Uriah, of the Washington Hebrew Congregation.

Captain Levy says not a word in his diary about what he did in North Carolina during this odd five-year interlude. But there is a record of some of the things he was up to in the *Journals of the Confederate Congress* at the Library of Congress and in the *Official Records of the Union and Confederate Armies* at the National Archives.

We know that Jonas Levy opened up a chandlery and hardware business in Wilmington. We also know that beginning in August 1861 he offered his services to the Southern cause in a series of letters to the Confederate Congress in Richmond and to several leading officials, including President Jefferson Davis and then secretary of war Judah P. Benjamin. These offers included building a twenty-gun ironclad ship in Europe and organizing a blockade-running operation.

Jonas Levy may have had an ulterior motive in pledging his allegiance to the South: getting control of Monticello. On April 16, 1862,

Jonas presented a petition to the Confederate Congress asking for a "modification of the sequestration law" to allow him—a resident of the Confederacy—to inherit Monticello. "I am a loyal citizen of this Confederacy," he said, in claiming to be Uriah Levy's only heir in the South.

The petition was referred that day to the Senate Committee on the Judiciary, and was reported to the full Senate on September 20. It was rejected on October 7.

A little more than two years later—on November 17, 1864—Jonas Levy showed up at the auction of Monticello. There are two versions of his behavior on that day. In *Monticello and Its Preservation*, the book published by Jonas's son, Jefferson M. Levy, the author George Townsend claims that Jonas Levy showed up at Monticello "to save it from confiscation" and "was held as a hostage, but told the people that the revolt would end and that they would have to restore the property." That version is almost certainly not true.

What does ring true are the details about the sale recounted in an article that appeared in the *New York Times* on December 1, 1864, based on an account in the Lynchburg, Virginia, *Republic*. That article makes no mention of any hostage situation.

It does mention that Jonas Levy spoke to the crowd before the auction began, saying "he did not come there to interfere with or prevent the sale in any way, and that while he for the present waived his rights in the premises, he intended to bid for the property himself." After the deputy marshal running the auction reminded the crowd that the Jefferson family graveyard was not part of the sale, Jonas Levy spoke up again.

"Captain Levy," the account says, "said his mother was also interred on the place, and he hoped whoever became the purchaser of Monticello would let her rest in peace."

First Monticello was auctioned off, with the bidding beginning at $20,000 and ending with Colonel Ficklin's winning $80,500 offer. Jonas Levy, while not the successful bidder, did come away with two of Uriah Levy's former possessions: a slave and a model of the *Vandalia*. Next came the auctioning of Uriah Levy's nineteen slaves. "The first negro man, Fuke, brought $7,000," the article says. "The next, Fleming, $7,450; Lewis, $7,350; John, sold to Capt. Jonas P. Levy for $5,400."

Colonel Ficklin bought a bust of Jefferson, "which stood in the hall on a fluted Corinthian pedestal," for $50. A pianoforte was sold for $5,000; a marble-topped sideboard went for $510. Jonas Levy got the *Vandalia* model for $100. Other items sold that day included a washstand, cows, oxen, shoats, and a threshing machine. The total take was $350,000.

Benjamin Franklin Ficklin, the new owner of Monticello, led an amazingly varied and adventurous life. He was born December 18, 1827, in Albemarle County and grew up in Charlottesville, the fifth of six children of Ellen Slaughter Ficklin and the Reverend Benjamin Ficklin II, a prosperous merchant and landowner. Benjamin went to the Virginia Military Institute in 1844 and is remembered there for his outlandish pranks. Among other things, Cadet Ficklin fired rockets on school grounds, buried the superintendent's boots in the snow, and painted white zebra stripes on his horse.

Ficklin interrupted his studies to fight in the Mexican War, then returned to VMI where he graduated in the class of 1849, fourth from the bottom. He briefly taught at a boys school in Abington, Virginia, then moved to Alabama where he got into the overland hauling business. From there, Ficklin headed west, and went to work as a route agent for the Russell, Majors and Waddell's freight company. In 1857 he signed on with federal troops under Albert Sidney Johnston—the future Confederate general—and took part in skirmishes with rebellious Mormons in the Utah territory.

Ficklin went back to Russell, Majors and Waddell's Overland California and Pike's Peak Express Company and was promoted to superintendent of Denver–Salt Lake City operations. In 1860 Ficklin, most historians agree, came up with the idea for a fast new overland operation that would deliver mail and news between St. Joseph, Missouri, and San Francisco. The company called it the Pony Express and gave Ficklin the job of organizing the huge operation. He set up 190 relay stations along the nearly two-thousand-mile route, bought five hundred horses and signed on eighty riders. The Pony Express got off the ground in April 1860. Ficklin quit the job three months later after a fight with his bosses.

On May 5, 1861, three weeks after the Civil War began, he was commissioned a major and became temporary quartermaster general of the Provisional Army of the State of Virginia. He was promoted to lieutenant colonel in August. A year later, Ficklin left his quartermaster job and joined the Fiftieth Virginia Regiment. He took part in several battles, including the bloody July 1, 1862, Battle of Malvern Hill near Richmond in which Gen. Robert E. Lee's forces suffered more than 5,300 casualties.

Ficklin subsequently left the regiment and took over the operation of three blockade-running ships, the *Virginia*, the *Coquette*, and the *Giraffe*. Historians believe that the $80,500 in Southern currency Ficklin laid out for Monticello came from profits he gained while shipping goods from Europe through the Union blockade to the South.

Shortly after the war ended, Ficklin was in Washington, D.C., where he was arrested—wrongly, it turned out—on April 16, 1865, for being involved in the assassination of President Lincoln. Ficklin later was in charge of U.S. mail operations in San Antonio, Texas. He died at age forty-four on March 10, 1871, while dining at the Willard Hotel in Washington when a fishbone lodged in his throat and the doctor who tried to remove it severed an artery.

It is not clear whether Benjamin Franklin Ficklin ever lived at Monticello during his brief ownership. Although the sale took place in November 1864, Ficklin did not receive title from the District Court until March 17, 1865, three weeks before Lee surrendered to Grant at Appomattox ending the war.

According to Ficklin family lore, Benjamin Ficklin, a bachelor, brought his aging father, the Reverend Ficklin, to live at Monticello, where he died. Other reports say that several other members of the family also moved into Monticello, including Captain Ficklin's youngest sister Susan and her husband Joseph Hardesty, and a brother known as "Dissolute Willie." One relative reports that Willie sold some of the Jefferson furniture left in the house to pay his gambling debts, and that the Reverend Ficklin died in Jefferson's bed.

. . .

WHEN the Civil War ended, Monticello reverted to the heirs of Uriah Phillips Levy. Those heirs were engaged in a lawsuit to overturn Uriah Levy's will—a lawsuit that would not be settled for fourteen years.

Uriah Levy signed his will on May 13, 1858, a few weeks before he and Virginia Levy shipped out on their Mediterranean cruise aboard the *Macedonian*. At the time of his death, in addition to Monticello and the surrounding acreage, he owned more than two dozen properties in New York, primarily rooming houses and other residential real estate in Greenwich Village. That property subsequently was valued at $330,600.

The Commodore bequeathed all of his city property to his wife, along with all his household furniture "either useful or ornamental." Upon her death or marriage, however, he directed that the furniture go to his favorite nephew, Asahel—referred to in the will as "Ashel"— S. Levy, a New York City lawyer, the son of his brother Isaac, and one of eight executors Uriah Levy named for his estate.

Uriah also willed to Asahel Levy his farmland in Virginia, along with "all my Negro Slaves, and all my horses, cattle, Stock and crops," $5,000 in cash, and the gold snuffbox he received from the City of New York in February 1834. He bequeathed $1,000 each to his brother Isaac, his nephew Mitchell (a son of Jonas Levy), and his sister Eliza Hendricks. Uriah remembered his nephew Morton Phillips with his gold hunting watch and $500, and bestowed personal items and smaller amounts of cash upon a not inconsiderable list of other relations, friends, and Navy colleagues.

Uriah Levy left specific instructions for the monument over his grave. He envisioned a full-length, life-sized statue of himself, either in iron or bronze, standing on a single block of granite sunk three feet in the ground. He was to be depicted in the full uniform of a U.S. Navy captain, holding a scroll in his hand. The scroll was to be inscribed: "Uriah P. Levy, Captain in the United States Navy, Father of the law for the abolition of the barbarous practice of corporal punishment in the Navy of the United States." He set a price for the monument of at least $6,000.

The large monument that his heirs erected atop Uriah Levy's tomb does not contain a statue of him. The monument, instead, consists of a tall column with a cloth draped over it. The inscription Levy wanted is engraved on the side of the monument, which also features a fierce eagle and a Navy sailing ship.

James A. Bear, the former curator at Monticello, correctly characterized Uriah Levy's will as "a compassionate and strange document." The compassionate parts of the will were the generous bequests to family and friends. The strange part was what Uriah Levy envisioned for Monticello after his death.

"I give, devise and bequeath my Farm and Estate at Monticello in Virginia, formerly belonging to President Jefferson" along with a significant chunk of New York City real estate, the will said, to "the People of the United States" for "the sole and only purpose of establishing and maintaining" there "an Agricultural School for the purpose of educating as practical farmers children of the warrant office of the United States Navy whose Fathers are dead." The funds to run the school were to come from the leasing revenues of his New York City properties.

Neither Bear nor anyone else who has studied Uriah Levy's life has figured out what was in his mind when he decided to turn Monticello into a farm school for Navy warrant officers' orphan boys. The explanation in the will—"My intention in establishing this School is charity and usefulness and not for the purpose of pomp"—is vague, at best. Uriah Levy did not address how he fell upon the idea of a farming school, nor why he singled out Navy warrant officers' orphans for his largesse.

Nor has it been explained exactly why he directed that, failing Congress's approval of the plan, Monticello should go to the state of Virginia for the same purpose. If Virginia refused, Jefferson's mansion was to go to the Portuguese Hebrew congregations of New York, Philadelphia, and Richmond to be used as an agricultural school for orphans, both Jewish and non-Jewish.

Thomas L. Rhodes, who was the superintendent at Monticello under Jefferson M. Levy, offered the theory that Uriah Levy was influenced by the unpleasant experience that John Augustine Washington, Jr. had had in disposing of his great-uncle George's farm at Mount Vernon. In the

1850s he decided to sell Mount Vernon, but did not want it to fall into private hands. His goal was for the historic house and its grounds to be preserved as a national shrine to the nation's first president.

Washington offered the mansion and some two hundred acres of land to the federal government and then to the Commonwealth of Virginia for $200,000. Neither Washington nor Richmond was interested. One reason was that no American government entity had ever purchased property for historic preservation purposes. On April 6, 1858—the year Uriah Levy wrote his will—John Augustine Washington, Jr. sold George Washington's home for $200,000 to the private, nonprofit Mount Vernon Ladies' Association of the Union, which had been formed five years earlier by Ann Pamela Cunningham of South Carolina. The association, the nation's first historic preservation organization, has run Mount Vernon ever since.

Another theory is that a family dispute, stemming from Uriah Levy's late-in-life marriage to his young niece, influenced him to cut many family members out of his will and to bequeath Monticello to none of them. "A matter of family interrelations with which the public has no concern introduced discord and the will was written under its influence," John S. Patton and Sallie J. Doswell said in their 1925 book, *Monticello and Its Master*. "If the old Commodore had lived twenty-four hours longer, it would have been made to accord with his original intent." That intent, Patton and Doswell said, was to make Jefferson Levy, Uriah's brother Jonas's oldest son, his heir.

It may well have been true that some family members let Uriah Levy know they were unhappy that he married his teenaged niece. But the idea that he meant to leave Monticello to Jefferson Levy was written in hindsight. And the fact that Uriah Levy died nearly four years after writing his will makes the argument that he would have changed it had he lived one more day specious.

Congress did not take up the matter of Uriah Levy's unprecedented bequest to the nation until March 3, 1863, nearly a year after his death. It was the last day of the third session of the Thirty-seventh Congress and it took place during the darkest days of the Civil War. Republican senator William Pitt Fessenden of Maine introduced a joint resolution to authorize the attorney general of the United States to investigate the bequest and make a recommendation on the matter to the next Congress. The debate in the Senate was short.

"It is very necessary to pass it immediately," Senator Fessenden said, pointing out that the bequest amounted to "a considerable amount of property . . . about $300,000 including an estate at Monticello and a considerable estate in the city of New York." Senator Ira Harris, Republican of New York, warned that if Congress went ahead with the matter it would also be accepting a lawsuit. Levy's heirs, he said, "are contesting the validity of the will." Both houses of Congress approved the resolution that day. That action put the ball in the court of the attorney general of the United States.

Senator Harris was correct. On October 31, 1862, four months after Uriah Levy's will was admitted to probate, a lawsuit was filed by Asahel Levy and the other executors against Virginia Levy, the other Levy heirs, the people of the United States, the people of the State of Virginia, and the three Hebrew congregations. Because of the war, no representative from the state of Virginia nor the Richmond Hebrew Congregation appeared in New York during the trial's argument phase. E. Delafield Smith, the U.S. district attorney for the Southern District of New York, represented the people of the United States.

The case was heard at a special term of the New York Supreme Court. The executors' aim was to get what was termed a judicial construction of the will; that is, to try to settle the difficult legal questions Levy's complicated Monticello bequest entailed and to clarify the duties of the executors.

It took more than a year for Smith to get started on the case. On March 16, 1864, he sent a copy of the proceedings of the lawsuit then being heard in the New York State Court of Appeals to the Virginia-born U.S. Attorney General Edward Bates (1793–1869). In his transmittal letter, Smith said he found the terms of the will "so onerous" that he believed the court "might conclude to decline availing themselves of the provisions of this will. . . ."

Smith received a reply from acting attorney general T. J. Coffey two days later, saying that the federal government had no role to play in the lawsuit because Uriah Levy's bequest had not been accepted by Congress. The government completely opted out when Bates, in a March 29 letter to Vice President Hannibal Hamlin, said he would not advise the government to get involved in the matter "which, beginning in troublesome and expensive controversy, may end in complete failure." Even if the will were ruled valid, Bates said, he questioned whether it would be "sound policy" for the government to get involved in running "purely charitable trusts, however laudable their purpose and ample the funds provided for them."

On April 21, 1863, the New York Supreme Court special term had declared the will invalid. The defendants appealed that decision to New York Supreme Court's general term. On November 30, 1863, that court reversed part of the earlier decision. Both the plaintiffs and the defendants (except for the state of Virginia and the Richmond Hebrew Congregation) appealed, this time to the New York Court of Appeals. That court heard the case in June 1865 and reversed the general term decision. Again, the will was declared invalid and void.

The original 1863 decision, in Virginia Levy's words, "was in the heirs' favor." Then, she said, "it went to the highest law of the state, the Court of Appeals in Albany, where the decision was passed in favor of the heirs." With the will's Monticello provisions voided, ownership of Thomas Jefferson's mansion went to Uriah Levy's next of kin, his widow.

That did not sit well with other members of the family, especially after June 28, 1866, when Virginia married William John Ree, described by Uriah Levy's biographers as "a young Danish Jew." According to the Ketubah (the Jewish marriage document) at Shearith Israel synagogue, Ree was thirty-three years old and the son of Isaac Phillip Ree and Sarah Warburg Ree of Denmark. He was living on West Ninth Street in Greenwich Village when the wedding took place. Virginia Levy resided on Fifth Avenue.

Two years after the wedding, in July 1868, a group of Levy family members, led by Uriah's brother Jonas, entered into a partition suit in the Circuit Court of the City of Richmond. The suit was filed against Mrs. Ree, the other heirs, the three Hebrew congregations, and the Commonwealth of Virginia.

Even though he had no children, Uriah Levy had many heirs. They included his wife, who was twenty-seven years old when Uriah Levy died in 1862; his sisters Eliza and Amelia; and his brothers Joseph, Isaac, and Jonas. Uriah Levy's sister Fanny, Virginia Lopez Levy Ree's mother, had died in 1857. There also were many nieces and nephews, including Virginia's siblings, George Washington Lopes (Lopez) and Abigail Peixotto, and Jonas Levy's five children: Isabella, Jefferson Monroe, Louis Napoleon, Amelia, and Mitchell Abraham Cass.

The Richmond court heard testimony from plaintiffs and defendants and made its decision on November 30, 1868. The court agreed with the New York opinion and ruled invalid Uriah Levy's bequest that Monticello become an agricultural school for Navy warrant officers' orphans. The court ordered that Jefferson's mansion, instead, should be auctioned off on the premises. The proceeds would be partitioned among Uriah Levy's many heirs.

George Carr, Uriah Levy's Charlottesville lawyer who also was an executor of the estate, was named commissioner for the sale. Carr was charged with advertising the sale in newspapers in Richmond, in Albemarle County, and elsewhere, at his discretion. Carr was anxious to put the house up for auction as soon as possible. But no auction would take place. What happened, instead, was that the legal wrangling continued and Jonas Levy took over the disposition of Monticello. In the early 1870s he turned his energies into insuring that his oldest son, Jefferson Levy, would be the owner of the estate.

At the time of the Richmond court decision, Jefferson Monroe Levy was sixteen- and- a- half years old.

Jonas Levy was very much in charge of Monticello matters from 1868 until his son took over a decade later. Jonas was sixty-one years old in 1868 and had retired from his maritime career. He had returned from his Civil War sojourn in North Carolina in 1866, and from that point until his death in 1883 lived with his wife Fanny and their children in a series of houses in New York.

In addition to being the family's point man on Monticello, Jonas Levy also was involved in real estate, insurance, mortgage, and other business ventures in New York. He traveled on business on occasion to Washington.

Jonas Levy carried on a steady correspondence with George Carr in Charlottesville beginning soon after Carr was named commissioner for the sale of the estate at the end of November 1868. The letters show that Jonas Levy was concerned with several issues regarding the property. They included what would happen to his mother's grave in the event of a sale; the exact number of acres conveyed with Monticello; and Joel Wheeler's responsibilities as overseer. Underlying the entire correspondence was the assumption that Jonas Levy himself was the rightful heir to the property and that he would either take control of Monticello or make sure that it was sold for a lucrative price.

In a letter dated December 18, 1868, Jonas Levy addressed the issue of Rachel Levy's grave at Monticello. "When the sale is made, a specific clause must be made in relation to the reservation of the piece of ground where my mother is buried for my family," Jonas said, "as it cannot be disturbed under any consideration whatever."

Carr wrote back five days later updating Jonas on the situation with respect to Joel Wheeler, Uriah Levy's Monticello overseer. "I have seen Mr. Wheeler," Carr said. "He is willing to remain at Monticello until the day of the sale and take care of the property without compensation. To get some other person to go there and take care of the property would require pay."

Carr then gave a pessimistic report about the potential sale of Monticello in the economically depressed Reconstruction South. The prospect of selling Monticello at a "fair price" to anyone "living in Virginia at this time is rather gloomy," he said. "Can't you find some person in the North where money is more plentiful who would be willing to purchase?"

Jonas Levy wrote back to Carr on December 28 saying he favored a sale no later than February. He also returned to the Joel Wheeler situation, telling Carr that the family blamed Wheeler for selling off Uriah

Levy's possessions at Monticello after the November 1864 Confederate auction.

"All of his conduct has been so repugnant to our family that we are very desirous to get rid of him," Jonas said. "We are satisfied to pay a good man to take charge of the property. . . . Wheeler we do not want." He asked Carr to have Wheeler off the premises by January 1.

Carr did not fire Wheeler. To the contrary, in subsequent letters Carr spoke favorably of Wheeler's management of Monticello, and recommended that Wheeler continue there.

Carr's next communication to Jonas Levy on January 22, 1869, dealt mostly with the best time for the Monticello auction. Carr suggested May. "The winter is a bad time to sell land," he said. "Everything in this country looks dreary. Land buyers from the North come south in the Spring or summer." The "view from Monticello," he said, "is much better in the spring and summer than in winter."

William J. Robertson (1817–1898), a prominent Charlottesville attorney who represented Jonas Levy in the ongoing family partition lawsuit, also kept him in the loop on Monticello matters. On March 18, 1869, Judge Robertson—he had sat on the Virginia Supreme Court of Appeals from 1859 to 1865—sent Jonas Levy a clipping of Carr's newspaper advertisement offering Monticello for sale at public auction on May 13. The judge also gave a gloomy assessment of the state of Monticello, saying there was "no doubt that the place is very much neglected and in a most dilapidated condition."

Four days later George Carr notified Jonas Levy that he had placed ads in the Charlottesville *Chronicle* and in the *Richmond Dispatch* for a May 13, 1869, sale. "The improvements are a large brick dwelling, planned and built under the direction and supervision of Mr. Jefferson himself," Carr's ad said. "It is situated on an eminence about three miles from Charlottesville, and four from the University of Virginia, commanding a view of all the surrounding country, one of the finest in Virginia."

Jonas Levy asked Carr to put off the sale, evidently so that he and his nephew Asahel Levy would have time to make the trip from New York to Charlottesville and be present at the event. Carr wrote to Judge Robertson on March 30, saying he was amenable to Jonas's suggestion to postpone the sale. He had received proposals, Carr said, to buy Monticello from "a gentleman from Richmond" and from two people from New York.

Carr had, indeed, received letters of inquiry in February from A. J. Ford of Richmond and on March 8 from Edward Blair Smith in New York. Smith's letter and subsequent correspondence on the matter indicate that Virginia and William Ree wanted to divest themselves of their share of the estate, but were uncertain how to proceed because of the pending legal action.

Smith also told Carr that the Rees were considering selling their interest in Monticello to members of the Randolph and Jefferson families "residing in the North" who had "expressed a desire some months back" to buy Monticello. But two factors, Smith said, prevented him from doing so: the lawsuits and Monticello's "very uncertain value." Smith asked Carr, therefore, to let him know the house's value, the amount of land that would be sold with it, the condition of the house, and what it would cost to repair and maintain Monticello.

"According to my recollection, the house would be an expensive one to keep up," he said. Smith also asked Carr to tell him what Mrs. Ree's exact share of the estate was and whether there would be any legal barriers to the Jefferson heirs buying out her share. Virginia Lopez Levy Ree had bought at least one heir's share of the estate. In June 1866, just before she married William Ree, she paid $6,476.61 to Uriah Levy's brother Joseph for his share of the Commodore's estate.

T. Jefferson Coolidge of Boston (1831–1920), the son of Thomas Jefferson's granddaughter Ellen Wayles Randolph Coolidge, was the family member most interested in buying Monticello in the late 1860s. Coolidge, who would later become president of the Atchison, Topeka and Santa Fe Railroad and then serve as U.S. minister to France, was dissuaded by the legal morass surrounding Monticello, as well as its price.

"If the title were perfectly good I should not feel like giving as much as the property will bring," Coolidge told Carr in an April 29, 1869, letter from Boston. "But the condition of the title is a still stronger bar to my doing anything."

Carr received other serious inquires about sale. They included an offer made by M. W. Tanner of New York in a July 2, 1869, letter and a second inquiry from A. J. Ford of Richmond on October 19, 1870. On April 1, 1869, Carr had notified Jonas Levy that he had rescheduled the sale and it would be held in May. Carr, however, subsequently canceled the May sale, probably because around that time Thomas R. Bowden, the Virginia attorney general, appealed the November 30, 1868, Richmond Circuit Court ruling to the Virginia Supreme Court.

There was no more talk of an auction until 1873. In January, the Virginia Supreme Court, following New York's example, ruled against the state in the matter of accepting Monticello. In another multifaceted and complex ruling, the court agreed that New York had properly ruled the Monticello bequest was "indivisible," and could not be broken up into pieces. The decision meant that Carr was again free to sell Monticello.

In March 1873, Carr wrote to Jonas Levy, saying he thought that May or June would be a good time to sell Jefferson's mansion. "The appearance of the lands in the country at that time is much better than in the winter and in the early part of the spring," he said. "I presume it will sell for a fair price."

In April, Carr continued to push for the sale, reporting to Jonas Levy that he thought Monticello "would bring a high price," and recommending that he place ads for the sale to be held on June 5. Jonas Levy replied in an April 7 letter saying that he "and those I represent" desired "that the whole business of that estate shall be closed."

However, Jonas then brought up several facts that strongly indicate he was in no hurry to see Monticello auctioned off. First, he pointed out that the acreage question was still unsettled. He also told Carr that Asahel Levy did not speak for all of Uriah's more than four dozen heirs, saying that Asahel represented only a forty-ninth share of Uriah Levy's estate. Jonas also expressed concerns about the condition of the house under Joel Wheeler's care.

"It was reported to me that Wheeler had made the front portico of the mansion a coach house," Jonas said, "and the house was much destroyed. Have you been up there of late years? And what is the state of the premises?"

Carr wrote back three weeks later. "I went to Monticello," he said. "The house is in bad repair, from not having been repaired for a long time. It needs painting and the windows new glass." Carr continued to support Wheeler, however, saying that the house "is as well taken care of by Mr. Wheeler as it would probably be by any tenants." Carr saw "no signs," he said, that the front portico had been converted into a coach house. "I presume the report to you of its having been so made is incorrect."

Monticello, Carr said, "is still in demand." He then offered to place an ad, with Jonas Levy's approval, for a sale in July.

On May 2, Jonas Levy wrote to Carr with more complaints about Wheeler. "You state the house is in bad order and some glass [is broken]," he said. "I think that Mr. Wheeler should be made to have all the glass put in [because] it was his duty to protect it from destruction and he alone occupied the house to live in. . . ." Jonas Levy accused Wheeler of plowing up part of the lawn and holding wild parties on the estate. Wheeler also "made the house an exhibition for which he received from 25 to 50 cents for each person who he allowed . . . in the house and premises. . . ."

In June, Carr wrote to Jonas Levy, saying he wanted to resign as commissioner. He also reported that Wheeler had agreed to continue to take care of Monticello "without charge and without paying any rent." Until then, Carr's letters indicated that Wheeler had been paying rent of between $130 and $260 a year.

The proposed July 1873 sale did not take place. Carr's application to the court to resign as commissioner was not accepted. Wheeler signed on to renew his lease on Monticello in the fall of 1873 for $150 a year. Carr continued to support him.

"I consider him the most laudable person I can get to take care of the property," Carr said in a November 21, 1873, letter to Jonas. "He is nearly blind but [is] careful and [has a] wife and a young man by the name of Clarkson living with him. I consider the property in as good hands as it now can be placed in."

Sometime late in 1873 Jonas Levy came up with a plan to sell Monticello to Congress. He lobbied for the idea at the same time that he spearheaded his ultimately successful campaign to have Congress take the David d'Angers sculpture of Thomas Jefferson off the White House lawn and bring it back into the Capitol. Jonas Levy's effort to interest the U.S. government in buying Monticello, however, did not meet with success.

Rep. Robert Milton Speer, a Pennsylvania Democrat, introduced a bill (HR 1250) on January 19, 1874, in the House that would have given the green light to federal ownership of Jefferson's home. "The Bill authorizes the President of the United States to contract for the purchase of Monticello, in the State of Virginia, formerly the homestead of Thomas Jefferson," Speer said on the House floor that day. The bill was referred to the House Judiciary Committee.

Jonas Levy explained the reasons why he wanted a sale to the government in a letter he wrote to Speer on January 21. "We have no desire to part with the property," he said. "Our dear mother is buried there. The only cause of sale is for partition, with my nieces and nephews. The only direct heirs now living is [sic] my sister and self. There is no inducement for us to part with the property, accept [sic] that our government would buy it and make an Institution to the memory of the great Apostal [sic] of Liberty, Thomas Jefferson. Under these circumstances, I will be pleased to [deal] with our government when the time comes in the most favorable manner. Reserving the small burial ground of my dear mother, a native born American for their [sic] to rest in peace."

The House bill to purchase Monticello was reported out by the Judiciary Committee on February 19, and referred to the Public Buildings and Grounds Committee. It never came out of that committee.

With the sale to the government dead, Jonas Levy continued to press Carr to get rid of Wheeler. In a November 19, 1875, letter written on the stationery of his twenty-three-year-old son's law office—"Offices of Jefferson M. Levy, Counsel at Law, No. 23, Park Row"—Jonas Levy asked Carr when Wheeler's lease was up and what he paid in rent.

At "the expiration of his term," Jonas said, "I will take the premises at the same rent and take proper care of it until we dispose of it. I understand that Mr. Wheeler is nearly blind and is not a proper person to have charge of Monticello as he allows visitors to destroy the property and takes shingles off of the roof of the main house, etc."

Wheeler did not leave when his lease was up. In fact, he stayed at Monticello for four more years, until shortly after Jefferson M. Levy purchased the property on March 20, 1879.

"It seems to me," Jefferson Levy said after he closed the deal, "that he is trying to ruin the place." Wheeler, he said, "has placed colored people" in the house, and "has not in my estimation expended any more than $75 on the place." It "is very important," Levy said, "that I obtain possession this spring as the whole place will be destroyed" if Wheeler were allowed to stay on.

. . .

THERE is little doubt that Monticello suffered greatly during the nearly two decades Joel Wheeler was in charge of the property. It appears that George Carr, as the Levy family's representative on the scene, also was culpable in the serious deterioration of Monticello during the Wheeler years.

"Jonas Levy at first, and then Jefferson Levy, tried their best to get Wheeler out because he was looting the property," Ira Dye says. "He rented it out to a black family. He let visitors go all over the place. He charged a quarter, which he kept. He did everything which, if you were the owner of that property, you would be dead set against."

Jonas and Jefferson Levy, Dye believes, "were always telling Carr to get rid of Wheeler. I know for a fact that if a man like George Carr in 1868 wanted a man like Joel Wheeler out of Monticello at nine in the morning, Wheeler would be out of the county by noon."

There's "no doubt in the world," Dye says, "that George Carr was screwing over the Levys."

Deterioration of Monticello's house and grounds began in earnest after Uriah Levy's death in 1862. By 1865, the house was "an absolute ruin," according to R. T. W. Duke, Jr., the prominent Charlottesville lawyer and jurist, who was recalling in 1914 a visit he paid to Monticello when he was twelve years old.

"The roof leaked," Judge Duke said. "The floor of the porch . . . was absolutely broken to pieces. When you entered the house you found it was begrimed and dirty and dusty." "Relic hunters," he said, had taken "parts of the ornamental friezes."

Judge Duke, who was Jefferson M. Levy's lawyer, laid the blame for Monticello's sad condition squarely on Joel Wheeler. Wheeler, Duke and many others pointed out, charged admission to the house. He also gave visitors—many of them free-spirited college students from the University of Virginia—the run of the place.

"I can remember my first years as a student [at UVA] when Monticello was wide open to anybody," William M. Thornton, the dean of the university's engineering department, said in 1916. "There was an old fellow named Wheeler who would give a right of way all over Monticello." College students, Thornton said, "were allowed to parade all up through the house, and we went wherever we wanted, and a lot of the boys would go up and watch the sun set from the roof."

Another University of Virginia student of that era, David M. R. Culbreth, said that during an 1872 visit he found Monticello to be "a total wreck," with a leaking roof, broken windows, missing shutters, mould-encrusted terraces, and a vandalized front portico. Monticello "is in a semi-ruinous state," another visitor, Frank Woodman, wrote in 1875.

Democratic Representative Augustus Albert Hardenbergh of New Jersey paid a visit to Monticello in April 1878, and had a similarly distressing report. "Desolation and ruin mark everything around the place," Hardenbergh said during a House floor debate on congressional funding of a monument for Jefferson's grave. "There is scarcely a whole shingle upon [the house], except what have been placed there within the last few years. The windows are broken. Everything is left to the mercy of the pitiless storm. The room in which Jefferson died is darkened; all around it are the evidences of desolation and decay."

Thomas Rhodes, Jefferson Levy's Monticello superintendent, said that during "the many years that the Levy estate was in litigation Monticello . . . went into decay and near ruin." He reported that the terraces had gone to rot, the outbuildings "had fallen," and the lawns "had become overgrown and dug up by swine."

Wheeler, Rhodes said, "permitted the young people of Charlottesville, in the early days of his occupancy, to use the mansion for balls and entertainments, and the lawns for picnic parties, always charging a fee for use." The Monticello Guards, the local National Guard unit, Rhodes said, "used to come to the place for target practice and were quartered in the mansion." On the "spacious west lawn," he said, "Wheeler had a shabby vegetable garden, and at one end a pen for his pigs. Cattle were stabled in the basement during the winter, and in the beautiful drawing salon [the parlor] with its handsome parquet floors, Wheeler had a granary where he set up a hand-fanning mill and winnowed his grain."

The east front steps, Rhodes said, "were broken and decayed, while those on the west side were covered with earth. The gutters of the house fell away, the roofs rotted, allowing the basement to fill with rain water and the entire house was subjected to the ruin of the elements without any semblance of repair."

Monticello under Wheeler's management, Rhodes concluded, "was wantonly desecrated."

. . .

DURING this period of wanton desecration, Jonas Levy's oldest son, Jefferson Monroe, came of age. He turned twenty-one on April 15, 1873. Not long after his father's unsuccessful effort in the spring of 1874 to lobby Congress to buy Monticello—and with the family partition suit still not completely settled—Jefferson Levy turned his attention to acquiring Monticello.

Jefferson Monroe Levy was born in New York City when his parents were living on Bank Street. He attended New York City public schools, and received a law degree from New York University in 1873. He then studied law at the offices of noted New York attorney Clarkson N. Potter (1825–1882), who later served four terms as a Democratic representative from New York in the House of Representatives.

The man who would own Monticello from 1879 to 1923 was tall, square-jawed, and sternly handsome, with a full moustache and receding hairline. In adulthood, he "was a man of great distinction in appearance," an acquaintance, Anna Barringer of Charlottesville, said, "well over six feet tall, well built and Bond Street [of London] tailored."

George Townsend, in the book Jefferson Levy published, compared his patron favorably with the Sage of Monticello. Levy is a of Jefferson's figure, slender and tall," Townsend wrote, and talks "with unvarying support of the maker of Monticello."

Frederick H. Rhodes, the son of Jefferson Levy's Monticello superintendent, described his father's employer as a very elegant man who often wore a morning coat, a giant pearl scarf pin, cufflinks made in Europe, and gaudily colored cravats. Levy smoked the best cigars, Rhodes told a Levy descendant in June 1976, and liked to eat in bed before going to sleep at night.

In addition to his older sister Isabella, Jefferson Levy had three other siblings: Louis Napoleon, who was two years younger and became Jefferson Levy's law and business partner; Amelia, who was born in 1862 and became his unofficial hostess during his ownership of Monticello; and Mitchell Abraham Cass, born in 1863 and, like Jefferson Levy, a life-long bachelor.

Jefferson Levy usually is identified as a lawyer, which he was. But his main business, from the time he left law school, was real estate and stock speculation. Family lore holds that he began dabbling in real estate in 1869 when he was seventeen years old. His business dealings earned Levy large sums of money, and he used that money to obtain Monticello by buying out Uriah Levy's other heirs.

According to the deed books in Albemarle County, Jefferson Levy purchased the Monticello inheritance shares of Virginia Lopez Levy Ree and those of her husband William J. Ree on June 26, 1875; of his mother and father, Jonas P. and Fanny Levy on March 22, 1876; and of Virginia Ree's brother George Washington Lopez of Spanishtown, Jamaica, on October 20, 1876.

"I own about one half of Monticello," Jefferson Levy wrote to Carr on April 2, 1877, and advised him not to put it up for sale, saying it "would be injudicious to sell the place at present." Levy asked Carr to repair the roof and "to see the place is well cared for." He also asked Carr what he thought Monticello was worth and what it "would bring if it was put up and sold at auction at the present time."

Jefferson Levy's lawyer, Judge Duke, testified on several occasions before Congress on the matter and was vague on the details of how much money Jefferson Levy paid the other heirs to gain control of the estate. With Jefferson Levy sitting beside him at a 1914 Senate hearing, for example, Duke said that Jefferson Levy bought "about five of the seven interests." When asked how much Jefferson Levy paid for the other interests, Duke replied, "probably as much" as the $10,050 that he paid for Monticello on March 20, 1879.

Jefferson Levy came from New York to Charlottesville to inspect Monticello in September 1877 where he met with Carr. It was clear by that time that he was the family member in charge. It took eighteen additional months, however, for Levy and Carr to finalize the transaction.

On February 5, 1879, George Carr placed an advertisement in the Charlottesville *Jeffersonian* announcing that Monticello and 218 acres of land would be offered "for sale at public auction, to the highest bidder on the premises between 11 o'clock A.M., and 2 o'clock P.M., on Thursday, March 20th." The terms were "one third cash; another third on twelve months credit; and the remainder on two years credit." The proceeds of the sale would be distributed among Uriah Levy's heirs.

The *Jeffersonian* reported on March 12, 1879, that the county assessor valued Monticello and its 218 acres at $4,360. Total annual state and local taxes on the property were $47.89.

It appears that Jefferson Monroe Levy was the only bidder at the March 20 auction. His winning bid was $10,050. That money went to the sale's commissioner, Thomas J. Evans, who took a small percentage and then distributed the balance to the heirs. Since Jefferson Levy had bought out most of the heirs, he received a good percentage of the purchase price.

Jefferson Levy had just bought Monticello from himself.

The new owner immediately began turning his attention to repairing, renovating, and restoring Jefferson's mansion. "Monticello will this Summer go through a thorough state of repair," the Charlottesville *Jeffersonian* reported on July 16, 1879. "The old home of Jefferson has for many years been suffered to go down, but we are glad to know that Mr. J.M. Levy, since he became sole owner of it, intends to put it in a thorough state of repair, keeping close as possible to the original plans and style."

Like his uncle, Jefferson Levy did not live full time at Monticello. But during the next few years he made regular visits to the place from his home in New York to oversee the renovation. There is evidence that Levy had a difficult time evicting Joel Wheeler. Several sources say that in 1879 a senile Wheeler considered himself the owner of Monticello and refused to leave. As John S. Patton and Sallie J. Doswell put it in 1925: Wheeler "had been in charge so long that he imagined himself the rightful occupant and resisted removal."

That is an exaggeration. What is certain is that Wheeler was more than a little reluctant to leave the place he had been living in since before the Civil War. Eventually, Levy prevailed and Wheeler departed.

The young lawyer and budding real estate speculator soon made enough headway in the repair department that by the summer of 1880 he felt comfortable playing host to friends and relatives at Jefferson's mansion.

"Mr. Levy is now restoring the interior of the irregular old Monticello mansion and will make it both in finish and furniture as nearly what it was in Mr. Jefferson's time as possible," the gossip columnist "Miss Grundy" wrote in the June 27, 1880, *Washington Post*. Levy, she said, "will begin this week a series of entertainments to his friends, as he intends having successive parties of visitors throughout the summer."

Miss Grundy also reported that Jefferson Levy had instituted a policy of not allowing uninvited visitors into the house "without a printed permit." She also said that many people continued to visit Jefferson's family graveyard on the property and to take away souvenir chippings from the grave markers. The graveyard, she said, "is a desolate, weed-overgrown place, and the tombs, especially that of Mr. Jefferson, have been woefully mutilated by relic collectors."

Virginia Trist, a Jefferson granddaughter, visited Monticello in 1880 when she was seventy-nine, and reported that the new owner "has done a great deal in the way of cleaning both house & grounds. . . ." It "is so gratifying to see the beloved old place in the hands of a person who appreciates it," she said, "and whose wish appears to be to restore the whole house to its former condition—he renovated the dining room and over the mantel is hanging a beautiful picture which Mr. Levy calls a Vandyke."

The Levy family partition suit, which had begun in July 1868, finally was settled on July 7, 1881. That summer several members of Jefferson Levy's family—his parents Jonas and Fanny; his youngest brother Mitchell, who was eighteen; his youngest sister Amelia, nineteen; his older sister Isabella (known as "Belle"), her husband Marcus Ryttenburg, and their infant son Clarkson Potter Ryttenburg—spent significant amounts of time at Monticello.

Fanny Levy wrote seven letters that survive from Monticello between June and October 1881 to her sons Louis (whom she addressed as "Lewis") and Jefferson, and to her son-in-law Marcus Ryttenburg in New York. Monticello, she said in a July 4 letter to Louis Napoleon Levy, "is looking elegant," the "grounds and scenery [are] magnificent." Fanny Levy enjoyed a staff of "splendid servants," she said, including "a good cook and waitress." Jonas, Fanny reported, "is happy. [He] takes a good hour to his meals and everything is plentiful."

The family put Monticello in the care of black employees when they returned to New York. "We have the colored man and his family in the place, already stationed for the winter," Fanny Levy wrote to Louis on September 23, 1881.

On May 1, 1882, three years after purchasing the place, Jefferson Levy received the final deed to Monticello and its 218 acres.

"Mr. Levy expects to have one day during the week when the citizens of Charlottesville and Albemarle will be invited to visit this historic mansion," the *Jeffersonian* reported on June 14. The article also said that Monticello had "been thoroughly overhauled and made to present a neat inviting appearance." The paper said that Jefferson Levy had spent "about $30,000" to fix the place up.

That figure is probably an exaggeration. However, it is a fact that Jefferson Levy easily could afford to lavish money on Monticello. Soon after he purchased the place he began amassing a fortune, primarily through real estate dealings in New York City and, to a lesser but significant degree, in Charlottesville.

The early 1880s was a propitious time for real estate investors, even in Charlottesville, where economic conditions still were less than healthy fifteen years after the end of the Civil War. "Possibly the only business in Charlottesville that reached what might be termed boom proportions during the eighties and nineties was that of real estate," one economist observed. By the late 1880s, lots in Charlottesville were selling for a healthy $600 an acre, and property was in strong demand in many parts of the city, including along the road to Monticello.

In 1887, Frank Stockton reported that Jefferson Levy had made great strides in repairing and restoring Monticello. "The whole establishment has been put in excellent order by the present owner," Stockton wrote in a magazine article, "and is now as sound and substantial a country mansion as it ever was. There is modern air about its furnishing and fittings which is not Jeffersonian, but the house is still Monticello."

Much restorative work, though, remained to be done on the grounds, Stockton said. Jefferson's "orchards and terraced gardens, the serpentine flower-borders on the western lawn . . . and the beautiful 'walkabout' walks and drives have all disappeared," he noted.

In January of that year Jefferson Levy, whose goal, he later wrote, was to restore Monticello "as nearly as possible to its condition in Jefferson's time," had made the first of three land acquisitions of property surrounding Monticello. He purchased a seventy-six-acre parcel known as the Monticello Mountain Tract—also known as the Farish Tract—from Charles H. Harman on January 21.

The Charlottesville establishment in general looked favorably upon the new owner of Monticello. On at least one occasion, in September 1881, the Levys were invited by the Randolph family to pay a visit to Edgehill. The Jefferson descendants "were delighted to see us," Fanny Levy wrote to her son Louis. Jefferson Levy was among the "prominent distinguished gentlemen," the Charlottesville *Chronicle* reported on December 16, 1887, invited to the University of Virginia's commencement that year.

Some in the community, however, were not happy. George Blatterman, in his handwritten memoir, had particularly unkind things to say about Jefferson Levy. Blatterman, who was under the impression that the owner of Monticello was named "Thomas Jefferson Levy," believed that Levy was passing himself off as a Jefferson descendant and referred to him as a "first-class fraud."

Blatterman wrote that he could not abide by the idea of a Jewish man "mixing" his name with Thomas Jefferson's. "The Jews never take modern names, but always such names as . . . Israel and never modern Anglo Saxon names," he said. Blatterman concluded: "I became so indignant at this scamp for daring to assume the name of Thomas Jefferson! No possible right to it, whatsoever!"

. . .

AFTER Jefferson Levy evicted Joel Wheeler he went through six overseers at Monticello. In 1889, Levy hired his seventh, twenty-six-year-old Thomas L. Rhodes. That turned out to be a very fortuitous event in the history of Monticello. Rhodes would stay on as Monticello's overseer for some five decades. He is given credit for being a tireless worker and a passionate advocate for the preservation and protection of Jefferson's architectural masterpiece.

"Monticello profited for over half a century from the inspired, devoted, indefatigable labor and financial sacrifice of Tom Rhodes," Theodore Fred Kuper, a founder and former national director of the Thomas Jefferson Memorial Foundation, said in 1955.

Thomas Rhodes was born June 11, 1863, at Rhodes Mill, six miles outside of Charlottesville, the son of Madison and Harriet Marr Rhodes. Madison Rhodes was a barrel manufacturer who served for four years in the Confederate Army during the Civil War. His son had a rudimentary education and began working full time at the age of twelve. He specialized in farm management. For fourteen years he was the manager of Morsebrook Farm in Albemarle County. Then, in 1889, Jefferson Levy hired him at Monticello where Rhodes found his life's work.

Shortly after he came to live and work at Monticello, Rhodes married Jeanette Cressey. They had one son, Frederick Hall Rhodes, who was born July 19, 1891, and brought up at Monticello. Thomas Rhodes was in charge of the house, grounds, and farming operations at Monticello. The latter included a cattle operation and crops of corn and oats. Rhodes also maintained a large vegetable garden, berry patches, and grapevines.

In the same year that Levy hired Rhodes, 1889, he received an offer for Monticello from a Jefferson great-great-grandson, Archibald Cary Coolidge (1866–1928). Coolidge was the nephew of T. Jefferson Coolidge of Boston (one of Jefferson granddaughter Ellen Wayles Randolph Coolidge's sons) who had considered buying Monticello in 1869. Archibald Cary Coolidge was a Boston-born, European and Harvard-educated diplomat and historian who was a founding executive officer of the Council on Foreign Relations in 1921. He had spent two years of elementary school, 1875–1877, studying at Shadwell in Virginia, a private school run by his Aunt Charlotte Randolph, where he took a strong interest in his illustrious ancestor.

In 1889, two years after graduating from Harvard, twenty-three-year-old Archibald Cary Coolidge put up $5,000 of his own money and attempted to borrow $30,000 from his father, Joseph Randolph Coolidge (1828–1925), and other family members to induce Jefferson Levy to sell Monticello. That effort failed, as did another one two years later.

Archibald Cary Coolidge later became an active member of the Monticello Association, the Jefferson family organization that formed in 1913 to administer the family graveyard. He was the group's president from 1919 to 1925. After his family purchased Tuckahoe, the old Randolph family estate on the James River in 1898, Coolidge was a frequent visitor to Virginia, and became active in the Virginia Historical Society. He is buried at Mt. Auburn Cemetery in Cambridge, Massachusetts, not at Monticello.

There has long been a debate over Jefferson Levy's Monticello restorations. His supporters claim that Levy saved the house from ruin, restored it as close as possible to Jefferson's design, and searched far and wide to reclaim Jefferson's scattered furniture and artwork, and that he did so primarily because of his admiration for the founding father. His detractors say Jefferson Levy did little more than repair and maintain the house and that he bought it for the prestige of owning a famous historical mansion, not because of any special affinity he had for Thomas Jefferson.

Jefferson Levy himself was forced to be the leading voice defending his ownership during the 1912–1916 movement to take the property away from him and turn Monticello into a government-owned shrine. In 1916 Levy said that for thirty-seven years he had spent a fortune "restoring the house and park" out of devotion to Jefferson.

"I have kept it up," he said, "at my own expense, not as a place of residence, but as a place where admirers of Jefferson could go and find, as near as possible, the conditions which obtained at the time Jefferson lived there." His goal, he said, was "to restore it as nearly as possible to its condition in Jefferson's time and to carry out Jefferson's ideas."

R. T. W. Duke, Jr., Jefferson Levy's lawyer and his staunchest ally in the debate, gave an example of how Jefferson Levy went to great lengths not to—as Duke put it while testifying in a 1914 Senate hearing—"alter the original building." Amelia Mayhoff—Jefferson Levy's sister who spent many summers at Monticello—one day asked Judge Duke, he said, "about cutting an oriel window in one part of the house, in order that air might be let into one of the rooms, which was very close." Duke brought the matter up with Levy who "said he would not allow a brick in the original house to be touched.

"He said: 'I do not care what the discomfort is. Mr. Jefferson got along with it, and his people got along with it, and we will have to get along with it.'"

In that same 1914 Senate hearing, Jefferson Levy gave a passionate defense of his work at Monticello and of his and his family's devotion to the life, ideas, and work of the Sage of Monticello. "We are thoroughly Jeffersonian, and I have always been trying to uphold the principles of Jefferson," Levy said. Monticello "has been my hobby, and has been my hobby throughout my entire life. I have never even married, and my whole life has been wrapped up in it."

Another Levy ally, W. K. Semple, described the lengths Jefferson

Levy went to to reacquire furniture, furnishings, and artwork that had once belonged to Jefferson at Monticello. Levy, he said, obtained the court records of the 1864 Confederate sale and then "began a systematic recovery of the relics." Levy "notified all who had purchased Monticello articles that he would insist upon his legal rights in the matter; that in view of the circumstances he would pay for these articles the amount the purchaser had paid at the auction if they were returned voluntarily, but in case of refusal or failure to do so he would bring legal action for recovery and prosecute those refusing to make restitution."

Jefferson Levy, Semple claimed, also made a thorough search of family records and documents, "as well as getting information from living friends and relatives who had known the home when Jefferson lived." From that research Levy "attempted to get in his many trips abroad exact duplicates of the works of art, furniture and ornaments originally brought from France by Jefferson."

Semple said that Levy "succeeded with considerable accuracy" in making Monticello look like it did in Jefferson's day—so much so that Jefferson "might step in the home in spirit and find it familiar with objects intimate with his earthly residence."

Levy, however, succeeded in purchasing only a few Jeffersonian objects. One was an eighteenth-century coffee urn Jefferson had brought back from Paris. Jefferson's grandson George Wythe Randolph had inherited the urn and, in turn, bestowed it on his son Francis Meriwether Randolph, from whom Jefferson Levy purchased it. Levy also purchased a pair of Jefferson's American-made Sheraton-style mahogany and rosewood veneered card tables and a marble-topped side table, although it is not certain from whom Levy acquired them.

Levy, true to his word, replaced Jefferson's Wedgwood insets in the dining room mantel, which had been destroyed by vandals during the Wheeler years. He replaced the broken tiles, Rhodes said, "with replicas made from the original designs which he found in the possession of the Wedgwood factory in England where the originals were made for Jefferson."

The rest of the furniture, furnishings, and works of art that Jefferson

Levy brought to Monticello had no relation to Jefferson, although most came from France. If anything, they reflected the taste of Jefferson Levy.

"Mr. Levy had the mansion done over by Sloan's of New York when he acquired it and on the whole it wasn't badly done, albeit not Jeffersonian," Anna Barringer, the daughter of Dr. Paul Barringer, the chairman of the faculty (the equivalent of the president) of the University of Virginia from 1895 to 1903, and a frequent visitor to Monticello, said in a 1970 reminiscence.

Make that Sloan's of New York by way of France. Levy, "mindful of the tastes of [Jefferson], turned to France as the source of what he needed" to furnish Monticello, John S. Patton, the University of Virginia librarian, wrote in 1914. "Sofas and chairs of the style of the Louis furnish the rooms, beautiful in gilt and white, with upholstery of white and rose. Their royal descent is well attested, since they came from the palaces of France, and the visitor who knows his France feels that he is in a miniature Fontainebleau."

. . .

ANNA BARRINGER provided a detailed inventory of Monticello's interior circa 1900. The entrance hall, she remembered, featured a full-length, gold-framed portrait of Jefferson as president, standing by a table upon which sat a copy of the Declaration of Independence. Facing that portrait, she said, was one "of equivalent size and prestige" of Uriah Levy—the same portrait that hangs in the U.S. Naval Academy Museum today.

Jefferson Levy later removed the Uriah Levy portrait, she said, and replaced it with a "very distingué" one of himself with one hand caressing a greyhound. The room also contained a smaller Jefferson portrait by Thomas Sully and featured classic Tole lamps with round glass shades.

Semple, writing in 1914, characterized the entrance hall as "a cool, stately room where formal tranquility is evident in the unusual height of the ceiling, an air of spaciousness and general atmosphere of refinement." Semple said the hall, as it was in Thomas Jefferson's day, was crammed with so many "curios and relics" they could "stock a good-sized museum." Semple reported that Thomas Jefferson's old walnut music stand stood in a corner of the room, upon which was placed a piece of paper that contained Jefferson's signature.

Next to the music stand was a column, which Semple described as one of "the original casts of the model designed by Jefferson, from which the pillars of the Capitol [in Washington] were fashioned." A bust of Jefferson was placed atop the column. The coffee urn that Levy acquired sat in another corner covered by a glass case that sat on an ornate table shaped "like a Greek amphora with graceful handles."

The room also contained a brass chandelier and a large Louis XV ormolu table. "This table," Semple said, "was a gift from Napoleon the First to his physician. Later it was owned by a member of the French nobility." Later still, presumably, Jefferson Levy purchased it in France, and had it shipped to Virginia.

Semple said there was a collection of first-rate artwork in Jefferson Levy's entrance hall. In addition to the Uriah Levy portrait Barringer mentioned, there was a Joshua Reynolds portrait of Lady Noel, said to be a Levy relative; a Van Dyck portrait of a Spanish grandee, Señor Miosa; and busts of Washington, Franklin, and Hamilton.

During Thomas Jefferson's time the plaster walls in the parlor were unpainted. Levy had them painted a pale yellow green. The pier mirrors from Jefferson's time remained in place. Levy decorated the room with gilt furniture and French curtains, Barringer said, referring to it as the salon. That room, she said, "with Jefferson's favorite octagon end, was one of the pleasantest and most livable rooms in the house, blending into the country about it. It was an enjoyable place for afternoon tea or after dinner coffee and chat."

Semple waxed euphorically over the parlor, which he called the grand salon. "Here the impression is felt at once of delicate but luxurious refinement," he said. "Priceless treasures of art, relics of Jefferson and heirlooms of the Levy family are stored in this high-ceilinged room." In the center of the room, Semple said, was a French gilt and black and white marble stand upon which stood two candelabra he said were used by Jefferson. Also in the room was a table carved from a solid block of malachite, a gift from the Czar of Russia, which was so heavy "it usually requires six men to move it."

The room also contained an elaborately carved clock from Louis XV's palace, a portrait by Sichel and two ornate Sevres vases. The furniture in the room, as Barringer remembered, was upholstered in gold brocade. The room contained a gold and glass curio cabinet, Semple said, filled with family treasures such as Uriah Levy's Navy epaulettes, belt, buckle, shoulder straps and embroidered vest, and the gold snuff box he received from the City of New York in 1834. Also in the cabinet: a gold locket containing a lock of Thomas Jefferson's hair.

The dining room, Barringer remembered, had "conventional" mahogany furniture and Chippendale chairs and a serving table to display Levy's silver. Jefferson had filled that room with copies of Old Master paintings and depictions of American architectural monuments and natural scenes, including Natural Bridge and Niagara Falls. Jefferson Levy adorned the dining room with what Barringer called "an oblong Rubenesque picture" across the mantelpiece.

Semple said that room, which he called the "state dining room," was "another storehouse of antique curios and relics of Jefferson." The elaborate gilt chandelier, which once hung at Fontainebleau, had not belonged to Jefferson, nor did any of the furniture, which, Semple said, Levy had reproduced "as nearly as possible to resemble the original." The room had a Sevres clock that, Semple said, Napoleon gave to King Joseph of Spain and two large Sevres vases.

The paintings in the dining room included one depicting the sea battle between the *Argus* and the *Pelican* during the War of 1812. There also were busts of George Washington, Henry Clay, and Benjamin Franklin, and an array of French antiques.

Jefferson Levy used Thomas Jefferson's ground-floor bedchamber as his own. It was the most ornately decorated room in the house, according to Barringer. Levy covered the walls in "Nattier blue damask," she said. Matching blue velvet carpets covered the floor. On a dais was a gold Louis XV bed, "upholstered in the same damask, while voluminous blue damask curtains draped to each side fell from a gold coronet that hung from the ceiling." The draperies were held "in puffs by gold rope and tassels." The room also contained two Louis XV armchairs done in that same blue damask. Thomas Jefferson, Barringer said, "had never foreseen this."

In an adjoining room Jefferson called the cabinet, Jefferson Levy hung several family portraits, including one of his great-grandfather, Jonas Phillips, one of his uncle Uriah Levy outfitted in a tight-fitting Napoleonic-type lieutenant's uniform, and one of his uncle Morton Phillips Levy. Uriah Levy's sword also was displayed in this room. A model of Uriah Levy's ship, the *Vandalia*, was displayed upstairs.

An upstairs room that Barringer incorrectly identified as Jefferson's bedroom was used by Jefferson Levy as a dressing room and clothes closet. The twin-sized bed in the room was painted pale green, as were the dresser and a set of chairs. The headboard was emblazoned with a French-style coat of arms that consisted of two laurel sprays enclosing an 'L' with a motto in Latin: *Hanc coronam facta dant* ("Deeds gave this crown").

Outside, Jefferson Levy had "low bushes" planted around the house, Barringer said, and kept "a beautiful lawn in the Virginia pattern." He placed two huge white marble lions with the letter "L" carved on their chests on the brick retaining walls beside the steps leading up to the house from Mulberry Row. A second pair of large lions—without the "L"—sat on either side of the west front entrance. On the lawn were three marble statues "known colloquially as 'Miss Venus' and 'Marse Apollo' and in the distance, 'Mistah Jupiter.'"

"Half a dozen English spaniels sport on the green lawn," said Edward C. Mead, who visited Monticello in 1898. The deep green lawn also featured benches, statuary, vases, and urns filled with flowering plants.

In addition to filling the house with French antiques, family mementos, and works of art, Jefferson Levy also introduced modern conveniences to Monticello. He installed running water, toilets, and, in 1902, a coal-burning furnace.

In 1879, soon after purchasing Monticello, Levy replaced the roof, a huge undertaking. Jefferson's first roof, which he had installed in 1809, was a complex combination of chestnut wood shingles, sheet iron, copper, and lead. Jefferson designed the highest surfaces of the roof in an elaborate zigzagging pattern of hips and valleys. Monticello's roof "was certainly the most complex of any dwelling built in America at that time," said John Mesick, an architectural preservationist who drew up the plans to restore Monticello's roof in 1992. "It may well have been the most complex of any building in existence at that time."

That complex roof leaked. In 1824 Thomas Jefferson had replaced it primarily with tin-plated wrought iron shingles. Those shingles were in turn replaced sometime during Uriah Levy's ownership. Jefferson Levy completely replaced that roof and covered it with standing-seam sheet metal. He later covered over Thomas Jefferson's original skylights (which were leaking) with dormer windows to help prevent future roof leakage, and added a new roof railing.

Preservationists have praised Jefferson Levy for making only minimal changes to Jefferson's mansion. "Except for the painted surfaces—superficial things, you might say—the house wasn't tampered with inside," says William Beiswanger, an architectural historian who is the director of restoration at Monticello. "The roof was changed and the dormer windows [put in], but all within ways that could easily be restored."

There is evidence, however, that Jefferson Levy on at least one occasion tried to alter the appearance of Monticello radically. It happened in 1895 after a fire at the University of Virginia destroyed the centerpiece of the campus, the Thomas Jefferson–designed Rotunda overlooking the Lawn.

The university hired McKim, Mead and White, one of the nation's top architectural firms, to rebuild the Rotunda. Stanford White (1853–1906) himself—the designer of the old Madison Square Garden who was considered the premier American architect of the late nineteenth century—took charge of the project.

While White was in Charlottesville working on the Rotunda restoration, "he was approached by Mr. [Jefferson] Levy," according to William M. Thornton, who was then the dean of the university's engineering department. "Mr. Levy told him that he wanted, very often, to entertain a number of guests at Monticello. It has thirty-odd rooms, but, still he needed more rooms. Now, he said, 'I want you gentlemen to take up the question of adding to Monticello.'"

White did not give Levy an immediate answer, Thornton said. Instead, he sent one of the firm's New York architects to Jefferson's mountain to "have a careful survey made of Monticello." After doing the study, White declined to do the enlargement.

There is no evidence that Jefferson Levy ever entertained any other ideas after 1895 to change Monticello. But that episode has given fuel to those who argue that Jefferson Levy did not venerate Jefferson as much as he claimed and that he did little more than simply put the house in good order and stock it with furniture and furnishings of his own taste.

"He put it in pretty good shape. He tore the roof off and replaced it. But, hell, it was his own house," James A. Bear, Monticello's former curator says. "They claim that he went around and bought a lot of furniture. But he bought very few Jefferson things. I don't think he was doing any more than fixing his own house up—no more than you and I would do. He was not there but a few months in the summer. I think he gets more credit for doing the restoration than he really did."

The fairest assessment is that Jefferson Levy, for whatever reasons, wound up making only minimal changes in the architecture. He may not have made as thorough a search for Jefferson's artwork and furniture as he and his supporters claimed, but Levy did purchase several Jefferson items and he did make a conscious effort to replicate much of Jefferson's French furniture and furnishings.

Much more importantly, Jefferson Monroe Levy stepped in and spent a good deal of money repairing—and saving—Monticello. It is not overstating the case to say that the young entrepreneur used his fortune to save Jefferson's mansion from ruin.

CHAPTER FOUR

Claiming Monticello

I will sell Monticello under no circumstances. I have repeatedly refused $1,500,000 for the property. My answer to any proposition seeking the property of Monticello is: "When the White House is for sale, then I will consider an offer for the sale of Monticello, and not before."

JEFFERSON M. LEVY, 1912

B eginning in the early 1890s Jefferson Levy's real estate and stock dealings began paying huge dividends. By the early 1900s he was one of the richest men in New York. His political career also blossomed. An active member of the conservative wing of the Democratic Party, Levy was anointed his party's candidate for Congress from New York's Thirteenth Congressional District in the fall of 1898. Levy got nearly 60 percent of the votes and handily defeated Republican James W. Perry and two minor candidates. In March 1899 he went to Washington as a first-term member of the Fifty-sixth Congress of the United States.

Jefferson Levy was not afraid to spend his newly acquired riches. He lived a lavish lifestyle, traveling often in the spring and summer to England, France, and Italy, and hobnobbing there with royalty and others in his exalted income bracket. He spent many summer weekends and Thanksgivings at Monticello, where he had a large staff of servants at his disposal. Levy also brought his own New York servants—including his valet, butler, and laundress—to Monticello, which the historian Merrill Peterson referred to as Jefferson Levy's "bachelor hall and summer estate."

He played host to many visitors. After his mother's death in January 1893, Levy asked his sister Amelia Mayhoff—who used the name "von

Mayhoff"—to be his hostess at Monticello, a position Mrs. Mayhoff relished. The two—like Thomas Jefferson and his daughter Martha before them—regularly hosted long visits from friends and relatives who often arrived at Monticello with children and servants.

Uninvited visitors also continued to stream through. To control them, Jefferson Levy charged admission to the grounds—funds he donated to charities in Charlottesville. An admission ticket most likely from the early 1890s was discovered in 1975 during restoration work at Monticello. On one side are the words:

"Upon presentation to the person in charge of the Monticello Estate, this ticket will admit bearer to a view of the grounds but will not entitle holder to admission to the mansion or buildings. Visitors to the Graveyard will not be charged any fee whatsoever."

On the reverse it says: "Visitors are requested not to mark or injure monuments, buildings or trees. The admission fee is distributed to Charity in Albemarle County, Virginia. The permission to visit the grounds may be revoked at any time and entrance fee returned."

Only a favored few were allowed into the house itself. After complaints about the fee to visit the grounds, Levy stopped charging admission in 1895.

Levy added significantly to his real estate at Monticello in the 1890s. On April 9, 1890, he purchased the Brennan Tract (also known as the Carlton Estate), consisting of 120 acres contiguous to Jefferson's mountain. Two years later, on May 2, 1892, Jefferson Levy bought 173 ½ acres from George C. Eakins. On November 1, 1897, he acquired one final contiguous parcel, the 112 ¼–acre Keller tract from Thomas S. Keller and his wife. After subsequently selling some 45 of those acres, Jefferson Levy brought the total of acreage around Monticello to 663.

On March 9, 1905, Levy bought two more tracts of land—of 961 and 142 acres—three miles from Monticello. Those parcels formerly belonged to President James Monroe. Jefferson Levy sold that property between 1912 and 1913.

Jefferson Levy's first significant purchase of property in the city of Charlottesville came in 1887 when he bought a building at the corner of

Park and High Streets known as the Town Hall, which had been built in 1852. The large, three-story Georgian style brick structure was used as a gathering place for local groups, traveling speakers, and touring theatrical companies. By the mid-1880s, though, it had fallen into disuse.

Jefferson Levy remodeled Town Hall and in 1888 renamed it the Levy Opera House. He enlarged the stage and put in a new orchestra pit with dressing rooms below it, inclined the floor to improve sight lines and installed a horseshoe-shaped gallery, new opera chairs, and two boxes on the sides of the stage.

The Levy Opera House hosted the first symphony orchestra that played in Charlottesville, the Boston Symphony, which came to town in 1891. That year Jefferson Levy leased the Opera House to Jacob ("Jake") Leterman and Ernest Oberdorfer, sons of the founders of Charlottesville's German Reform synagogue. Leterman and Oberdorfer brought in other symphony orchestras, minstrel shows, and various types of theatrical productions.

In 1907, Levy leased the building to the Jefferson School for Boys, a small boarding and day prep school, for $400 a year. An addendum to the lease stipulated that if any theatrical performances were given in the Opera House, it "shall be advertised as the Levy Opera House," and that Jefferson Levy retained the right to his box there. The school moved out in 1912. Two years later Levy sold the building, and it was subdivided into apartments. Today it has been remodeled into office space.

Levy—described in the November 28, 1896, Charlottesville *Daily Progress* as "a large owner of property in Charlottesville"—bought and sold many other commercial and residential properties in town during his years as the owner of Monticello. That included the People's National Bank Building, the Maupin House, the Early House, the Redlands Club, and the Central Hotel. In 1911, he owned seventeen properties in the city.

Jefferson Levy began contributing to Charlottesville-area charities in the early 1880s. In April 1893, the *Daily Progress* reported that he sent $93 to the mayor for the Piedmont Hospital. Forty-three dollars of that amount represented three months' gate receipts from Monticello. "This is only one of the many contributions Mr. Levy has made to this and other worthy causes," the newspaper reported.

A month later, Levy donated $40—April's Monticello gate receipts—to Piedmont Hospital. He sent $66 to the hospital in August. In February 1895, he donated $50 to the city's Ladies' Benevolent Society to disburse to needy families. A few days later he sent $100 from New York.

Levy also contributed financially to the Monticello Guard, which, on January 11, 1895, elected him a contributing member of Company D. He gave money as well to Charlottesville's Men's Reading Room and Library Association, and to the city's Citizens Band, which regularly played at Monticello gatherings. In April 1899, in commemoration of Jefferson's birthday, Levy gave the University of Virginia a large regulator clock for its library, two 56-inch steel clock dials for the Rotunda (to replace the originals that had been destroyed in the 1895 fire), and a device that electronically controlled the bells in all the University's lecture rooms.

Amelia Levy Mayhoff, Jefferson Levy's youngest sister, did not waste any time taking over the role of mistress of Monticello after her mother died in January of 1893. Amelia, who was born in 1858, had married Carl Mayhoff, a New York City cotton broker, in 1890. They lived most of the year in New York City at 66 East Thirty-fourth Street, on the same block as Jefferson Levy. The Mayhoffs' only surviving child, Monroe, was born in 1897. (A daughter, Virginia, born in 1892, died in infancy.) Amelia became her brother's Monticello hostess for the first time in the summer of 1893, and occasionally accompanied Jefferson Levy on his travels to Washington and to Europe.

During the seasons when she was in charge of Monticello, Amelia Mayhoff played host to innumerable social events, with and without her brother present. She and her husband occupied a suite of rooms on the first floor. Saturdays most often were set aside for receiving guests.

One of the first large events was held on October 2, 1892, a year before Fanny Levy's death, when Jefferson Levy hosted a fund-raising Colonial Ball at Monticello to benefit the Albemarle County chapter of the

Daughters of the American Revolution. *College + Topics*, a Charlottesville weekly newspaper, in its October 15 issue called the event "one of the most brilliant entertainments ever given in Albemarle County."

Fanny Levy "came down from New York to be his hostess," Anna Barringer—who was among the guests—said, "wearing a colonial outfit of lavender in which she had her portrait painted later." Jefferson Levy brightened up Monticello for the occasion, stringing Japanese lanterns from the gatehouse all the way up the road to the front entrance. More lanterns were festooned on the front porch where Levy greeted arriving guests.

The event featured thirteen young women representing the original colonies in period dress draped with the names of their states. Nora Moran, representing Virginia, was dressed as Queen Elizabeth I, for whom the state was named. Elizabeth Bryan, representing Massachusetts, was decked out as a Puritan maid; Winnie Sears, representing Pennsylvania, dressed in Quaker style. A group of costumed dancers did the minuet in the parlor and in the upstairs dome room. Former Virginia governor Fitzhugh Lee addressed the gathering and then read the Declaration of Independence from Jefferson's music stand.

On September 21, 1899, some 150 guests gathered at Monticello for what the *Daily Progress* called "a brilliant affair" given by Amelia Mayhoff and Jefferson Levy. The host and hostess had help from several young women, including Lulu Noel of New York, who newspapers linked romantically with Levy. The guests were treated to a lavish luncheon and were entertained by the Citizens Band of Charlottesville.

Amelia Mayhoff presided at countless smaller dinner parties at Monticello, playing hostess to visiting members of Congress, university professors, and friends from Charlottesville, New York, and elsewhere. She hosted a cotillion in September 1902 to honor Arabella Adams Moran on her wedding to Navy Lt. John Melton Hughes. In October, there was a reception for fifteen members of the National Daughters of the American Revolution, who were escorted to Monticello by Fitzhugh Lee. She regularly entertained the Keswick Whist Club and held a reception on September 14, 1904, for E. A. Alderman, who had recently been appointed president of the University of Virginia.

Carl Mayhoff occasionally joined his wife at Monticello. In October 1904, for example, a visitor from Ohio reported that Mr. and Mrs. Mayhoff were "occupying the residence this fall." Mr. Mayhoff "was most courteous and kindly in his treatment of me," the visitor said. "He showed me into the house and gave me much local history of the place."

The most famous guest during Jefferson Levy's tenure at Monticello was President Theodore Roosevelt, who arrived on horseback from Charlottesville on June 17, 1903. Roosevelt was in Charlottesville attending commencement ceremonies at the University of Virginia. He had arrived the day before by special train from Washington.

Accompanied on horseback by a group of local men who had supplied the horses, by Dr. Barringer of the University, by Mrs. Roosevelt, and by his Secret Service men, Roosevelt set out for the forty-minute ride to Monticello at 3:30 in the afternoon.

"The President wore riding britches, puttees, an easy coat, and well beaten hat," Anna Barringer—who rode with the group in an open car—reported.

A large group of guests, invited by Jefferson Levy and Amelia Mayhoff, were on hand to greet the president. Secret Service men asked the other guests to leave the house when the presidential party arrived so that Roosevelt could get a private tour of the mansion. After the tour, the reception line that greeted the guests included Jefferson M. Levy, Amelia Mayhoff, President and Mrs. Roosevelt, and Dr. and Mrs. Barringer.

"It is a pleasant memory to have seen 'Monticello' *en fête* on a lovely June day," Anna Barringer remembered, "the lawn dotted with pretty women with big hats and fluffy skirts at their decorative best for our most distinguished citizen and his charming wife, and as many diplomats and cabinet officers as were fortunate to be invited."

After Roosevelt rode off, she said, Amelia Mayhoff "enthusiastically hugged my stunned mother saying, 'Now, she has got to invite us both to the White House!'" Amelia then took the chair that TR sat in and had an American flag sewn in its seat.

Another memorable social event at Monticello was a May 1897 luncheon gathering of 250 U.S. senators, congressmen, and their wives hosted by Jefferson Levy with help from a female friend, Miss R. Stuart Wilson of Philadelphia, and from his older sister Isabella Ryttenburg, and from three Jefferson descendants: Dr. and Mrs. W. C. N. Randolph and their daughter Carrie. The congressional party arrived in Charlottesville, as TR did, by special train, and immediately were whisked by carriage up to Monticello.

They had a tour of the mansion, followed by lunch on the lawn. The entire party was photographed on Monticello's front steps—a photograph that unfortunately has not survived.

Another visitor of note was Jules Jusserand, the French ambassador to the United States, who was given the royal treatment at Monticello by Jefferson Levy in November 1904. Levy made a special trip from New York to open Monticello to Jusserand and his wife, who arrived at Jefferson's mountain with members of the local Alliance Française. Levy met the group at Jefferson's graveyard, where the ambassador placed a laurel wreath on Thomas Jefferson's tomb as the University of Virginia Glee club sang "America."

Monticello, the *Daily Progress* reported on November 30, was then "thrown open and the French tricolor [waved] in the breeze from the flagpole on the mansion's roof. The Stars and Stripes were to be seen from a staff on the lawn." Levy then hosted a luncheon party.

In 1901, Jefferson Levy played host at Monticello to 250 members of the Jefferson Democratic Club of St. Louis who came to dedicate a granite monument at the Jefferson graveyard. Levy threw open the house to the visitors, giving the group a guided tour of the mansion. "I hope all citizens of our country will continue to visit Monticello, for I am sure it cannot but help to insure our people with a love for our republican form of government," Jefferson Levy said in his speech. "I am sure pilgrimages of this character cannot fail to inspire and unite our party."

Aside from the Mayhoffs, the other family members who spent the most time at Monticello were Jefferson Levy's brother L. Napoleon, his wife Lillian Hendricks Wolff, and their four daughters. When that family came to Monticello from New York they brought along two nannies. The L. Napoleon Levy family spent many summer months visiting

what they called the "farm," according to one of the daughters, Florence Levy Forsch, who was born in 1897 and who was interviewed
about her childhood memories of Monticello by her niece, Annabelle
Prager, in the mid 1970s.

The family would travel by train to Charlottesville and then continue
by carriage. "One was an elegant fringed landau pulled by two horses,
Black Beauty and Prince," Mrs. Forsch remembered. "The roads were
always muddy and the beautiful carriage would get to its destination
splattered with dirt."

At the entrance to Monticello, the carriage would stop at the gatehouse, which was manned by Eliza, an elderly black woman. "She would
ring the bell, which alerted those on the mountain top that people were
coming," according to Mrs. Forsch. "The road up the mountain top was
narrow and winding. It took half an hour to reach the summit." Many of
Eliza's and the other black servants' families, she reported, had "been at
Monticello for generations."

The Levy nieces and their cousin Monroe Mayhoff were forbidden
to enter many of the rooms in the mansion. That included Jefferson
Levy's bedroom. They were allowed to play outside, however, and often
took rides in wagons pulled by ponies.

"This morning we racked the hay and in the afternoon we are going
to pile the hay in Monroe's wagon and bring it to the barn for the ponies
and horses," another daughter of L. Napoleon Levy, nine-year-old
Frances Wolff Levy, wrote in a May 31, 1902, letter from Monticello.

The children stayed in their own wing of the house on the second
floor with their nannies, who were called "nurses," and ate together at a
table in the bay window of the dining room.

As for Jefferson Levy, Mrs. Forsch remembered him as "very austere
and serious. Children were in awe of him but he wasn't interested in
children." He made a point of raising the American flag every morning
and lowering it at night.

"The children like to help. This was one activity when they saw him,"
Mrs. Forsch said. He "had lots of lady friends," she remembered, including "countesses and other titled people. He admired pretty women."

Nearly every Fourth of July Jefferson Levy made a point of appearing at Monticello and hosting Independence Day ceremonies. He would assemble the farm employees and guests and read the Declaration of Independence from Jefferson's music stand on Monticello's front steps. After 1889, Frederick Rhodes built catapults and scaffolds for displays of fireworks. Often, a band came from Charlottesville to play patriotic tunes.

. . .

IN 1897, the first shot was fired in what would become a twenty-six-year battle for control of Monticello. The salvo came at a time of a renewed interest among Americans in Thomas Jefferson's life and ideas. One result of the new widespread adulation was a large influx of admiring tourists. By the turn of the twentieth century, Merrill Peterson noted, "as Monticello became better known and more accessible, the number of visitors doubled to forty or fifty thousand annually."

That number likely is an exaggeration. Still, large numbers of visitors came to Monticello, and it is indisputably true, as Peterson said, that by around 1900 "conditions were ripe for the first concerted campaign to make Monticello a national shrine."

The start of that campaign was a brief, one-man mini-crusade undertaken by William Jennings Bryan, the populist politician and venerator extraordinaire of Thomas Jefferson. Bryan, seemingly out of the blue, wrote to Jefferson Levy in April 1897 suggesting that he sell Monticello to the federal government, which would turn it into a national shrine. Six months earlier Bryan, the Democratic Party nominee, had narrowly lost the 1896 presidential election to William McKinley.

On April 9, 1897, the *New York Herald* reported that Bryan had "begun an agitation to get the Government to buy Monticello, the house of Thomas Jefferson, for a national memorial." The newspaper said that Bryan would ask Congress to pass a bill to buy and maintain the estate. If that failed, he would "start a popular subscription, to which Democrats will be invited to contribute."

The paper pointed out a "slight drawback" to Bryan's plan: the fact that Jefferson Levy happened to own Monticello and had no inclination whatsoever to sell it. Levy, the paper said, "takes so great a family pride in it that he does not care to part with it for any amount of money."

Bryan, it was reported, sent Levy a letter, asking him to name a selling price for Monticello and outlining his idea for turning the house into a national memorial. Jefferson Levy's reply to Bryan was brief.

"The gist of his answer," the *Herald* said, "was that not all the money in the United States Treasury would induce him to part with it."

The paper also reported that Levy wrote that he had had other offers for Monticello and had refused large sums of money for it.

"Mr. Bryan knows this," the paper said, "but hopes that if the project is taken up by the nation the owner may change his mind."

In an April 16, 1897, editorial, the *Herald* advised Bryan to give up his plan, and strongly endorsed Jefferson Levy's stewardship of Monticello. "It must be admitted, and happily so, Mr. Levy is keeping up the estate better perhaps than the government would do," the *Herald* said. "Mr. Levy does not live there. He rarely, indeed, visits the historic spot, but he spends annually a good deal more than a senator's salary in keeping the house and grounds intact. His chief pride is maintaining [Monticello] exactly as it was in Jefferson's day. The mansion itself is most carefully preserved."

The Bryan campaign faded. There is no evidence that Bryan had any success in asking Congress to take action to buy Monticello. Nor does it appear that he started any type of private fund. But Bryan's solitary, unsolicited mission was a foreshadowing of a much more determined and widespread effort that did make it to the halls of Congress in 1912.

After fending off William Jennings Bryan, Jefferson Levy went about his business, raking in money on Wall Street, traveling to Europe, and enjoying the good life. After making a killing on wheat futures in September 1897, Levy celebrated in London by buying what the New York *Mail and Express* characterized as a "famous picture," an oil painting by Nathaneal Sichel called "The Lady in the Empire Gown." The subject of the portrait was Prussian Queen Louise, the great grandmother of Kaiser Wilhelm.

Levy continued to lavish attention on Monticello. On April 28, 1898, the *Daily Progress* reported favorably on recent work he had done on the grounds. "The banks on either side of the drive from the porter's lodge to the mansion have been sewn with grass seed, and at intervals rare and beautiful flowers have been planted, which are now blooming," the article said. "The lawns are in perfect sod and on them are late acquisitions of flowering shrubs."

The paper reported that Thomas Rhodes had planted large crops of wheat, oats, and corn, and that he was overseeing construction of a driveway on Monticello's river side. "There are to be many more costly improvements which will further beautify this magnificent estate," the paper said. "Everything about the place gives evidence of excellent management."

On August 24, 1898, the *Daily Progress* reported that Jefferson Levy was at Monticello, enjoying the company of several guests, including "a noted beauty," Lulu Noel, who lived in Washington Square, New York. Two weeks later the Citizen's Band of Charlottesville gave an open-air concert for Levy and a group of guests. In November, he won his first election to Congress.

A few weeks later, Levy made a rather startling announcement for a prospective first-term House member. He would run for the top leadership position in the House, the speakership, when Congress convened in January.

"I have received," he told the Fredericksburg *Free Lance*, "a large number of letters and telegrams urging me to become a candidate for the Speakership on the Democratic side, and I have decided to stand for it."

In Washington in January 1899, the congressman-elect of New York City gave a banquet for several of his friends in Congress, including members of the Virginia congressional delegation. Levy, the *Daily Progress* reported January 24, "has gained a reputation as a hospitable host, having gained much fame from his gathering of prominent Democrats at Monticello."

Levy's pricey lobbying campaign for the speakership failed. When Congress convened, Jefferson M. Levy took his place as a first-term member with no seniority. He held no leadership position in the Democratic Party, much less the speakership.

In May, Levy was at Monticello to greet a special visitor: Peter Fossett, an eighty-five-year-old African-American Baptist minister. Fossett had been a slave at Monticello whose freedom had been bought in 1850. He left Virginia and joined family members in Cincinnati, Ohio, where he owned a prosperous catering firm. Members of his church raised the funds for the trip back to Monticello, where Jefferson Levy and Amelia Mayhoff greeted Fossett at the front door "with most gracious hospitality."

That summer Levy spent two months in England and in France, returning to New York early in September of 1899. In December 1899 he made an issue on the floor of the House of Representatives over the pronunciation of his name. When the Clerk of the House called the roll on December 11, the *Daily Progress* reported, he pronounced the name "lee-vee," rather than "leh-vee."

"At the first opportunity and before the next roll call," the paper said, "Mr. Levy had a short talk with all the clerks at the desk who take turns in calling the roll and explained to them how he pronounced his name."

Jefferson Levy introduced several measures in Congress in 1900. They included a resolution directing the secretary of the treasury to inform Congress of the cost of the Spanish American War and a resolution directing the secretary of war to send copies to Congress of correspondence relating to the safety of the Long Bridge across the Potomac.

In the fall of 1900, the New York Democratic Party, which was dominated by the Tammany Hall machine, did not renominate Jefferson Levy for his congressional seat. Oliver Hazard Perry Belmont (1858–1908), the son of the prominent New York Democratic Party leader August Belmont, got the nomination and won the Thirteenth District seat in the November election.

Again, in the summer of 1901, Levy took an extended tour of Europe. He spent most of September and October of that year at Monticello, where he hosted the large Jefferson Club of St. Louis gathering on October 11.

In 1902 and 1903 Levy's social life, his many six-figure real estate deals, his high-stakes stock speculating, and his political views were regularly and prominently reported in newspapers in New York, Washington, Charlottesville, and throughout the country. In the summer of

1902, *Jewish World* magazine listed Levy as one of 115 Jewish million-aires in the United States, and one of 38 in New York City. The maga-zine estimated that there were a total of four thousand men in the country who were millionaires.

On April 21, 1902, Monticello lost a long-time resident when Willis Sheldon, who had been the gatekeeper for nearly a half century, died on Jefferson's mountain. Sheldon "had been blind for years, and was always found at the post until a few days ago [when] he became too feeble for duty," the *Daily Progress* reported on April 22. "'Uncle Willis doubtless was one of the most extensively known colored men in Virginia. The position he occupied brought him in touch with thousands of people who visited Monticello within the last forty years."

On May 5, 1902, Levy privately published the book *Monticello and Its Preservation Since Jefferson's Death, 1826–1902,* which was written in the form of correspondence of the noted journalist, novelist, and lecturer George Alfred Townsend (1841–1914), who often wrote under the pen-name of "Gath." Townsend made his journalistic name as a Civil War correspondent for the *New York Herald,* the *New York World,* and as a ghostwriter for *The New York Times.* He is also known for building, near the Antietam Battlefield in Maryland, the nation's only memorial to Civil War correspondents.

Monticello and Its Preservation is a paean to the Levy family, and in all likelihood was Jefferson's Levy's response to what Townsend called "late frivolous biographies" that denigrated the Levy family's role in preserv-ing Monticello. That was a reference to Amos Cummings's 1897 New York *Sun* article, "A National Humiliation," which attacked both Uriah and Jefferson Levy.

Townsend criticized James Turner Barclay's treatment of Monti-cello, bemoaned the disrepair it fell into during and after the Civil War, and praised the work of Uriah and Jefferson Levy. "For over two gen-erations," he said, "the Levys, uncle and nephew, have worked at this property, to regain and restore its Jeffersonian reality." Townsend char-acterized Jefferson Levy as "mild, constant, patient, but of discrimina-tion." It is difficult, he said, "to see how a property like this could have been conserved in one family 70 years, under only two possessors with no mistakes . . . to refurnish it, like Mount Vernon, in the verisimilitude of Jefferson's day, and restore the Library."

Jefferson Levy went to Europe again in the summer of 1902. The man the *Washington Post* described as "one of the most conspicuous bachelor hosts of the London season" gave a dinner at the Carlton Hotel in August and then got a glimpse from a hotel window of the newly crowned King Edward VII. Levy repaired to Monticello early in September, where he threw a big party for the artist George Burroughs Torrey (1863–1942), who had painted a portrait of Levy that he had placed in Monticello.

He then went to Washington where a reporter spotted the loquacious, sportily dressed former congressman at the city's top hotel, the Willard. "The Honorable Jefferson M. Levy," the reporter said, "the well-known financier and former Tammany Congressman, was chatting with friends in the lobby." Levy "was clad in a suit of blue serge and a broad-brimmed Panama came well down over his forehead. He looked in splendid health and was as courteous and full of information as in the days when he used to give pointers on the market and confide inside tips about the doings of Congress to his circle of friends. . . ."

Levy was in Washington again in January 1903, where a reporter described him as "the same agreeable gentleman and fluent talker as in the day when he represented a New York City district in Congress." Levy, the reporter said, "is considered an authority on matters related to finance, and his business career has been one of remarkable success. Though he has piled up thousands by clever speculation and big real estate deals, there are other things beside money making that interest him." The main "other thing," Levy said, was Monticello.

Levy was interviewed by a reporter for the *Brooklyn Eagle* on January 27, as he was leaving 1600 Pennsylvania Avenue after meeting, he said, with President Theodore Roosevelt. Levy was quoted as saying that the White House was "getting to look more and more like Monticello" because "recent extensions to the [White House] emphasized the resemblance between the two fine old homes."

Jefferson Levy told the reporter that the architects in charge of remodeling the White House had asked to buy Monticello's pier mirrors.

"I replied that I did not feel at liberty to part with them, even for so laudable a purpose as letting them go to the White House," Levy said. "I wrote to the architects saying that I had no objection to having the mirrors copied, and I understand that this will be done. The mirrors at Monticello are beautiful specimens of the Louis XVI period, and were purchased by Jefferson in France."

In February 1903 Jefferson Levy was appointed a vice president of the newly formed Thomas Jefferson Memorial Association, which was organized to lobby for building a memorial to Thomas Jefferson in Washington. Levy made a special trip to Monticello in April to observe the 159th anniversary of Jefferson's birth at a large ceremony at Jefferson's tomb organized by Albemarle County chapter of the Daughters of the American Revolution and the Sons of the American Revolution.

In June, the U.S. naval hero George Dewey and his wife paid a visit to Monticello. Admiral Dewey's visit was followed four days later by President Roosevelt's. On the Fourth of July 1903, during ceremonies at Jefferson's tomb, the full text of the Declaration of Independence was read by a Captain Mikajab Woods.

After another trip to London, Levy returned to Monticello early in October 1903 and a few days later attended the Richmond Horse Show with Amelia. He and Amelia did not open Monticello again until the following June, although Levy spent most of that month in New York City. In July he went to St. Louis to attend the World's Fair that was held to commemorate the one-hundredth anniversary of the Louisiana Purchase.

He was back in Charlottesville in mid July and sounded off to the local newspaper about the breaking of shrubbery at Monticello. "Visitors do not seem to realize that they are on private property and allowed to enter the grounds only by the courtesy of the owner, and do not hesitate to break a flower or branch from any plant or shrub they desire to mutilate," the *Daily Progress* reported July 19. "The practice must be stopped or Mr. Levy will refuse admission to visitors. His courtesy should be rewarded by courtesy and consideration on the part of visitors."

In September 1904 Levy was in Paris, staying at the Hotel de Londres. He then journeyed to Biarritz before returning to the United

States from London. On the ocean journey home on the liner *St. Paul*, Levy made headlines after he sold a plot of land containing fifty lots fronting the Harlem River at 201st Street in New York City by wireless.

"Nothing remarkable about it," Levy told *The New York Times*. "I just used the wireless on shipboard, so that all the details of the deal were out of the way, and all that I had to do when I arrived was to put my name on the contract. They use the wireless for everything else, so I thought I'd try it on real estate."

On September 17 he and Amelia gave a reception at Monticello for Edwin A. Alderman, the recently elected president of the University of Virginia. On November 29, he played host to the French Ambassador, J.J. Jusserand, at Monticello. During his visit, Jusserand told Levy that the city of Angers regretted not having a copy of the David statue of Jefferson that Uriah Levy had commissioned. Levy promised that he would have a copy made and presented to the David museum in Angers. Two days later Levy returned to New York.

The rich speculator got immensely richer in January of 1905 when miners at the Premier Diamond Mine in Pretoria, South Africa, unearthed the largest diamond ever discovered. Jefferson Monroe Levy was the largest American stockholder. The stone weighed about a half a pound, and was valued at $5 million.

That state of events prompted the *New York American* on January 30 to ask: "Will Jefferson M. Levy, former Congressman, capitalist and owner of Monticello, be the diamond king of America? Will his ownership of a large share of the great Premier diamond mine of the Transvaal from which a 3,032-carat stone was taken a few days ago, make the New Yorker a rival of the late Cecil Rhodes . . . ?" Levy, the paper said, "will not say, but he does admit that luck has showered wealth upon him from an unexpected source which may exceed the wildest dreams of his fancy."

"I really got into this thing quite by accident," the paper quoted Levy as saying. "Constantly I am making investments, and when the diamond shares were offered me at what I considered a very low price, I took them. But even with my real estate and other large holdings, I almost forgot the Premier stock."

In February, Jefferson Levy and Carl Mayhoff spent a few days at the Willard Hotel in Washington. Then they took off for Palm Beach, Florida. Levy was back in New York on March 18 where he gave a dinner at the Waldorf Astoria for the theatrical producer Sir Charles Wyndham and the actress Mary Moore. Sir Charles and Miss Moore were in a good frame of mind that night, the newspapers reported. They had made $40,000 in a stock deal with Levy's help. A day earlier Levy had purchased 1,100 acres of land three miles from Monticello.

His success on Wall Street gave Levy a national reputation. The St. Louis *Globe Democrat*, for example, identified Jefferson Levy—along with Charles M. Schwab and several others—as "big speculators" who had made "enormous profits" during "the recent rise in the stock market." Levy's wealth, the paper said on March 19, "has materially increased recently. His accretions have been due largely to the rise in Canadian Pacific of which he is the heaviest individual holder."

The big speculator came to Monticello for Jefferson's April 13 birthday, where he put on a luncheon for E. A. Alderman of UVA. That evening there was a large fireworks display. Levy was in London in June, where Amelia and Carl Mayhoff and their son Monroe joined him. He spent the Fourth of July at Monticello, then went back to Europe.

Near the end of his summer of 1905 sojourn in Europe, Jefferson Levy was the guest of honor at an elaborate ceremony put on by the city fathers of Angers. The occasion was his presentation to the Musée David in Angers of a replica of the David d'Angers statue of Thomas Jefferson. Levy had made good on his promise to French Ambassador Jusserand, and had had the statue reproduced earlier in the summer.

The city began preparing for Levy's arrival the day before. Museum officials placed the statue in the center of the Musée David's Great Gallery surrounded by French and American flags. Special carpets were put down, hundreds of chairs were brought in and busts by David of George Washington and James Fenimore Cooper were placed next to the newly donated Jefferson statue.

Levy arrived at two o'clock on the afternoon of September 16, accompanied by the American ambassador to France, Robert Sanderson McCormick (1849–1919, a nephew of the inventor Cyrus McCormick), and the artist George Torrey and his wife. The railway station was decked out for the occasion with American and French flags.

The Levy party stopped briefly at the Grand Hotel, which also was decorated with the Stars and Stripes and the French tricolor, then repaired to the *Grand Gallery David*. As the party, accompanied by the mayor of Angers, entered the gallery, an eighty-member military band played "La Marseillaise." Henry Jouin, David's biographer and the secretary of the Ecole des Beaux Arts in Paris, greeted them.

The ceremonies began with children presenting bouquets to the honored guests. The Jefferson statue was unveiled by Mrs. Torrey. Levy then addressed the gathering with a short, flowery speech, in which he praised the city of Angers, the nation of France, the Marquis de Lafayette, Uriah Levy, David d'Angers, and, of course, Thomas Jefferson, whom Levy called "the greatest statesman and philosopher of modern times." He ended his speech with these emotional words to the mayor, the city council, and the citizens of Anger: "I am one who ever will love you as a people, and as a Republic."

The mayor then thanked Levy, the band played "Hail Columbia," and Henry Jouin made a long speech in which he said the David Jefferson statue would be "the gem of this wealthy collection." A letter was then read from Jusserand—who was unable to attend because of illness—announcing that Jefferson Levy would be presented with a Sevres statuette (a reproduction of Paul Dubois's "Military Fortitude") and two Sevres vases "to preserve at Monticello as a souvenir of your visit to France and as a token of gratitude for your kind gift."

After a round of champagne and cake, the mayor gave the Levy party a tour of the museum as the band played "Yankee Doodle." A tour of the town followed and that evening Levy was the guest of honor at a banquet at the Grand Hotel. The next day he and the Torreys had lunch at the American consulate and then took a train back to Paris.

Levy was back in New York by the end of September. He did not go to Monticello until late November, where he and his sister hosted a Thanksgiving Day dinner. Jefferson Levy was on the Riviera in March, where an English-language newspaper described him as "an ardent motorist" who was "daily enjoying the beautiful excursions along this coast." He spent most of that summer in Paris, then extended his European stay, apparently due to an unspecified illness. He returned to Charlottesville in November, accompanied by Amelia. The two then drove to Monticello where they spent Thanksgiving.

Jefferson Levy soon returned to New York, but was back in Virginia early in March 1907 in Richmond visiting his old friend Claude Swanson, who was then the state's governor. In April, Levy and Amelia threw a dinner party for Republican senator John C. Spooner of Wisconsin and his wife at Levy's house, 39 East Thirty-Fourth Street in New York City. The guest list included secretary of the treasury L. M. Shaw and his wife.

Levy was at Monticello in April. He spent much of the summer of 1907 in Europe, and much of the fall at Monticello. In October he hosted a dinner there for the Bishop of London. Among his guests was Frances Evelyn Greville, the Countess of Warwick (1861–1938), a well-known Edwardian beauty, socialite, and writer. The Charlottesville *Daily Progress* described Levy as the countess's "legal adviser." Later that month seventy-five visitors from Brooklyn came to Monticello on their way back from the Jamestown Exposition, a seven-month world's fair-like event held near Norfolk to commemorate the three-hundredth anniversary of the settlement of Jamestown in 1607.

Jefferson Levy's political career revived in the spring of 1908 when he regained the favor of Tammany Hall, the powerful New York City Democratic political machine. One sign of his political reemergence was his appointment to an important Tammany Hall legislative committee in March.

"It is understood that Mr. Levy will take [Rep. William Bourke] Cockran's place in Congress at the next election," the New York *American* reported on March 19. Levy, the paper said, was newly desirable because of his expertise on financial matters.

"When in Congress several years ago, Mr. Levy was a leader among the Democrats whenever any matter of financial importance came before the House," the paper said. Levy was described as "one of the largest land owners in the State of Virginia," and "a descendant of Revolutionary stock [who] has been prominent in the financial world for years both here and in London."

Levy did not receive the nomination.

Earlier that year, on March 2, 1908, Ohio Republican congressman Isaac R. Sherwood had introduced a resolution in the U.S. House of Representatives that called for the creation of a commission to look into the "practicability" of the government buying Monticello and preserving it as a public museum. Congress took no action on the measure.

. . .

ON APRIL 13, 1909, the noted trial lawyer and famed orator of the day, Martin Wiley Littleton of Long Island, New York, was in Charlottesville to deliver the Founder's Day speech at the University of Virginia on Thomas Jefferson's birthday. Littleton had earned a national reputation the previous year when he skillfully defended the playboy millionaire Harry K. Thaw who had shot and killed the renowned architect Stanford White in the first media-celebrated American "trial of the century."

Martin Littleton was accompanied in Charlottesville by his wife, the former Maud Wilson, a Texas native and an ardent admirer of the founder of the university. Maud Littleton, thirty-seven, had been dreaming of visiting Jefferson's home since she was a child.

After the ceremonies at the university, Mr. and Mrs. Littleton went to Thomas Jefferson's grave where they took part in a commemoration led by the Albemarle County chapter of the Daughters of the American Revolution and a group called the Descendants of the Signers of the Declaration of Independence. That night Jefferson Levy invited the Littletons to dinner at Monticello.

Levy was a kind and hospitable host, Mrs. Littleton later said. But the visit to the home she had dreamed about for decades was a severe disappointment. "Somehow it did not enter my mind that I was going to visit [Jefferson Levy]," Mrs. Littleton said three years later at a congressional hearing. "Thomas Jefferson was uppermost in my mind. I could think of no one else. Somehow I had never connected Mr. Levy with Mr. Jefferson and Monticello. He had not entered my dreams."

Maud Littleton's long-nurtured dreams of the Sage of Monticello were dashed, she said, the second she entered his mansion. "I can remember nothing now of the house and my visit, except that I have a vivid impression of portraits—big, oil portraits of the Levys—and ships—models of ships in which Uriah Levy was supposed to have sailed," she said in 1912. "I did not get the feeling of being in the house Thomas Jefferson built and loved and made sacred and of paying a tribute to him. I did not seem to feel his spirit hovering around those portals. My dream was spoiled."

Thomas Jefferson, Mrs. Littleton said, "seemed detached from Monticello. He seemed to have been brushed to one side and to be fading into a dim tradition. Somebody else was taking his place in Monticello—an outsider. A rank outsider."

Everything, she said, "was disappointing. I had a heavy-hearted feeling. There was nothing of Jefferson to me in Monticello. He had dropped out and the Levys had come. One could hear and see only the Levys and the Levy family, their deeds of valor, their accomplishments, their lives. I wished I could get them out of my mind, but when I left Monticello Thomas Jefferson was but a disappearing memory, run out into and mixed up with the Levys. I made up my mind to find out how it all came about."

While Mrs. Littleton, as she was referred to in newspaper accounts, was researching how the Levy family came to own Monticello, Jefferson Levy was experiencing increasing difficulties with uninvited visitors. On Wednesday afternoon, July 7, 1909, with the Levy family absent, a party of men and women tore down the ivy on the walls of the mansion, pried open the shutters, destroyed the shrubbery, and otherwise conducted "themselves in such a manner that had any one of the family been present, would at once have been compelled their ejectment from the premises," as the *Daily Progress* put it.

Jefferson Levy subsequently announced a new set of rules for large parties of visitors. He ordered that no large groups would be admitted to Monticello unless they sent a list of their names in advance either to Levy himself or to Thomas Rhodes, the superintendent. In addition, all groups would need a letter of introduction written either by a professor at the university or by someone known to Jefferson Levy. The owner warned that he would close the grounds to the public for thirty days if there were another similar incident of destruction.

There were no recorded instances of visitor destruction at Monticello after Levy's dictum. In 1910, Jefferson Levy turned his attention to politics again. Back in favor with Tammany Hall, he was named in the fall as the Democratic candidate for Congress in the same congressional district he had represented for one term in 1899–1901. Levy defeated two-term Republican Herbert Parsons in November in an election in which the Democrats wrested control of the House of Representatives from the Republicans. Among the many other Democrat House winners in 1910 was Martin W. Littleton of New York's First District. In January 1911 Littleton joined Jefferson Levy in the House of Representatives, where Levy once again represented New York's Thirteenth Congressional District.

During that session Levy spoke out strongly against legislation that would strengthen antitrust laws. In April, Levy played host at Monticello to the College Men's Democratic League, which celebrated Jefferson's birthday there. In May, Levy was proposed for membership in the Metropolitan Club of Washington, but was barred by the elite club's governing board because he was Jewish. The club also refused to admit Martin W. Littleton because he was a self-made man.

"President Taft freely expressed his indignation at the narrowness and injustice of the policy of exclusion," one newspaper reported, and "has made it a current topic of discussion throughout the United States."

Levy spent many weekends at Monticello during the spring of 1911, bringing along groups of his Washington friends. Amelia continued to act as hostess. At the end of May he left for Europe, returning in mid-June aboard the Cunard liner *Campania*.

Maud Littleton spent the first half of 1911 furthering her knowledge of the history of Monticello. What she found spurred her into action. Her first move was to write "One Wish," a pamphlet Republican Representative Richard W. Austin of Tennessee called "a patriotic labor of love." That sixteen-page tract, which Mrs. Littleton wrote under the pen name of Peggy O'Brien, was mailed out to influential friends around the country in August.

"One Wish" was an emotional plea for public ownership of Monticello. Its publication signaled the start of a bitter, contentious, two-year battle between Mrs. Littleton and her allies and Jefferson Monroe Levy and his supporters over Levy's ownership of Monticello.

"One Wish" was not subtle. In it, Mrs. Littleton made her case for government ownership of Monticello in hyped-up, breathless prose. She effusively praised Thomas Jefferson for his many selfless patriotic acts, including his role in making Washington, D.C., the nation's capital.

"What a precious gift to the South!" she exclaimed over the geographic choice. "May it never cease to be grateful to Thomas Jefferson!"

She praised the capital's builders: "Washington! Jefferson! [Pierre] L'Enfant! Laborers! Master builders! Master minds." She bemoaned the fact that Washington did not contain a memorial to Jefferson, saying: "In all this glorious temple of trees and marble there was no niche reserved for him." She wrung her hands over the condition of his gravesite at Monticello.

Then she got to her wish. Instead of erecting a monument in Washington, Mrs. Littleton said, "the Nation whom he loved so well" should "purchase and preserve forever to his memory the house and grounds and graveyard at Monticello, now owned by Mr. Jefferson Levy, of New York." Jefferson, Mrs. Littleton scolded, "is not one man's man. He belongs to the people who love him, for that he first loved them. He belongs not only to us and our people but to the people of all the world wherever liberty is. And their one wish is to be free to lay upon his grave a Nation's tears. It is my one wish, too."

Maud Littleton then made a case that her wish also was Uriah Levy's wish, as expressed in his "wonderful will" which aimed, she pointed out, "to secure Monticello to the people of the United States." But Uriah Levy's wish, she said, was thwarted by the executors' lawsuit, which was decided "on the technical ground of 'indefiniteness.'" That meant, she said, that "Uriah P. Levy's wish must go for nothing," and that Monticello "came into the possession of Jefferson M. Levy, instead of the people of the United States, to whom it had been left in trust."

Early in 1912, Mrs. Littleton began organizing a national organization, the Jefferson-Monticello Memorial Association, to lobby to turn Monticello into a Jefferson shrine. Jefferson Levy, meanwhile, was busy in Congress.

Mrs. Littleton later said that she approached Levy three times during this period, asking him to sell Monticello to the government, but he rebuffed her on each occasion. She said she even had a Tiffany tablet designed that praised Levy for his public spirit and generosity in turning Monticello over to the government. Levy was not impressed, she said, and turned her down.

Levy first responded to Mrs. Littleton's offensive in a February 3, 1912, letter he wrote to Martin W. Littleton from Monticello. In it, Levy offered hollow-sounding praise for "One Wish."

He called it "a very entertaining sketch by a charming and accomplished lady." While "it contains much that is interesting, I am only sorry that the accomplished author did not consult those who could have given exact information on many points referred to."

He went on to refute what Mrs. Littleton had written about the condition of Jefferson's graveyard, saying that her description was far out of date. "The author of the booklet could have ascertained, with little or no inconvenience, that for a generation and more—ever since I arrived at maturity—Jefferson's grave and the monument erected by Act of Congress, have been most carefully and zealously protected."

Levy congratulated himself on his stewardship of Monticello itself and added his own spin to Mrs. Littleton's wish motif. "Thousands of people from different parts of the country have visited Monticello including many men in public life," Levy said, "and I have been complimented repeatedly and in the most extravagant terms on the manner in which Monticello has been maintained. As you yourself must have discovered, to preserve Monticello in accordance with its traditions has been the wish nearest my heart."

Levy said he was "shocked" by being named as the selfish owner of Monticello and invoked his uncle's name to refute the charge. Uriah Levy bought Monticello "solely out of patriotic feeling and out of reverence for Jefferson," Jefferson Levy said. "If I have ever failed to be ac-

Taken around 1870, this is the oldest known photograph of Monticello and is attributed to William Rhodes. From Uriah Levy's death in 1862 until 1879, while his will was contested, Monticello suffered greatly under caretaker Joel Wheeler. It was in serious disrepair when Jefferson Monroe Levy bought out the other heirs and took control of the property in 1879. (*Manuscript Print Collection, Special Collections Department, University of Virginia Library*)

George Wythe Randolph, Thomas Jefferson's youngest grandchild, at the Jefferson gravesite at Monticello circa 1871. Visitors who came to honor Jefferson routinely took souvenir chippings off the monument. In 1882, Congress appropriated $10,000 for a new monument and for improvements to the site, which is owned by Jefferson's descendants. (*Manuscript Print Collection, Special Collections Department, University of Virginia Library*)

(top) In February 1826, the Virginia legislature approved a state lottery plan, which Jefferson devised, to sell at least 11,000 Monticello lottery tickets at $10 each. Jefferson would keep Monticello for the rest of his life, then it would go to the lottery winner after his death. When Jefferson died on July 4, 1826, no lottery tickets had been sold. (*Monticello/Thomas Jefferson Memorial Foundation, Inc.*)

(below, left) James Turner Barclay (1807–1874), a Charlottesville pharmacist, bought Monticello from Jefferson's heirs in 1831 for $7,500. He lived there with his family while he tried, without success, to cultivate silkworms. He sold Monticello to Uriah Phillips Levy in April 1834. (*Monticello/Thomas Jefferson Memorial Foundation, Inc.*)

(below, right) Thomas Jefferson was $107,000 in debt when he died. His heirs auctioned off his household furnishings in 1827, then decided to sell Monticello. Their first attempt, which found no takers, was this notice in the July 12, 1828, *Richmond Enquirer*. (*Monticello/Thomas Jefferson Memorial Foundation, Inc.*)

JEFFERSON LOTTERY.

Register No. 1979 Combination No. 3 15 31

MANAGERS.
John Brockenborough,
Philip Norb. Nicholas,
Richard Anderson.

This Ticket will entitle the holder thereof to such prize as may be drawn to its numbers in the JEFFERSON LOTTERY.

Richmond, April, 1826.

For the Managers,

Wm. Grattan, Printer.

$25,000 in part discharge of it. There is, therefore, at this time, the sum of $72,000, remaining unpaid, to pay which, the lands of Mr. Jefferson are now offered for sale.

Valuable Lands for Sale.

The Lands of the Estate of THOMAS JEFFERSON, deceased, lying in the Counties of Campbell and Bedford, will be offered on the premises, if not previously sold privately, on Monday, the 22d of September next.

Likewise, MONTICELLO, in the County of Albemarle, with the Lands of the said estate adjacent thereto, including the Shadwell Mills, will be offered on the premises, if not previously sold privately, on Monday, the 29th of September next. The whole of this property will be devided to suit purchasers. The sale being made for the payment of the testator's debts, the desire to sell is sincere. The terms will be accommodating, and the prices anticipated low. Mrs. Randolph, of Monticello, will join in the conveyance, and will make the titles perfect.

TH. JEFFERSON RANDOLPH, Exec'r.
of THOMAS JEFFERSON, dec'd.

July 12, 1828.

Uriah Phillips Levy (1792–1862) was the first Jewish American to serve a full career as an officer in the U.S. Navy. His long, sometimes controversial fifty-year Navy career stretched from the War of 1812 to the Civil War. An ardent admirer of Thomas Jefferson, Levy purchased Monticello in 1834 from James Turner Barclay for $2,700 and repaired and restored the mansion and the grounds. He is pictured in the dress uniform of a U.S. Navy captain. (*Courtesy of the U.S. Naval Academy Museum*)

(above, right) Jefferson Monroe Levy (1852–1924), a New York City lawyer, stock and real estate speculator, and three-term U.S. congressman, who was Uriah Levy's nephew, bought Monticello in 1879. He poured hundreds of thousands of dollars into repairs, renovations, maintenance, and furnishings. He sold Monticello to its current owner, the Thomas Jefferson Memorial Foundation, in 1923. (*American Jewish Historical Society, Waltham, MA and New York, NY*)

The Rotunda at the University of Virginia today. Jefferson Levy donated a new outside clock after the Rotunda—designed by Thomas Jefferson as the centerpiece of the university's campus—was destroyed in an 1895 fire. (*Michael Keating*)

(top) Rachel Phillips Levy (1769–1839), Uriah Levy's mother, had ten children who survived infancy. She died at Monticello and is buried not far from the house along Mulberry Row. (*American Jewish Historical Society, Waltham, MA and New York, NY*)

(bottom) Rachel Levy's gravesite today, with the plaque added by the Thomas Jefferson Memorial Foundation in 1985. (*Michael Keating*)

Monticello's east front, early 1870s. This photo provides a clearer look at Monticello's state of disrepair during Joel Wheeler's time. Aside from the broken windows, dangling shutters, and weeds growing in the gutters, Monticello's roof was leaking badly, the lawn, gardens, and groves of trees were all but destroyed, and the interior suffered from decades of neglect. Wheeler stabled cattle in the basement during the winter and stored grain in the parquet-floored parlor. One visitor in 1875 said Monticello was in a "semi-ruinous state." *(Monticello/Thomas Jefferson Memorial Foundation, Inc.)*

Amelia Mayhoff, Jefferson Levy's sister, and her son Monroe on the lawn of Monticello in the early 1890s. *(Courtesy of Harley Lewis)*

Agnes and Frances Levy, nieces of Jefferson Levy, in carriage, with their cousin, Monroe Levy, on the lawn at Monticello circa 1890. *(Courtesy of Harley Lewis)*

A view of Monticello's east front circa 1890 in which Jefferon M. Levy's repair work is evident. Levy did not live at Monticello, but spent summers there and entertained lavishly with his sister Amelia Mayhoff acting as his hostess. *(Manuscript Print Collection, Special Collections Department, University of Virginia Library)*

A group of Monticello visitors, including Appleton Lawrence (seated, in suit), in 1911. The group posed with a Monticello employee (standing, left) next to one of the marble lions that sat at the west front entrance. Jefferson Levy placed another pair of lions, emblazoned with the letter "L," on the brick retaining walls beside the steps leading up to the house from Mulberry Row. The lions were the only significant additions Jefferson Levy made to Monticello. *(Courtesy of the Lawrence family)*

The back of the 1929 two-dollar bill featured an engraving of Monticello with the Levy lions. After receiving complaints that the lions were not part of Jefferson's Monticello, the Treasury Department said the design was meant to represent Monticello as it appeared in the present day, not in Jefferson's time. The lions remained on the back of the two-dollar bill until 1976, when a scene depicting the signing of the Declaration of Independence replaced Monticello. *(Monticello/Thomas Jefferson Memorial Foundation, Inc.)*

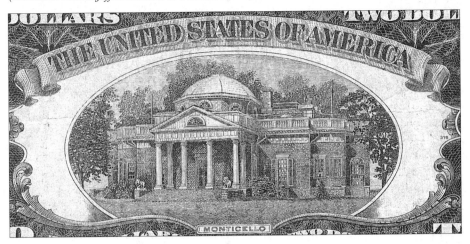

(above, right) Monticello today. (*R. Lautman/Monticello*)

(above, left) The Jefferson-designed Great Clock framing Monticello's Entrance Hall, along with the ladder used to maintain it, is one of the few items that has been at Monticello continuously since Jefferson's death. (*R. Lautman/Monticello*)

The Jefferson family graveyard at Monticello today. Thomas Jefferson's congressionally furnished grave marker is the large obelisk at the rear. (*Michael Keating*)

tuated by the same sentiments, I can conscientiously say that I have searched my heart and am not conscious of any such failure."

He pointed out that the public had had free access to Monticello "during all my life," and promised to spend whatever amount of money it would take to make Monticello into something "more in keeping with Jefferson's character."

. . .

ON MARCH 19, 1912, Senator James E. Martine, a New Jersey Democrat, introduced Senate Joint Resolution 92 on the floor of the U.S. Senate calling upon Congress to provide "for the purchase of the home of Thomas Jefferson at Monticello, Virginia." The resolution was sent for action to the Senate Committee on the Library. In an editorial a week later headlined "Let the People Own Monticello," the *Richmond Times-Dispatch* endorsed the idea.

"There can be no doubt of the wisdom of this proposal," the editorial said, and went on to praise Jefferson Levy's "patriotism and devotion." Levy, the paper said, "has done well to preserve the beauty of this estate, and doubtless as far as was possible, he has opened his private residence to the demands of visitors. . . ." However, the editorial said the time had come for Levy to "be relieved of his stewardship and Monticello [to] belong to all the people to be cared for by them and to be opened to them at all times." The paper said that if the federal government did not buy Monticello, the Commonwealth of Virginia should.

Jefferson Levy fought the rising sentiment to take Monticello from him with a statement he issued on April 2, 1912, written on the stationery of the House Committee on Claims. "I shall not assume the right to question the motives of those who are attempting to create public sentiment favorable to the purchase of Monticello by our government, distasteful as the idea is to me," he said, "but no one will deny me the privilege of correcting misleading statements."

Levy voiced his objections to statements that appeared in newspapers "tending to create the impression that I was a party to the law-suit instituted some 47 years ago, under which Monticello reverted to the numerous heirs of my uncle. That statement was clearly misleading."

Levy pointed out that when Uriah Levy's executors brought the suit he was a minor. (In October 1862, when the suit was filed, Jefferson Levy was ten and a half years old.) The lawsuit itself, he said, "was more akin to an application for instructions from the court than an attempt to fight the will." Such cases, he said, "are brought with great frequency by Executors and others acting in a fiduciary capacity."

Levy also sought to correct the impression, he said, of "a mystery" surrounding the ownership of Mr. Jefferson's grave. "No mystery exists," he said. "The records dispel any uncertainty. The heirs of Mr. Jefferson reserved their right to burial in the deed conveying the estate and have since from time to time exercised the same without question or hindrance. . . ."

He recounted with pride his stewardship of Monticello. In the thirty-five years he owned the property, Levy said, "Monticello has been carefully guarded and appropriately maintained. This will be testified to by hundreds of men in public life and others who have visited there. All visitors are freely admitted to the Estate upon application for a card of admission. Every year thousands from all parts of the world have enjoyed this privilege. I have been frequently told that the property is kept in as good, if not better, condition than it would have been if owned by the Government. These conditions have been maintained by me and my Uncle before me for over 80 years excepting the few years of said litigation."

Mrs. Littleton's plan to purchase Monticello, Levy concluded, "has no sound basis and I assume that, like other similar projects, it will shortly be abandoned for a new agitation promising a wider notoriety." Whether or not it was intentional, Levy misspoke when he said the will litigation lasted a "few years." The fact is that the executors filed their lawsuit in 1862, and the partition suit was not cleared up until 1879— a period of nearly seventeen years.

Jefferson Levy's lawyer, R. T. W. Duke, Jr. of Charlottesville, became his client's chief spokesman on the Monticello issue. Duke, known to his friends as "Tom," would be Levy's strongest and most persistent advocate during the sometimes turbulent events of the next several years.

Duke (1853–1926) was descended from one of Albemarle County's oldest families, and one that had a long and close relationship with the

Jefferson and Randolph families. Judge Duke (he had been Char-lottesville's first judge) took up Jefferson Levy's Monticello cause in April 1912. "I do not see why Mr. Levy should present the property to the Government, or even sell it," he said in an April 6 letter to Martin Littleton. "He took the property after it had been bought by him under a partition sale of his uncle's estate, with only a small amount of land at-tached to it. At great expense and trouble he began purchasing back the original part of Monticello until he now has it all."

Monticello, Judge Duke said, "was practically a ruin" when Jefferson Levy took possession of the property in 1879. "With singular good taste," he said, Levy "restored it so as not to interfere in the slightest way with its original form, spending a large amount of money to get it in good shape. He has allowed free ingress and egress to the public and has taken greater care of the property than I believe ever would be taken if it belonged to the government.

"I think he deserves the thanks of all patriotic citizens for the way in which he has preserved the place and for the way in which he has al-lowed the public access to it, and I am not at all in sympathy with the criticism of Mr. Levy in the public press. I have the highest personal re-gard for him."

Duke then hinted that Jefferson Levy might be willing to part with Monticello—if approached in the proper manner. "I believe if he were let alone he would probably be much more amenable towards a proposi-tion for sale to the Government than if he were found fault with and his motives misjudged in the public press. I believe it would be much better to approach Mr. Levy directly than by attempting to take it through the public press."

Judge Duke then took the Littletons to task—as Jefferson Levy did—for using dated information about the state of Jefferson's graveyard. "You are entirely mistaken in supposing that the monument has been broken," Duke said. "The Government some years ago erected an obelisk and surrounded the graveyard with a very high and handsome iron fence. Mr. Levy has time and again offered the Randolph heirs his services to keep the graveyard in complete and thorough repair, but there are so many of them and some of them did not like the idea of Mr.

Levy's having anything to do with the graveyard, under the mistaken idea that it might give him some rights in it, so his good wishes in this respect have not been carried out.

"The present monument and railing is in first class condition. Some vandal has chipped off a little piece of the monument, but it is hardly noticeable."

Judge Duke and Jefferson Levy's entreaties did nothing to stop Mrs. Littleton's juggernaut. On Jefferson's birthday, April 13, 1912, Rep. Richard W. Austin took to the House floor and heaped praise upon the Sage of Monticello. "I know of no public man to whom the American people owe a greater debt of gratitude than Thomas Jefferson," Austin said to a round of applause. He then called for the government to take two steps to honor his memory: procuring Monticello and erecting a monument to Jefferson in Washington.

After another round of congressional applause, Austin was granted permission to insert Mrs. Littleton's "One Wish" into the *Congressional Record*. On June 15, he introduced a joint resolution (House JR 330) identical in wording to Senate Joint Resolution 92, Senator Martine's measure that called for the government to purchase Monticello.

Six days later, on Friday, June 21, 1912, the House Committee on Public Buildings and Grounds held a hearing on a proposed resolution introduced by Democratic Representative Benjamin G. Humphreys of Mississippi to rename the House Office Building "Jefferson Hall" in honor of the nation's third president.

Humphreys invited Maud Littleton to address the committee, and she took the opportunity to make her case for governmental ownership of Monticello. Mrs. Littleton began her testimony by saying she supported Rep. Humphreys's resolution because it paid tribute to Jefferson, "a man whom I think has been very sadly neglected." Then she launched into a prepared speech on the subject "that is nearest my heart . . . the ownership of Monticello—the estate and resting place of Mr. Jefferson."

She praised Jefferson. She lamented the fact that there were no outdoor memorials to him in the nation's capital. She was interrupted by John L. Burnett, an Alabama Democrat, who argued that naming the

House Office Building—he called it "a mere workshop"—would be "very humiliating and degrading" to Jefferson's name. That got Mrs. Littleton off message a bit and she made an impromptu speech against spending public money on erecting memorials.

"I think," she said, "it would be more useful to build a road or to build a hospital, or something that would be of use and the people could enjoy."

After Barnett and Humphreys sparred briefly over the office building naming, Mrs. Littleton returned to her Monticello script. "It is a sacred place," she said, "not one of national but of international importance." Her wish, she said, was that Monticello "will become forever a shrine, a place where our children and our children's children may go to learn lessons of history and freedom. It is too sacred a trust to be left in the care of one individual."

She gave the impression that Jefferson Levy controlled access to the Jefferson family graveyard. "The right to go to and from his grave belongs to the unnumbered generations, and the right can not be narrowed down to the rights of one individual whose proprietorship rests upon naked purchase." Then she scolded Levy for his selfishness. "However much this proprietor may venerate the memory of Mr. Jefferson and rejoice in the ownership of his old home, he should not appropriate to himself, even in this spirit of veneration, that which is common to every human being in the Republic. . . ."

Monticello, she said, was in physical danger because Jefferson Levy did not live there year round. Monticello "should not be used as a summer house," Mrs. Littleton said, "but should be absolutely guaranteed against loss by fire, or otherwise, under the vigilant eye and in the affectionate solicitude of the whole nation." She faulted Levy for using Monticello as "a personal exhibit," and intimated that his wealthy and luxurious social life there was "grotesque."

Those inflammatory words were merely a preview of what came next: two bombastic congressional hearings that made front-page headlines in newspapers across the country in July 1912 in which Maud Littleton went head to head with Jefferson Levy and Judge Duke over the future of Levy's ownership of Thomas Jefferson's Monticello.

. . .

AT TWO o'clock on the afternoon of Tuesday, July 9, 1912, the thermometer outside the U.S. Capitol in Washington registered 110 degrees. Moments before, a taxicab pulled up to the Senate side of the Hill. Maud Littleton stepped out, alone, and walked through the stuffy corridors of the Senate to the small room where the Senate Committee on the Library was about to hold a hearing called "Public Ownership of Monticello."

She was clad, the Washington *Herald* reported the next day, "in a white fluffy lace dress, a black hat and white slippers." Armed with a long prepared speech and with a large stack of letters she had received in response to her "One Wish" mailing, Mrs. Littleton faced a friendly group of senators.

"I feel a trifle nervous," she said as she prepared to give her testimony. Her nervousness vanished as she launched her blistering, all-out attack on Jefferson Levy's ownership. She began, as was her pattern, by reminding the senators that there was no memorial to Thomas Jefferson in Washington, and by singing his praises and extolling Monticello. Mrs. Littleton also praised John Augustine Washington and the descendants of Robert E. Lee and Andrew Jackson for "patriotically surrendering their historic houses as national memorials."

Mrs. Littleton expressed indignation that Monticello was in private hands. "It is not a pleasant thing to be obliged to go upon private property to pay a visit to the tomb of Jefferson," she said. Characterizing Monticello as a "poor, neglected, forsaken home," Mrs. Littleton accused Jefferson Levy of making it a memorial to Uriah Levy.

She then offered her version of the "complete history" of Monticello, going back to 1735 when Peter Jefferson gained title to the land. When she got to Uriah Levy's 1834 purchase, Mrs. Littleton repeated the unsubstantiated story that had Uriah Levy stealing Monticello from another buyer.

Mrs. Littleton then reviewed, in laborious detail, Uriah Levy's will, the congressional debate over whether to accept the bequest, and the executors' lawsuit. She again said that the New York Supreme Court decision voiding the will was based on "the technical ground of 'indefiniteness.'" That technicality, she said, meant that "Uriah Levy's wish, which was solemnly written in his will," that Monticello be used as a school for the orphans of Navy warrant officers, "must go for nothing." Worse, she said, was the ultimate outcome: "that Monticello came into the possession of Jefferson M. Levy, instead of the people of the United States, to whom it had been left in trust."

She repeated, in detail, the story of Uriah Levy's gift of the David d'Angers Jefferson statue and the forty-year wait before Congress officially accepted it. She quoted from a Jefferson Levy–friendly (and probably Levy-written) biography in the 1892 edition of the *National Cyclopaedia of American Biography* in which Jefferson Levy was identified as Thomas Jefferson's grandson.

"This is not true," Mrs. Littleton said. "J. M. Levy is not the grandson and he did not inherit Monticello. These mistakes have always done so much harm, and it is a good thing to have them straightened out."

Mrs. Littleton went into more detail about the condition of the Jefferson graveyard. She recounted proceedings in Congress in 1878 that resulted in a $5,000 congressional appropriation to pay for a new monument—providing Jefferson's descendants gave title to the graveyard to the government. She took care to point out that Jefferson Levy, who had gained title to Monticello the year before, objected to the appropriation.

In a July 13, 1878, letter to Secretary of State William H. Evarts, Jefferson Levy had mistakenly claimed that he owned the graveyard. After the attorney general of the United States looked into the matter, Levy was forced to face the reality that the graveyard did not convey to him when he purchased Monticello.

The descendants did not accept Congress's conditions in 1878. Four years later, in April 1882, Congress—with no strings attached—appropriated $10,000 for the erection of a monument over Jefferson's grave and for other improvements to the site. A new, eighteen-foot granite monument was placed on Jefferson's grave that fall. Repairs were made to six other graves, a new iron fence was installed, and the entire site was graded, reseeded and resodded. The family donated the old monument from Jefferson's grave to the University of Missouri in 1885.

Mrs. Littleton did not mention the federally funded refurbishment in her testimony. And she gave what can only be described as untruthful testimony when she told the committee that Jefferson family members "have not much heart to go to Monticello, and I believe they rarely visit the place. . . . I think it is very mortifying to them. I believe they are in the habit of making occasional visits there to make sure of their owner-ship [of the cemetery]; that it was not escaping from them."

Jefferson Levy, she said, "persistently refused" to give the public ac-cess to the Jefferson family graveyard. "Mr. Levy owns all the surround-ing grounds, the Government built the monument, and Mr. J. M. Levy is the only one who has access to the grave of Thomas Jefferson, except the Jefferson heirs. . . . No human being has the right to go there, except Mr. Levy and the Randolph family."

Showing photographs she said she had recently taken, Mrs. Littleton again decried the condition of the graveyard. "As you can see by these pictures, the graveyard is in a very dilapidated condition," she said. "There is no path in it and the weeds are very bad. The Randolphs feel keen chagrin and mortification and do not like to go there at all because they have to pass through property which they do not care to pass through."

Not all the Randolphs felt that way. In a letter that appeared in the July 15, 1912, *Washington Post*, Cornelia Jefferson Taylor took Mrs. Lit-tleton to task for mischaracterizing the condition of the graveyard and the family's feelings about Jefferson Levy and Monticello.

"Most of the graves, except those of very recent date, have monu-ments," Taylor—the granddaughter of Jefferson's favorite grandson, Thomas Jefferson Randolph—said. "A man is employed to cut and trim the grass at intervals during the year. Probably Mrs. Littleton saw the place after a rainy season and when some weeks had passed since the man's last visit.

"The tomb is not 'shamefully neglected,' as Mrs. Littleton asserts. With its surroundings, it is watched over, cared for, and constantly vis-ited by those to whom it is sacred as the resting place not only of a great man, but of a long list of loved ones of whom he was the ancestor."

Cornelia Taylor said she spoke "with authority, as the graveyard is cared for my myself and Mrs. William Mann Randolph, granddaughters of Col. Thomas Jefferson Randolph." She also had kind words for Jefferson Levy.

"I have found him always most deferential in manner to me and mine and exceedingly hospitable and kind," she said in a 1904 family letter.

W. N. Ruffin, of Danville, Virginia, a great-great grandson of Jefferson, also spoke out on Levy's behalf. "As one of the oldest descendants of Mr. Jefferson and speaking, I believe, for a large majority of them, we not only disapprove of Mrs. Martin W. Littleton's proposition that the Government shall condemn Monticello and take it from Mr. Levy, but believe that such a move is diametrically opposed to all of Mr. Jefferson's ideas of right, justice and fair dealing," Ruffin told *The New York Times*.

"Mr. Levy came by this property honestly and is entitled to enjoy it as to him seems best. We do not believe and cannot comprehend that any right-thinking man can approve or sanction such a high-handed proceeding on the part of the Government."

At the committee hearing, Mrs. Littleton wound up her presentation with more heavy ammunition: photographs of the entrance to Monticello, which proved, she said, that the property "is not well kept up." Being well kept, she conceded, "is a matter of opinion," but, she said, "I have met a great many people who do not consider [Monticello] to be very well kept up. I do not believe many good housekeepers would consider it well kept up."

As for the house itself, Mrs. Littleton said she did not take any photographs of it because "I did not feel I was at liberty to do so." This did not stop her from giving a negative description of the house's condition. It is "closed most of the time," she said, and "needs nails here and putty there. The painting is gradually fading away. Lack of personal attention is the impression one receives upon looking the place over—except the vegetable garden; it seemed prosperous."

There was little truth to those allegations. From all other accounts, Jefferson Levy and Thomas Rhodes kept Monticello in excellent condition, inside and out.

"Monticello itself is well cared for and kept in order by the owner, so there is no need for anyone's sensibilities to suffer," Cornelia Taylor said in her letter.

"To say that [Jefferson Levy] fails to keep up the house and grounds properly is unjust," the Charlottesville *Daily Progress* said in a July 17 editorial. "The house and grounds have never been better kept since the death of Mr. Jefferson, and probably were in no better condition in the life of the statesman. The truth is, they could not be better cared for than they are."

Mrs. Littleton ended her prepared testimony with a presentation of hundreds of letters of support for her cause.

Cornelia Taylor, among others, came to Jefferson Levy's defense concerning keeping uninvited visitors out of the house. Levy, she said in her *Washington Post* letter, "has always kindly allowed visitors on the grounds, and any thoughtful person can sympathize with him in not admitting them to the house, when we realize the destructive propensities of the American sightseer. . . ."

The *Daily Progress* editorial agreed, saying "it is equally unjust to say that people have trouble in obtaining permission to enter. There are no restrictions of this kind that ought not to be imposed. In spite of the fact of vandalism and general disregard of the rights of the owner, Mr. Levy still allows all comers to visit the grounds, and on special occasion admits visitors to the house."

The editorial did not mention that Mrs. Littleton herself had been Jefferson's Levy's dinner guest on one special occasion. The editorial concluded: "At a great expense to himself, Mr. Levy is the host of those admirers of Jefferson who visit the old estate. There is nothing selfish in his ownership."

Judge Duke spoke up at the hearing on this point, as well. "I live at Charlottesville," he said. "I have never known of anybody being refused admission to [the grounds at] Monticello."

As for the interior, Judge Duke criticized Jefferson Levy's decorating scheme—"It is very bad taste," he said—but defended his upkeep. "The house is in very nice repair in the interior," Duke said. "I agree that it needs a coat of paint, but they have made preparation for doing that."

Duke then directly confronted Mrs. Littleton, asking her if she was certain that she was correct in saying Monticello was not well kept up. She shot back: "Mr. Duke and I are diametrically opposed. He is attorney for Mr. Levy and he and I could not possible agree."

Mrs. Littleton vehemently denied not telling the truth as she saw it about Monticello. "I have stated nothing but the exact truth," she said, "and I have shown everything—records and pictures—to prove it."

When asked specifically by committee chairman George P. Wetmore whether she believed Monticello was well kept up, Mrs. Littleton said: "No," but shifted the argument to Jefferson Levy's alleged selfishness.

"The question is," she said, "Is Mr. Levy the only person in the whole world who has the right to Monticello and access to the grave of Thomas Jefferson?"

When asked what Jefferson Levy's attitude was about selling, Judge Duke said: "I think he would just as soon sell the kingdom of heaven as to sell Monticello. If properly approached, I think he might take the patriotic view of it and sell it to the United States Government. But he looks at the place as the apple of his eye."

Senator Albert Cummins, an Iowa Republican, brushed off Levy's wishes on the subject and, as Senator Martine did, raised the condemnation specter. "When we build a railroad, if we find it necessary to take a man's property . . . we can take it by condemnation proceedings," he said. "And if the Government of the United States wants Monticello, it can take it."

Mrs. Littleton then introduced a letter from James W. Beck, the former solicitor general of the United States, in which he made a case that government condemnation of Monticello would be legal. Soon thereafter, around four in the afternoon, the committee went into executive session. Fifteen minutes later the senators reassembled and Senator Wetmore announced that they had voted in favor of Senator Martine's resolution.

The next day's three-column headline in the *Washington Herald* read: "Mrs. Littleton Scores Victory in Her Fight for Monticello."

Jefferson Levy did not appear at the July 9 hearing. He gave several newspaper interviews following the hearing, though, disputing Mrs. Littleton's contention that Monticello was not well kept up and that the public did not have access to the Jefferson gravesite. Mrs. Littleton answered those charges in a scathing statement that appeared in the July 12 *New York Post*, in which she repeated many of the arguments she made in the Senate hearing.

"Oh, fudge!" she said. "This talk of Mr. Levy about not answering the facts I presented to the Library Senate Committee is wearisome. It was a public hearing . . . to which Mr. Levy should have appeared, and made these statements which he now is feeding to the public through the press." She then misrepresented Judge Duke's statements, saying he "did not dispute any facts I presented" at the committee hearing. Levy, she said, "cannot answer the facts which were presented to the committee by being absent and assuming the air of injured innocence."

The question at hand, she said again, was not Levy's upkeep of Monticello. It hinged instead on other more important questions: "Is Mr. Levy the only human being in the whole world who has a right to enjoy Monticello? Is he the only human being in the whole world who should have the right of access to the grave of Thomas Jefferson? And are the people of the United States willing to let him retain that right for the purchase price of $10,050, which he paid to his relatives to get it when they succeeded in breaking Uriah Levy's will?"

Jefferson Levy, she argued, was trying to get "the world to accept [Monticello] as a memorial to the Levy family," saying "they have begun to bury there" and "they delight to immortalize their late ancestor as the 'father and author of the abolition of flogging in the navy.'"

It is true that the Levys often proudly pointed to Uriah Levy's role in abolishing flogging in the Navy. But Mrs. Littleton's contention that the family was starting a Levy graveyard at Monticello was a complete falsehood. The only Levy family member buried at Monticello is Uriah Levy's mother Rachel, who was put to rest there in 1839. Between 1839 and 1912 the Levy family members who had died—including Uriah Levy himself and Jefferson Levy's parents, Jonas and Fanny—were buried elsewhere.

On July 17, the U.S. Senate took up a slightly reworded version of Senator Martine's resolution. Senator Cummins introduced the modified resolution, which was designed, he said on the Senate floor, to "remove every objection that has been or could be suggested to it." He deleted the resolution's preamble, which could have been viewed as an endorsement of congressional seizure of Monticello. That left a resolution simply calling for a joint Senate-House committee to "inquire into the wisdom and ascertain the cost of acquiring Monticello . . . that it may be preserved for all time in its entirety for the American people."

Republican Senator Henry Cabot Lodge of Massachusetts initially was not convinced that the new resolution did not give Congress permission to take Monticello. It is "apparently a scheme to take the property of somebody who does not want to sell it, as I understand," Lodge said on Senate floor.

Cummins reassured Lodge that he was mistaken, and that the resolution would simply call for the "appointment of a committee to inform the Senate and the House." There was no further debate, but the Senate decided to postpone action on the resolution.

Then, on July 24, the House Rules Committee held a hearing on a companion Monticello resolution to the one the Senate had considered a week earlier. Mrs. Littleton was the first witness. She gave another long presentation, touching on most of the same points she had testified about two weeks earlier. She once again lionized Thomas Jefferson and demonized Jefferson Levy, accusing him of turning Monticello into "a memorial" to Uriah Levy.

Near the end of her long testimony Mrs. Littleton launched into an emotional attack, accusing Jefferson Levy once again of selfishness and a lack of patriotism. Levy, she said, "knows that Monticello should belong to all the people. He knows it should be public property." By what right, she asked, "must the people ask Mr. Levy's permission to visit the home and grave of Thomas Jefferson? Is it only through his favor that we can take our children up to the top of that little mountain to teach them lessons of history?"

She then presented the House Rules Committee with what she said were one thousand letters she had received in support of her cause. That included one from Governor Woodrow Wilson of New Jersey, who wished her project well "with all my heart."

Newspaper editorials weighed in on the subject, many endorsing

Mrs. Littleton's plan. The *Daily Progress*, a strong Jefferson Levy supporter, came out in favor of government ownership. "Our feeling is that
as Mr. Levy must one day go off the scene, there is uncertainty as to
what will befall the estate after he has departed," a July 30 editorial said.
"It cannot fall into better hands and it might fall into worse. National
ownership under conditions is very desirable. . . ."

The paper argued against government confiscation, though, saying in
an August 2 editorial that that "would be a poor reward for the generous
behavior of the man who owns the title." That editorial also contained
strong words of praise for the Levy family. The paper noted that Monticello had been in the family's hands for eighty years, that Uriah Levy
bought it "not as an investment or in the pursuit of selfish aims," and
that Jefferson Levy "has not trafficked with it nor sought any incre-
ment." Jefferson Levy's ownership "and stewardship are sincere expressions of his reverence for [Thomas Jefferson] and any attempt to bring
to bear upon him the compulsion of public emotional criticism is at best
ungracious and it amounts to unfairness when even incidental misrepre-
sentation enters into the game."

. . .

THE NEXT act in the congressional drama came on August 8 when the
House Rules Committee reconvened to give Jefferson Levy a chance to
give his side of the story. He took the opportunity to make an unforgiv-
ing, emotional pitch to keep Monticello, telling the committee: "Every
stone and every brick in the house of Jefferson, every tree, every nook
and corner, every foot of Monticello is dear and sacred to me. And
never will I listen to any suggestion for disposing of it, whether coming
from a private or public source."

Levy received support at the hearing from Republican Representative William Wedemeyer of Michigan, who told the committee he had
made an unannounced visit to Monticello and found no evidence of neglect. Eugene V. Daly of New York City, Jefferson Levy's legal counsel,
made an argument against the government's acquisition of Monticello
by condemnation.

Mrs. Littleton spoke last. She began with an unexpected change of
tactics. Mrs. Littleton, *The Washington Post* said, "surprised all by begin-

ning her remarks with a statement that she had no criticism to make on the way the property was maintained." She then launched into an impassioned speech pleading with the committee to make the property into a government-owned Jefferson shrine.

At the end of her testimony, she burst into tears.

At the end of the hearing, the committee voted to bring the resolution to the floor of the House of Representatives.

Mrs. Littleton's tears did not sit well with some people. Flora Wilson, a young woman whom gossip columnists had linked romantically with Jefferson Levy, was the most vocal about it. Wilson, a suffragist and the daughter of Agriculture Secretary James Wilson, wrote an article in the August 10, 1912, *Washington Post* taking Maud Littleton to task for her public emotional outburst.

"Is this the way women are to plead for what they want?" Flora Wilson said. "Can we ever achieve our purposes employing as does a spoiled child the last resort to get his own way?" She then listed a group of famous women who, she said, "unlike Mrs. Littleton, did not weep in battle for their causes: Clara Barton, Florence Nightingale, Jane Addams, Catherine de Medici, and Mary Queen of Scots."

Flora Wilson also criticized Maud Littleton along feminist lines for abruptly changing her tune on the upkeep question. "When, pray tell me, will committees take us seriously if we argue in that manner?" Wilson asked.

She went on make a strong pitch for Jefferson Levy. Monticello, she said, "can never serve more public benefit, utility, or advantage than is now true in the conduct of the place. It is open from sunrise to sunset." There "would be no incentive to recover Monticello," she said, "had not the Levy family guarded it as precious grounds belonging to the great Jefferson."

The *Post* carried a response from Mrs. Littleton in the same issue. "The only difference between Miss Wilson and myself," she said, "is that she is a friend of Mr. Jefferson Levy and I am a friend of Thomas Jefferson."

Jefferson Levy likely had a hand in crafting Flora Wilson's comments. It's likely also that he influenced the words in a letter to the editor from his brother. In the letter, which appeared on August 13 in both *The New York Times* and the New York *Herald*, L. Napoleon Levy spoke of Mrs. Littleton's many "misleading statements and innuendoes regarding Monticello." He refuted one such misstatement: that Jefferson Levy had neglected the place.

"My brother has always taken great pride in maintaining the lands in a high state of cultivation," he said, "and the mansion is in an excellent condition of repair, equal to, if not better, than at any time during its existence and the eighty-four years my family has owned it. All visitors have been and are welcomed, meeting with courteous treatment at the hands of the present manager, who has been on the estate some twenty-three years." A visit to Monticello, L. Napoleon Levy said, would prove what he said.

The day that letter appeared in the New York newspapers something strange happened on the floor of the House of Representatives. Jefferson Levy and Republican Nicholas Longworth of Ohio—who later became Speaker of the House—nearly got into a fistfight. According to an article in the August 12 Nashville *Democrat*, Longworth and Levy had "an altercation on the floor of the House today, during which Mr. Longworth invited Mr. Levy 'to come outside with him,' where they would settle their differences."

The contretemps arose during a vote to override a presidential veto on the wool bill. It was a contentious debate, with Republicans complaining that Democrats were unfairly attacking President William Howard Taft. Levy and Longworth denied the incident took place.

In August, the New York newspapers reported that because of severe redistricting, Levy and three other New York City congressmen would not be nominated by Tammany Hall to run for reelection in the fall. It appeared that Levy's political career, at least in the House of Representatives, would come to an end.

Rumors abounded in Washington that summer that Levy was engaged to Flora Wilson. Levy put an end to the speculation in a September 2 telephone conversation he had with a *New York Times* Washington bureau reporter. The *Times* reported on September 4 that Levy said such reports a "had no other basis than the possible desire of somebody to make capital out of the fact that Miss Wilson recently came to his rescue by publicly declaring against the federal acquisition of Monticello over his protest."

On October 11, Levy's political career was resurrected when he was named the Democratic candidate from the newly realigned Fourteenth New York Congressional District. He ran a modest campaign, spending only $100, according to figures released by the Clerk of the House on October 28. Levy won his third House race in the general election the next week, outdistancing the Republican E. Crosby Kindleberger and the Progressive candidate, Abraham H. Goodman.

Throughout the late summer and fall Mrs. Littleton carried on her letter-writing campaign. Her office was based in her New York City home, at 113 East Fifty-seventh Street. The elaborate Jefferson-Monticello Memorial Association stationery she had made up was emblazoned with renderings of Jefferson's gravesite and Monticello itself. Under the banner "Public Ownership of Monticello," was a quote from Jefferson: "Take care of me when dead."

Under the Monticello drawing were the words: "Monticello—which sheltered Jefferson—His home in life as it is now in death should become a shrine—a place set apart, where our children and our children's children go to learn lessons of freedom." An annotated chronology ran the length of both sides of the stationery. It began with Jefferson's birthday on April 13, 1743, and ended with the August 11, 1912, Rules Committee hearing.

The New York *Press* reported November 9 that Mrs. Littleton had won several influential people over to her cause. The group included J. P. Morgan, the financier whose famous Manhattan mansion (now a museum) was in Levy's congressional district; Charles F. Murphy, the leader of Tammany Hall; Secretary of the Treasury Franklin MacVeagh; John H. Finley, president of the College of the City of New York; the noted union organizer Samuel Gompers; and William F. McCombs, chairman of the Democratic National Committee.

In a speech to the Women's Democratic Club at the Waldorf-Astoria Hotel on November 8, the paper said, Mrs. Littleton "said that the hearty cooperation of women throughout the country is helping wonderfully." She predicted that the bill calling for government ownership of Monticello would be passed in the upcoming session of Congress.

Mrs. Littleton made the front page of the *New York Herald* on November 11 in an article headlined "Mrs. Littleton Fires a Broadside of 10,000 Letters in Fight to Get Monticello from Jefferson M. Levy." The Littleton home, the article said, "is the busiest place imaginable. It has all the appearance of the national headquarters of a political organization. The furniture in the dining room has been taken out and a dozen stenographers take dictation and work eight hours a day at typewriters."

The paper described Mrs. Littleton sitting "at a desk in the centre of a richly furnished parlor." The "heavy carpet" there was "littered with papers and mail of all description. Japanese screens are covered with posters and notices. Petitions and bills hang from the frames of oil paintings and small trucks are loaded with outgoing mail, and an index and letter filing cabinet occupies the place where the grand piano stood."

"My husband has been a perfect angel to me in this fight," Mrs. Littleton said. "He has never denied me a penny I asked."

The paper quoted Jefferson Levy as responding: "They must be spending at least fifty thousand dollars to take my home away. . . . I am going to fight to the last ditch."

The following day, November 12, 1912, *The New York Times* published an article containing a long statement by Jefferson Levy, in which he gave a spirited defense of his right to keep Monticello. "I feel it my duty to notify the public that [sending money to Mrs. Littleton's association] will be useless," Levy said. "The campaign to deprive me of the property which has been in my family for eighty years is without legal basis, as numerous Constitutional lawyers have advised me."

Levy said he might have considered parting with Monticello if it had been "founded on a real affection and reverence for the memory of Jefferson." But Mrs. Littleton's campaign, he said, "has been attended with numberless and wholly unnecessary misstatements about Monticello [and] about my Uncle, Commodore Levy." He attacked Mrs. Littleton for first claiming that he neglected Monticello and then abandoning that charge. Levy said that he "was not an active participant in the litigation that was begun after my uncle's death when I was a minor." He neglected to mention that he was the main participant in the last several years of the litigation.

"When the litigation was finished and my title confirmed by the courts, I set about as complete a restoration of the Estate as possible," he said. "To preserve Monticello in accordance with its traditions has been the wish nearest my heart. . . . I ask no gratitude from the public for my care of Monticello for it has been a work of love and I have always had the consciousness that I was carrying out the wishes of Commodore Levy." The public, Levy said, "has had as free access to the estate as its safety and preservation would permit and as any lover of Jefferson's memory could ask."

Then he lit into Mrs. Littleton. He called her "a self-appointed Director whose interest in the matter has been of the briefest, especially in view of the character of the campaign of abuse of my family, willful misstatement and absolute disregard of the care I have bestowed on the estate for a generation."

Mrs. Littleton, meanwhile, had produced a sequel to "One Wish." It was a fifty-two-page booklet titled "Monticello by Mrs. Martin Littleton" that repeated the story of Uriah Levy stealing Monticello, and contained a good deal of what she had told the Senate and House committees earlier in the year with much of the same emotional, flowery language. A letter that was sent with the booklet asked people to write to Congress asking for government ownership of Monticello, to try to get local newspapers to join the cause, to join her association, to form local branches, and to send contributions to the association's treasurer in New York City, her daughter Laura Littleton.

In late November, William Jennings Bryan joined Mrs. Littleton's cause. "Monticello ought to be public property," he told *The Washington Post* on November 20. "The care of it should be entrusted to those who have a patriotic, rather than a private interest in it." That same newspaper carried an article saying that Mrs. Frank Anthony Walke of Norfolk, Virginia—the custodian of the flags of the United Daughters of the Confederacy who also was a member of the Daughters of the American Revolution, of the Colonial Dames, and of the Society for the Protection of Virginia Antiquities—advised Mrs. Littleton that she opposed government seizure of individual property. Mrs. Littleton attended the UDC's convention in Washington, asking members to join her association, but met with little success and left the city without addressing the body.

The Albemarle County Chapter of the DAR at its monthly chapter meeting in November also came out against the government taking Monticello. The Richmond Chapter of the UDC followed suit, sending a letter to Levy saying they believed the matter was one of "individual rights."

Jefferson Levy was said to be very much upset by the campaign. Nevertheless, he announced December 1 from Monticello that he was a candidate for secretary of the Navy in the Democratic administration of Woodrow Wilson, which would take over the following month.

Levy "said that he believed New York should have a representative in the cabinet, and that it would be fitting if the navy portfolio went to that state," the *New York Herald* said on December 2. "'I'm a candidate,' said Mr. Levy."

. . .

THE FINAL act in the 1912 congressional drama came on December 8 when the House of Representatives debated the Rules Committee resolution calling for the formation of a committee to look into governmental ownership of Monticello. Mrs. Littleton was in the House gallery observing the proceedings. Representative Jefferson Levy was on the House floor, but did not take part in the debate over the future of his ownership of Jefferson's mansion.

Robert Lee Henry of Texas, the chairman of the Rules Committee—and the great-great-great grandson of Patrick Henry—led the fight for the resolution. "I have great respect for [Jefferson Levy] as my colleague," he said, "but it seems to me that the name and fame of Thomas Jefferson are far above any personal consideration in this day and generation. . . ."

Republican John Dalzell of Pennsylvania took up Levy's cause. Jefferson Levy owned Monticello, Dalzell said, and let it be known that it was not for sale. "This resolution, therefore, is unnecessary and inopportune, unless it has an ulterior motive," Dalzell said. He then identified the ulterior motive: "to compel a private citizen against his will to part with his property by means of legislation." Dalzell called that "an assault upon the fundamental right of private property," and said the resolution was "a disgrace to any civilized body, and especially to the House of Representatives of the United States of America."

Edward W. Saunders, a Virginia Democrat who represented Monticello's congressional district, made a similar argument. "The name and the fame of the dead are being used to oppress the living," Saunders said. "I am opposed to any movement that looks to the acquisition of this property by means of the power of eminent domain."

Joseph Hampton Moore, a Pennsylvania Democrat, agreed, saying that taking Monticello from its private owner would set a bad precedent. "Why not take the Betsy Ross house in which was made the first flag of the United States. . . . Why not take over the battlefield of Appomattox. . . . Why not take over Mount Vernon . . . Independence Hall in Philadelphia . . . the state house in Boston?" he asked rhetorically to a round of partisan applause.

Those who argued for the resolution included Henry Clayton of Alabama, the chairman of the Judiciary Committee, who said he was sure Congress would not trample on Jefferson Levy's legal rights. He then asked Levy voluntarily to "let the American people have free access, and not some sort of permissive access, to the shrine of the greatest statesman that ever graced American history." The House erupted in applause at that remark.

After the applause died down, Jefferson Levy said the only words he would utter during the debate: "They do have free access to it now."

Saunders then read a letter written to Jefferson Levy from Frank M. Randolph, a great-great grandson of Thomas Jefferson. Randolph spoke of his "abhorrence of the unjust fight Mrs. Littleton is waging to seize your home. I am sure that all my family, to whom you have always been so courteous and kind in offering the hospitality of Monticello, feel the same way." The family, he said, "all feel that it is a travesty of justice, a direct infringement on American liberty, and directly opposed to the principles and sentiments of the great builder of Monticello."

Randolph also put in a pitch for Jefferson Levy's upkeep of the house, grounds, and Jefferson family graveyard, saying he had "evinced always a desire and interest to care for Jefferson's tomb."

Augustus Owsley Stanley, a Kentucky Democrat, ended the debate by arguing that the resolution under consideration was legal and constitutional and that it merely would investigate government ownership, which, he contended, was the right way to proceed.

The House then took a roll call vote. One hundred and one members voted in favor of the resolution. One hundred and forty-one members, including Jefferson M. Levy, voted against it. Ten members answered "present." One hundred and thirty-eight members, including Martin W. Littleton, did not vote. The resolution was rejected.

Levy, *The New York Times* reported the next day, was "jubilant." He issued a statement saying he was grateful for the support he had received "during this trying ordeal." Representative Henry and Mrs. Littleton issued statements saying "the fight had just begun," and promising that the resolution would come up for a vote again.

Mrs. Littleton also said that a prominent Virginian, whom she would not identify, would soon make an offer, through Governor William Hodges Mann, to purchase Monticello at four times its assessed value and turn it over to the state of Virginia to be used as a shrine to Jefferson. Judge Duke, at a Senate hearing in 1916, identified the prominent man as Thomas Fortune Ryan (1851–1928), the aptly named Virginia-born New York millionaire industrialist.

When Jefferson Levy heard this news, he replied: "I will sell Monticello under no circumstances. I have repeatedly refused $1,500,000 for the property. My answer to any proposition seeking the property of Monticello is: 'When the White House is for sale, then I will consider an offer for the sale of Monticello, and not before.'"

Henry and Mrs. Littleton were correct. The battle over Monticello's fate by no means ended with the December 9, 1912, House vote in favor of Jefferson Levy. It continued throughout 1913 and well into the next year. It also was fought in the public press and in the Commonwealth of Virginia.

After the House vote, Jefferson Levy refused the offer for Monticello that came through the Virginia governor's office. He sent a telegram to Governor Mann on December 11, declining the offer—which he claimed was $750,000—for Monticello. In the telegram Levy let on that he interpreted the offer as an endorsement of his stewardship of Monticello, calling it a "commendation of my custody of Monticello and my efforts to preserve it intact, as a great shrine, fully accessible to all earthly persons."

Levy then trumpeted his achievements at Monticello and claimed he turned down the money because he could not "commercialize the sentiment of years by putting a price upon this noble property." Because of his "highest conception of patriotic feeling" toward Jefferson, and because of his "deep affection for the place itself because of long association, and in the full assurance that my care will continue to be both abundant and constant," he said, he was "not prepared to make or accept any offer depriving me of this cherished right."

At the same time Levy received a vote of support from another Jefferson descendant, H. Randolph Burke, a great-great-grandson who lived in Alexandria, Virginia. "I assure you that the most friendly feelings have always existed between my family and the owner of Monticello," Burke wrote to Levy. "My mother is grateful and has always appreciated your cordial and several times repeated invitations to her mother, Mrs. Virginia J. Trist [Jefferson's granddaughter], and herself . . . to visit Monticello at any time it was convenient to do so. . . ."

The family, Burke said, "has always had a feeling of obligation to you for the restoration and good care" of Monticello. "We view with surprise the attempt to dispossess you against your will of property which belongs to you. Certainly the former owner of Monticello would never have believed such a thing possible in our country."

Levy's longtime superintendent at Monticello, Thomas Rhodes, joined the fray against Mrs. Littleton in a letter to her dated December 16. "I have been informed that you have been making statements to the effect that an admission fee of ten and twenty dollars is being charged for admission to Monticello, and that servants are accepting tips from visitors to the place," he said. "I beg leave to say that I have been Manager at Monticello for the last twenty years. No admission fee whatever is charged for any purpose in regard to Monticello, and servants are prohibited from accepting tips."

Near the end of the year, Mrs. Littleton added a new piece of ammunition to her campaign against Levy's ownership of Monticello: the existence of a mortgage on the property. After discovering the fact in the Albemarle County courthouse, she made copies of the mortgage available to the press and sent out a mailing excoriating Levy to members of her Monticello acquisition association.

"When an offer was made to purchase the property at four times its assessed value, Mr. Levy replied: 'I cannot commercialize the sentiment of years by putting a price upon this noble property.' At the very time Mr. Levy made this statement, Monticello was covered by a mortgage to John Uppleby for $45,000," Mrs. Littleton told the New York *American* on December 28. "If Mr. Levy is embarrassed to such an extent as to be forced to put a mortgage on Monticello, and thus make it a commercial pawn, instead of a national shrine, will he not permit the American people to sweep away this encumbrance?"

Jefferson Levy denied there was such a mortgage, telling the *American* reporter that the only mortgage he had in Virginia was one on the large tract of land near Monticello that had formerly belonged to President Monroe. He then injected gender politics into the argument, saying, the paper said, "it was impossible for him to enter into a controversy with a woman." Levy also reiterated his contention that Monticello was not for sale.

In her letter to association members, Mrs. Littleton took a highly indignant stance and lashed out at Levy for daring to take a mortgage out on "this sacred shrine." "Shall we permit the shame of this mortgage to rest upon Monticello?" she asked. "Shall it be said to all the world that the sacred spot where Jefferson lived and died and is buried, which every heart reverences, shall be made a commercial pawn— mortgaged! . . . Surely, in our country, there is wealth and generosity enough to raise any amount of money, the need of which compelled

Mr. Levy to assail the sacred precincts of Monticello and compelled him to raise money by mortgaging this ground, where rests the author of the Declaration of Independence?"

In a letter dated December 31, 1912, to Downing L. Smith of Charlottesville, Mrs. Littleton said that the mortgage proved that Jefferson Levy "is a most unworthy occupant" of Monticello. She also lamented the fact that Jefferson's descendants were on the wrong side of the issue.

"If the descendants of Jefferson and the Randolphs would only be my friends, instead of Mr. Levy's!" she said. She confessed that she was "tired, body and soul," but was still working hard and looking forward to carrying out "our beautiful plans, to honor the birthplace of Jefferson."

The next step in the plan came in January when Mrs. Littleton printed thousands of huge, two-by-three-foot lithographed 1913 calendars featuring a color photograph of Monticello. She sent two copies of the calendar to every member of Congress—one for the office and one for the home.

Jefferson Levy, meanwhile, was feeling confident—and rich. The Washington correspondent of the New York *World* reported in mid-January 1913 that Levy was the proud owner of a $30,000 sable overcoat.

"Mr. Levy has promised to appear in it when the thermometer drops to a proper degree," the paper reported January 12. "The members of the New York delegation are waiting anxiously for the drop."

Levy, the paper said, bragged that it was the "finest piece of sable in existence," but would not say whether he had bought the coat or someone gave it to him. When asked, he said: "Ah, that is the question. If you only knew from whom I got the coat, you would be surprised." The paper speculated that it might have been a gift from J. P. Morgan, the Sultan of Turkey, or the Duke of Sutherland. The latter two were "gentlemen in whose acquaintance Mr. Levy revels."

On January 30, Jefferson Levy introduced a joint resolution in the House to make Francis Scott Key's "*Star Spangled Banner*" the official national anthem. Levy was years ahead of his time. Even though the song—for which Key, a lawyer, wrote the lyrics after watching the 1814

British attack on Ft. McHenry near Baltimore—had been in general use for nearly a century, it was not officially adopted as the national anthem until 1931.

On March 18, 1913, Maud Littleton rented New York City's Little Theater and delivered a lecture entitled "True Story of Monticello." *The New York Times* reported the next day that forty-three people showed up, including two reporters. Mrs. Littleton, the paper said, hung her association's signed petitions along the walls of the theater, in the foyer, and in the downstairs tearoom where she met with supporters after her lecture. During the lecture Mrs. Littleton hammered at Levy's refusal to part with Monticello and showed slides of photographs of letters of support from political figures such as President Wilson.

As "the slides showing their signatures appeared on the screen," the *Times* article said, "she would murmur with a delight that would be reflected in a sympathetic flutter in the auditorium."

Jefferson Levy took the occasion of Thomas Jefferson's birthday on April 13, 1913, to make a speech at Monticello in which he reiterated his case that the federal government had no right to take Monticello from him. The speech was printed in the next day's Charlottesville *Daily Progress*.

Levy began by saying he cordially welcomed those who wanted to visit Monticello—something, he said, he had been pleased to do "at all times" during his ownership. He spoke of Jefferson's "generous hospitality," and said that the "maintenance of that same atmosphere" had been the "life work" of his family at Monticello for "four score years." During that time, he said, "we have with zealous care united again these acres and gathered from two continents the scattered and priceless things of bygone days, and preserved them for your devotion as you see them today."

He ended with an emotional plea to keep Monticello. "Generations of my family have consecrated time and money to its restoration and preservation," he said. "Will not now the great American people see and understand that this stewardship has become a part of the heart and life of the present owner? Will a man fix a price upon wife or child?"

In the summer of 1913 Levy remained active in Congress, pushing his pro-business agenda. He introduced a bill to permit the Interstate Commerce Commission to authorize combinations or contracts between railroads, even if those agreements violated the Sherman Antitrust Act. He spoke out against a proposed income tax and for improving the conditions of Jews in Romania. He made headlines in July by strongly advocating that the House stop investigating business-lobbying practices.

In August, gossip columnists again linked him romantically with Flora Wilson. *New York Topics* magazine, for example, had this to say about the couple on August 14: "At Mr. Levy's parties at Monticello, as elsewhere, Flora Wilson is always in evidence, and so conspicuous are Jefferson Levy's attentions to her that everybody wonders why he does not make her the mistress of his home, as she evidently is of his heart."

In November 1913, a confident Jefferson Monroe Levy announced that he expected to be the Democratic candidate in 1914 for the New York Senate seat held by the famed Elihu Root (1845–1937), the former McKinley administration secretary of war and Roosevelt administration secretary of state who had been awarded the Nobel Peace Prize in 1912. Levy made the official announcement of his candidacy in Albany, New York, on January 5, 1914.

That "startling announcement," the *Washington Herald* said on January 23, was the latest example of Levy's self-aggrandizing headline grabbing. "Levy is a rich man, a bachelor, and represents a business element in New York State and city, not to mention a religious element, that would rejoice to see him filling a few pages of *Congressional Record* week after week on the slightest provocation," the article said.

The focus of the Levy-Littleton-Monticello battle shifted to Richmond in February 1914. On February 16, the Virginia General Assembly passed a resolution, at the urging of Mrs. Littleton, asking Congress to acquire Monticello. "Monticello is now private property to which the public has no right of access," the resolution stated. Technically, of course, the public did not have the right to enter the privately owned property, though, in reality, the grounds were pretty much open to all visitors, announced and unannounced.

Levy responded to the resolution with a letter to the editor that appeared in the February 24 Richmond *Times-Dispatch*. "I have heard, though I have not seen the statement in print, that Mrs. Martin W. Littleton stated on the floor of the House of Delegates of Virginia that I had offered Monticello for sale to some rich capitalist for $1,000,000," Levy said. "This statement is absolutely without foundation. I have never offered Monticello for sale at any price."

What Levy did say, he wrote, was "that I had been offered and had refused $1,000,000 for this place, which is as dear to me as it can be to any one in the world, and which has been in my own family longer than in the Jefferson family."

Levy complained about "the many cruel and unjust things which have been said of me in this crusade to try and take my property away from me." He also objected to the fact that he was not given the chance to rebut Mrs. Littleton's accusations in Richmond.

"It seems to me," Levy said, "that the Virginia legislature, in passing Mrs. Littleton's resolution, might have at least given me an opportunity to be heard."

An editorial in the February 26 Norfolk *Virginian-Pilot* took the state of Virginia to task for not purchasing Monticello after Uriah Levy died and strongly defended Jefferson Levy's right to keep the house. "The action taken by the Virginia House of Delegates the other day in response to hysterical prodding by a lady from New York will only serve to rivet public attention anew upon a chapter in Virginia's record which is little to her credit. . . ."

The U.S. Senate Committee on Public Buildings and Grounds held two days of hearings March 17 and March 19 on a resurrected Monticello resolution offered by Democratic senator James Alexander Reed of Missouri. The committee heard from just three witnesses, Jefferson Levy, R. T. W. Duke, Jr., and Maud Littleton. Things got testy many times during the two days of testimony, and on many occasions Judge Duke and Mrs. Littleton argued fiercely over Monticello's fate. There also was a lot of unfriendly give and take between Senator Reed and Judge Duke. Reed faced off against Jefferson Levy on both days as well.

The hearings began at 10:30 on Tuesday morning, March 17, with a warning from Senator Reed to Jefferson Levy. He said that Levy would have thirty days to make a proposal to the government to buy Monticello after the joint congressional committee called for in the resolution voted for such a sale. If Levy did not come up with a proposal, Reed said, "then the committee is authorized to direct the Attorney General to bring . . . condemnation proceedings. . . ."

Reed congratulated Levy for preserving Monticello "at least to a very large extent, in its original condition" and for "generously" opening it "for visitation by sightseers and by the public." But Reed then said that he believed Monticello should be "owned by the people of the United States." He characterized Mrs. Littleton's petitions as "the most remarkable . . . ever presented to the American Congress" because they contained the signatures of countless state supreme court justices, governors, state officials, university professors, clergymen, and lawyers.

"The movement is so universal that it may be said to embrace generally the enlightened sentiment of the people of the United States," Reed said.

When it was Judge Duke's turn to speak, he launched into a long defense of Jefferson Levy's right to keep Monticello. Judge Duke—characterizing himself as a "man of comparative obscurity . . . from a provincial town"—attempted to distance Jefferson Levy from the lawsuit over Uriah Levy's will. "When that will contest was instituted, Mr. Levy was a boy, eight years old," Judge Duke said. Actually, on October 31, 1862, when the executors filed the suit, Jefferson Levy was ten and a half.

Senator Reed interrupted at that point to ask Judge Duke who had contested the will. Duke conceded that Jefferson Levy's father Jonas was one of the contestees. Mrs. Littleton then spoke out, saying that she believed Jefferson Levy was "about twenty-one years old" at the time, and she and Judge Duke argued over Jefferson Levy's age. Levy himself remained silent on the age issue.

Judge Duke then skipped lightly over Jefferson Levy's role in the partition lawsuit, saying only that he bought up "the interests of a good many of the outstanding heirs." Duke spoke of the condition of Monticello when Jefferson Levy bought it and said that Levy "devoted himself to restoring Monticello to its original condition." He also went over

Uriah Levy's stewardship of Monticello and what took place on Jefferson's mountain during the Civil War.

Duke told the senators these stories, he said, "to show what a debt of gratitude the people of this country owe to Mr. Jefferson M. Levy." Levy, he said, "has been attacked in the most violent way because he wants to hold on to this property. The committee would be surprised to know what has been said about him. It has been represented that the property is a ruin at the present time."

He described how Jefferson Levy bought up the surrounding land at Monticello and spent "between fifty and seventy-five thousand dollars" since 1880 restoring the house and lands.

"A good deal more than that," Levy added.

Duke said Levy was losing money on Monticello, to the tune of some $5,000 a year, to which Levy added again: "It is a great deal more than that. I do not keep any book accounts at all of it."

The revenue from Monticello's crops, Duke said, paid only for Thomas Rhodes's salary. "He has one of the best men who can be had as manager there," Duke said of Rhodes. "He pays him high wages. The place is kept up in beautiful shape." Monticello, he said, "is in as fine condition as it is possible for anybody to put it in without altering the essential parts of the house." Levy, he said, "has taken better care of the property than the Government would take of it today."

As for admission fees, Duke said that when Levy first took possession of the property Joel Wheeler had been charging a twenty-five-cent fee, which he "never accounted for." Levy kept the admission fee, he said, "but turned over every penny . . . to public charities in Charlottesville."

Levy then said he kept the fee "only for six months." Duke added: "The people who went there raised such a cry about it that it was stopped."

He talked about the public's free access to Monticello, saying it was open to the public from nine in the morning to five during the week and until noon on Saturdays. "The public have as free admission to the place as they have to a public park in the city of Washington. Nobody is turned back from the grounds," he said.

"The house is not open. Why? Mr. Levy would have to have a guard in every room . . . if it were open to everyone" because of "relic hunters."

Reed and several other senators asked Duke many questions about the monetary value of Monticello. When Reed asked what the "actual value" was, Duke replied: "I know that Mr. Levy was offered one million dollars for that property . . . in 1889. I have no hesitancy in saying that it was offered by Cornelius Vanderbilt."

"He is dead, and where is your proof?" Mrs. Littleton injected. "You have made so many misstatements this morning, Judge Duke, so many misstatements that are wrong. . . ."

"I have made no misstatement," Duke said. "I am responsible for every statement I make here upon my integrity as a gentleman and a lawyer. . . . It is not my fault, sir, if this becomes a personal matter."

When asked whether Levy had ever set a price on Monticello, Duke said: "Never, sir. I have heard Mr. Levy time and again tell me that there was not a brick for sale in Monticello; that he would not sell any part of it."

The session went on with more questions about the property's worth when Mrs. Littleton asked to be "allowed to say a few words this morning." Duke, ever the gentleman, said he had not finished his presentation, but would yield the floor to her.

"I do not ask you to give way now," Mrs. Littleton said, "but I should like, if you will allow me, at some time to present this subject in an impartial way—not as a lawyer for Mr. Levy and not as a representative of the government, but just as a person who is deeply interested in the success of the cause."

It was decided to let Judge Duke finish his statement, but he couldn't resist getting in some patronizing remarks about Mrs. Littleton. "Regarding the value of Monticello, I know Mrs. Littleton calls my veracity into question," he said. "Ladies sometimes cannot help doing that sort of thing. I am sure Mrs. Littleton's heart is so deeply interested in the matter that she sometimes does not exactly realize the force of words."

He praised her patriotism and her zeal. "If Monticello is ever obtained, it is the duty of the United States Government to put up a statue there to Mrs. Littleton as the person who did the work," Duke said. "I assure her that I do not entertain anything but the kindest feeling in the world for her, as I do for all ladies like Mrs. Littleton. As you probably know from Senator Swanson, that is the weakness of the average Virginian."

After Duke's presentation, Republican senator George Sutherland of Utah asked Jefferson Levy if he would be willing to sell Monticello "under any circumstances or for any price." Jefferson Levy responded with emotion. "I have always opposed selling Monticello. It would be like pulling my heart out if I were ever to part with it. I am opposed to the entire proposition."

Senator Miles Poindexter, a Republican from Washington, then asked Levy what he would do if the government "by some definitive action should indicate its desire" to acquire Monticello. Levy's resolve seemed to soften.

"We are all fallible," he replied. "I mean to say, we must take the public into consideration. I am surprised at the resolution of the Virginia Legislature. It shocked me. . . . I cannot say what I will do from day to day. But as my mind is and has been, I have been opposed to the sale of Monticello."

"Will you sell it?" Senator Reed then asked. "Will you make an offer to the Federal Government so that the Government can take this property and preserve it for all future generations? Would you be willing to do that?

"Senator," Levy replied, "if you ask me now, I say, 'No.'"

Reed shot back: "This is the only opportunity I have had to ask you."

"I am opposed to the sale of Monticello," Levy repeated, and then launched into what can only be described as an uncharacteristic *cri de coeur.*

"It is my hobby and has been my hobby throughout my entire life. I have never even married, and my whole life has been wrapped up in it. I presented to France a replica of the statue of Jefferson which my uncle in 1833 presented to the United States—the statue now in the Rotunda. We are thoroughly Jeffersonians, and I have always been trying to uphold the principles of Jefferson."

Senator Sutherland then suggested that after Levy died Monticello might go to someone who did not revere Jefferson, and in that case perhaps the best thing would be for him to sell Monticello to the federal government. Again, Levy's resolve faltered.

"All these are serious things to consider," he said, "and if you ask me this minute for an answer I must say that I still feel the same way. Whether the Congress of the United States through the action of the House and Senate could change my mind, I do not know. I do not want to be antagonistic to the people of the United States. I think I am doing something for the people."

Levy said, under persistent questioning from Reed and Sutherland, that he would take the matter of selling Monticello "under serious consideration" if Congress passed Reed's resolution and "if there is no threat over me." The recent Virginia resolution, Levy said, "has changed my views somewhat, as well as shocked me. I thought they all loved me in a certain way."

Levy and Mrs. Littleton then got into a spat over the role in the December 1912 House floor debate of Rep. William Sulzer, a New York Democrat (and later governor) and then Senator Swanson adjourned the two-hour session, saying the committee would reconvene on the matter two days later on March 19.

That hearing began with Judge Duke continuing his statement. It was brief and centered on the Levy will litigation. When the question of Jefferson Levy's age at the time came up, Senator Reed asked Duke when Levy was born. Duke said, "Mr. Levy, you have to own up. In what year were you born?"

Levy replied: "I am not giving that away."

Then it was Mrs. Littleton's turn. She began with a dig at Judge Duke, who had introduced himself at the previous hearing by offering a brief Duke family history.

"I will prove my appreciation by not taking up your valuable time in telling you the history of my life," Mrs. Littleton said, "but I will talk about the matter before us today."

She went on to make her case along the lines she used in the 1912 hearings, by praising Jefferson, decrying the fact there was no memorial to him in Washington, and accusing Jefferson Levy of selfishness. She went over Monticello's post–Thomas Jefferson history, repeating the story of Uriah Levy, in essence, stealing Monticello from unidentified "friends of Martha Jefferson Randolph" who were trying to buy back the house for her—a woman "who had been left penniless with eleven little children."

She repeated her allegation that Uriah Levy's will was overturned on a "bare technicality." She said that Jefferson Levy charged admission until 1900. Levy shot back that he charged admission "for six months [in 1879] that is all, absolutely."

Mrs. Littleton then charged that Levy did not donate the admission fees to charities. "In getting the history of this place I have left no stone unturned, and on my frequent visits there I have tried to find a record in regard to the matter, but have found no such record." She said the fees only were rescinded in 1887 after then Rep. Amos Cummings made a visit, was outraged by the fee and "threatened to make it public on the floor of the House unless the charge was removed."

She hammered away at Jefferson Levy, accusing him and Sulzer of sabotaging the December 1912 House vote. She accused Levy of being a pawn of Tammany Hall, which, she said, "is responsible for Mr. Levy's appearance in the House of Representatives."

"Not a bit," Levy remonstrated, "the people are."

The two then got into an argument over the alleged Monticello mortgage.

"Has that anything to do with the matter?" Levy asked Senator Swanson, the committee chairman.

"It is pertinent," Swanson said.

"Putting in my personal affairs?" Levy replied.

"It is a public record," Swanson said.

"Yes, but I do not think you ought to go into my personal affairs," Levy said.

Swanson allowed Mrs. Littleton to add a copy of the mortgage to the hearing record. She criticized Levy for not accepting the offer to buy Monticello from the Virginia governor on the grounds that he couldn't put a price on the "noble" property.

"Then," she said, "immediately after that, I found that he had put a price upon it, that it was mortgaged in Wall Street, a pawn, for $45,000."

Judge Duke interceded, saying he had loaned the money to Jefferson Levy "and I have never been in Wall Street in my life."

Mrs. Littleton forged on, telling how she had been to see President Wilson "many times on this question," and reporting that he was strongly in favor of government ownership, even through condemnation proceedings. She went on to pillory Levy as a callous businessman who did not care what happened to Jefferson's legacy.

"I am absolutely certain that not much longer can Jefferson's grave be in the brambles and bushes," she said. "No longer can that place which holds his own dead body be mortgaged, a commercial pawn by a real estate manipulator."

She launched into a discussion of Monticello's worth and hinted Levy was holding out to make a huge profit. "In refusing the $100,000 for this property [from the state of Virginia], which was a fair price, some think the proprietor is taking advantage of a national feeling, for personal gain, to drive a hard bargain, and in the spirit of an auction to raise the bid and turn the immortality of Jefferson into gold. . . ."

She derided Levy's statements that the government was trying to take his home. "We do not propose that the nation take the home of the proprietor of Monticello," she said. "We all know his home is in New York." Monticello, she said, "is now no home. Its value is distributed among money lenders and it lies under the constant peril of foreclosure. . . ."

Levy and Duke were given a chance to speak after Mrs. Littleton ended her remarks. Judge Duke explained the mortgage situation, saying it was a deed of trust done through his office and represented money loaned to Levy by a client of Duke's. Levy—the man who owned a $30,000 sable overcoat—had already paid off five thousand dollars of the note, Duke said, and "has repeatedly told this gentleman, who begged him to keep the money, that he would pay him the $40,000 whenever he wanted it. Mr. Levy has always been borrowing money on real estate in Charlottesville. . . . He needs money very frequently, as most of us do, in his operations. But there is no discredit in that."

The hearing dragged on for three hours, during which Judge Duke and Mrs. Littleton skirmished on other matters, including the wording of the deed on the Jefferson family graveyard.

"I represent the Randolphs, although . . . I do not represent them on this matter," Duke said at one point.

"I represent them, too," Mrs. Littleton rejoined.

"Yes, ma'am," Duke said, "I have been paid fees to represent them, however."

"I have not," Mrs. Littleton said. "I represent them without it."

After Mrs. Littleton finished, Jefferson Levy was asked once again if he was still committed not to sell Monticello. His answer was similar to the one he gave two days earlier.

"No, I have not changed my mind," Levy said. "I stand by my previous determination not to commercialize Monticello, and will not consider an offer for its purchase. If, however, both houses of Congress pass this resolution asking me to turn Monticello over to the government, in that case I may take its sale under consideration."

The committee then went into executive session. When the senators returned, the chairman announced that they had voted unanimously to report Senator Reed's resolution favorably to the full Senate.

CHAPTER FIVE

Selling Monticello

I am convinced that I must put aside my feelings and yield to the national demand, and make what to me is the supreme sacrifice of lifelong association.

JEFFERSON M. LEVY, OCTOBER 5, 1914, LETTER
TO WILLIAM JENNINGS BRYAN

Jefferson Levy's determination not to part with Monticello weakened considerably in the next six months. In an interview in the Richmond *News Leader* on March 23, 1914, he used words similar to those he spoke at the March 19 committee hearing in hinting that the possibility of Congress enacting Senator Reed's resolution had an influence on him. If pushed by Congress, he said, he would give the resolution "serious consideration."

After saying he did not intend to sell Monticello "with any threat over my head," Levy left himself an out to do just that. "I regard Congress as representing the voice of the people," he said, "and under these circumstances I would give the resolution passed by it serious consideration."

Representative Henry kept the pressure on, announcing, also on March 23, that he would bring the matter up in the House as soon as the Senate acted on it.

The April 1914 *Good Housekeeping Magazine*—the popular women's monthly that had been in existence since 1885—contained an article by Dorothy Dix that was sharply critical of Jefferson Levy's proprietorship of Monticello. In the article, titled "Monticello: Shrine or Bachelor's

Hall?," Dix implied that Levy's refusal to sell was greedy, selfish, and unpatriotic.

Dix, a popular newspaper advice columnist whose real name was Elizabeth Meriwether Gilmer, praised Maud Littleton and "women's patriotic societies" in general for their work "to perpetuate and preserve the landmarks of American history." Dix then repeated the litany of arguments Mrs. Littleton used for government ownership of Monticello. In doing so, Dix put Levy's ownership in the worst possible light and embellished the truth to his disadvantage. Twice she referred to the Levy family as "aliens."

Dix said that Levy, "a private individual," owned all the land around Jefferson's "little graveyard," and that "none who visit it may do so except by special permission of Mr. Levy." She left the mistaken impression that Levy did not allow visitors to get close to Jefferson's grave and that they were allowed to stay but a short time. "Fifty to sixty thousand people a year visit Jefferson's grave," Dix wrote, "but none may stay more than twenty minutes, gazing from the top of the mountain above . . ."

"None may enter" Jefferson's house, Dix said. "The house that in Jefferson's lifetime was open to the meanest citizen of the great republic he had helped to found is closed to all except Mr. Levy's personal guests."

In telling the story of how Monticello passed "into alien hands," Dix derided Uriah Levy and repeated the "stealing Monticello" story Mrs. Littleton used in her pamphlet, "Monticello." Littleton's unidentified "young Virginian" who supposedly had raised $3,000 to buy back the house for Jefferson's daughter Martha Randolph in 1834 became an unidentified "young relative of the Jeffersons" in Dix's article. When he journeyed to Charlottesville from Philadelphia via stagecoach, Uriah Levy just happened to be in the same coach and the young man "confided his plan" to the Navy lieutenant. The young man then "became intoxicated and dallied," Dix said, implying that Levy plied him with drink in order to steal Monticello.

"The next day the repentant and sober young man arrived and besought Captain Levy to take the three thousand dollars that the generous Philadelphians had given for the purpose, and let Monticello go

back to the Jefferson family," Dix said. "The Captain [Levy was a Lieutenant at the time] refused to part with his bargain."

Dix did not mention a word about Uriah Levy's adoration of Jefferson, his commissioning of the David statue, or his restoration of Monticello. She repeated Mrs. Littleton's disparaging words—"it was finally
decided upon a technicality"—to describe the judicial outcome of the
executors' lawsuit. Dix said that "all the patriotic societies" had been
helping Mrs. Littleton's Monticello acquisition project. In fact, Mrs.
Littleton could make no headway, as we have seen, with the United
Daughters of the Confederacy and, as we shall see, received mixed results, at best, from the Daughters of the American Revolution.

Dix called Jefferson Levy "a rich and generous man," but pointed
out—as Mrs. Littleton often did—that after turning down Virginia's
$100,000 offer for Monticello, he "mortgaged it for forty-five thousand
dollars." The government, Dix argued, had every right to condemn
Monticello because of the "exceptional circumstances when the right of
one individual should give way to the good of the many." Jefferson's
home, she said, "is one of the shrines of history in this country, and it is
not fitting that any one man should be possessor of these sacred sou-
venirs."

Mrs. Littleton, Dix reported, was confident that "her long fight to
preserve the home of the Great Commoner is about to end in victory."
Dix said that Mrs. Littleton was predicting that President Wilson would
ask Congress to enact a bill to buy Monticello and give it to the nation.
"If he doesn't, why, then, we will go on with the fight," Dix quoted Mrs.
Littleton as saying. "Jefferson must not remain unhonored in his own
country and no other memorial is so fitting as his old home. Monticello
must belong to the people."

Dix ended her article with a dire and completely untruthful description of the state of Monticello and its grounds under Jefferson Levy's
ownership. "Soon, unless some action is taken, all the marks that Jefferson set upon Monticello will be swept away," she said. "The trees he
planted are rotting and falling down, the terraced garden is almost
obliterated, the house is decaying, and the little graveyard is overgrown
with weeds."

A reasonable argument can be made that the Dix article—along with Amos Cummings's attack on Jefferson Levy in the New York *Sun* in 1897 and much of Mrs. Littleton's campaign—contained more than a whiff of anti-Semitism. The 1890s marked the beginning of an era of widespread feelings of nativism and jingoism in this country in reaction to large numbers of newly arriving immigrants from Europe, including Jews. Between 1890 and 1920 the Jewish population in the United States grew from about 400,000 to some 3.3 million.

The era's anti-Semitism wasn't aimed only at Eastern European Jews, as Jefferson Levy and many other American-born Jews found out. During this time even Jews whose families had lived in this country for generations were subject to nativism. Levy, like other acculturated American Jews, faced being excluded from many of the nation's top hotels, resorts, colleges, residential areas, jobs, and social clubs. The references by Dix, Cummings, Littleton, and others to Uriah and Jefferson Levy as "aliens" and "outsiders" can be interpreted as expressions of this widespread anti-Semitism.

In the *Good Housekeeping* article, Dix portrayed the Levys as if they didn't care about Monticello, and as if all they wanted was money. Dix—and Cummings—painted portraits of greedy Jews who were not a part of American culture, and who therefore had no right to own an icon of American culture.

Theodore Fred Kuper, a New York City lawyer who was the national director of the Thomas Jefferson Memorial Foundation from 1923 to 1935, argued that anti-Semitism had played a role in Monticello matters beginning with Uriah Levy's death. "The unfortunate lasting effect" of the long family fight over Uriah Levy's estate, Kuper said, was "the canard against Jews [that] developed [in which] one Jew, U. P. Levy, had tricked an intending purchaser by sneaking ahead and buying Monticello himself and that his Jewish family broke the will and deprived Monticello of being an honor to Jefferson. Of course, all of this is false and vicious [and] as a Jew, I wish it had been dealt with differently. . . ."

Did anti-Semitism play a part in Maud Littleton's campaign? There was nothing overtly anti-Semitic in Mrs. Littleton's literature or in her public utterances. It's not difficult, though, to see a strong anti-Semitic subtext in Mrs. Littleton's campaign. Her congressional testimony, speeches, and newspaper interviews were filled with nativist-style rhetoric aimed at the Levys, spiced with the themes of greed, selfishness, and lack of patriotism.

Then there is this strange, biblically inspired (and wholly made up) passage in her "Monticello" pamphlet in which Mrs. Littleton described how Uriah Levy came up with the idea of donating the home to the nation. "He heard it in his dreams day and night, and was filled with it," Mrs. Littleton says. "As when the disciples of Judea looked with solemn awe at His tomb from whence came redemption—a Christian era dawned for the world—so when Uriah Levy, now a faithful old patriarch, heard the call of the people to sacredly care for its shrines—an age of patriotism had already dawned. And when he came, and with uncovered head stood on the consecrated soil of Monticello . . . he responded to the call of the people."

What is the point of comparing Uriah Levy to the Jewish disciples who revered Christ? And why describe Uriah Levy with "uncovered head" at Monticello? These can be interpreted as unfavorable—if oblique—references to Jews. On the other hand, they merely may have been Mrs. Littleton's way of praising Levy by comparing his choice of donating Monticello to the nation with great events in Christianity. It is of more than passing interest to note that Mrs. Littleton later embraced fundamentalist evangelicalism with the same fervor she brought to her Monticello campaign.

Members of the Levy family, including Jefferson Levy's niece Frances (Fanny) Lewis and her husband Harold, believed there was more than an anti-Semitic tone to Mrs. Littleton's campaign. Frances and Harold Lewis "said that she was violently anti-Semitic," says their daughter Harley. "The reason that she pursued [taking Monticello from Jefferson Levy] was that she objected that people by the name of Levy owned it and she [started] a tremendous campaign and rallied the country. It was all really on anti-Semitism and there was no other reason for it."

. . .

SENTIMENT around the nation in the first half of 1914 was by no means completely favorable toward Mrs. Littleton's plan. An editorial on April

1, 1914, in the Newport News (Virginia) *Times-Herald*, for example, lambasted her movement as little more than an idle rich woman's crusade for headlines.

"Mrs. Littleton is not averse to the applause, and she is winning," the editorial said. "Its agitation gives Mrs. Littleton something to do, which she can do brilliantly, and it draws upon her the attention of the nation, which she seems to enjoy with great complacency. Perhaps it's more fascinating than bridge."

Others attacked Mrs. Littleton's plan because of their strong feelings against the confiscation of private property by the federal government. "The federal government has no right to confiscate this property under the accepted interpretation of eminent domain," a Danville (Virginia) *Register* editorial opined. The editorial did not object to Jefferson Levy selling Monticello willingly, but "under no circumstances would we countenance the virtual seizure of private property as proposed in the legislative resolution embodying Mrs. Martin Littleton's demand."

In the spring of 1914 newspaper accounts indicate that Jefferson Levy was more concerned with the upcoming New York senatorial election than with Monticello matters. He was mentioned as a possible candidate for the seat in May at a New York City Democratic conference, along with secretary of the treasury William G. McAdoo (who was President Wilson's son-in-law), New York Governor Martin Glynn, and several others.

Levy's senatorial aspirations were the subject of a long article that appeared in the June 19 *Washington Herald*. The article, datelined New York, said that Levy was "a trifle troubled in spirit," not because of Monticello matters, but due to "suggestions from admiring friends that he is entitled to take a turn at the Senatorial game." His spirit was troubled, the article said, because Levy would have to choose either a longshot run at the Senate race or a virtually assured reelection from his congressional district. If he stayed in the House, Levy would become the ranking Democrat on the Foreign Affairs Committee, and would accede to the chairmanship if then chairman Henry D. Flood of Virginia ran for higher office as was rumored.

The article suggested Levy's age was another reason he considered running for the Senate in 1914. "Six years hence he might be a trifle old," the article said, and then pointed out that Levy consistently refused to reveal his age. "He has ever been careful to leave the date of his birth [April 15, 1852] out of his official biographies," the paper reported, "but he has passed the three-score mark and must get into the Senatorial contest this year or never."

The article went on to give a glimpse of Jefferson Levy's life in New York City. After spending most of the week in Washington, Levy often would make an appearance at the Waldorf Hotel where he would hold court in the downstairs restaurant or on the roof garden with some of the city's financial movers and shakers. Levy "is ever given much attention by the big financiers and business men who assemble at eventide to discuss not only operations in Wall Street, but to tell each other how the government really ought to be run down in Washington," the article said. "The financial coterie appreciates that Levy is a good deal in touch with the downtown financial district himself and unusually for a Congressman from New York or any other state."

Around that same time Mrs. Littleton announced that she had consulted with astrologists in this country and in Europe who bolstered her optimism about the pending governmental purchase of Monticello. "My psychological instinct tells me that the fate of Monticello is decided, and I am going back to my farm on Long Island," Mrs. Littleton said. "It is only a matter of weeks before the American people will own the deed. Astrologists have so advised me."

Jefferson Levy made headlines in July when he tried—and failed—to force the House of Representatives into an early adjournment to cut off debate on pending legislation that would have strengthened antitrust-laws. The next month he took part in another strange incident in Washington. This time it was on a streetcar. According to an article in the August 13, 1914, *Daily Progress*, a Washington streetcar operator physically threw Levy off his car because the New York congressman had refused to enter the car through the proper aisle and then got into a loud argument with the conductor.

Back in the House of Representatives, on July 11, Levy's fellow New York City congressman, Jacob A. Cantor, a one-term Democrat, intro-

duced a bill—more than likely at Levy's request—to appropriate
$25,000 to erect a "suitable" monument in Washington in honor of
Uriah P. Levy. The bill was sent to the House Committee on the Library where no action was taken on it.

William Jennings Bryan, who in April 1897, had been the first person
of note to ask Jefferson Levy to sell Monticello, made a similar plea in
September 1914. Bryan was then the Wilson administration's secretary
of state, and for reasons unrecorded, he sat down at his State Department desk on September 23, 1914, and wrote a letter to Levy that
changed the course of Monticello's history.

"You will remember that several years ago I suggested to you the propriety of selling Monticello to the national government. You then declined, on the ground that you did not like to have it go out of the
possession of your family," Bryan began.

The secretary of state said he had "never relinquished the hope" that
Levy "would some day yield to the popular desire that the government
should own Monticello and keep it in [Jefferson's] memory. . . ." Bryan
took note of the pending congressional legislation, and urged Levy
"anew to consider the advisability of selling the property to the government." He suggested that Levy could reserve a life interest in the place
when he sold it to the government so he could live out his days there.

Bryan ended the letter by appealing to Levy's Democratic Party loyalties. Selling Monticello to the government, Bryan said, "would commemorate the great Democratic administration of President Wilson,
which is being conducted on Jeffersonian principles, and the fact the
President is by birth a Virginian makes the present moment still more
opportune."

Levy gave the first hint that Bryan's letter had swayed him in an October 2 interview in Washington. "Mr. Bryan's letter makes it an administrative movement," Levy said. "It puts an entirely different aspect on
the matter of my holding out against selling. I will treat the idea more
seriously than ever."

Three days later, on October 5, 1914, William Jennings Bryan made
a startling announcement. He had received a letter from Jefferson M.

Levy in which he agreed to sell Monticello to the United States government. Levy's asking price: $500,000.

"I confess to you that your letter urging me to sell Monticello to the Government has very much unsettled a determination not to part with it, which I thought was unalterable," Levy said in the letter. "I am convinced that I must put aside my feelings and yield to the national demand, and make what to me is the supreme sacrifice of lifelong association."

Levy spoke of his patriotic adoration of Thomas Jefferson. As for Monticello, he said: "Its every nook and cranny, hill, spring, and tree belonged, through years of tenderest recollection, to the inner circle of my life." Levy said he did not want Monticello to become a museum, an idea he "abhorred." Instead, he wanted it to remain a home as he had maintained it—a summer home for presidents.

"Make it the home—the Virginia home—of the Presidents of the United States, and maintain it for their occasional occupancy," Levy said, "and I will be content."

Levy said he would therefore bow to Bryan's wishes "and those of the American people." He then set his terms. Levy said he had been offered a million dollars for Monticello and had expended that amount on it since he purchased it in 1879. "I designate a price of $500,000," he said, "which will make me more than half donor of Monticello and thus consummate the people's will."

The sudden announcement made no mention of the fact that on September 29—between the time Bryan wrote his letter and Levy answered it—the New York Democratic Party had held its primary elections. Jefferson M. Levy had decided to forgo the Senate race and stood for re-election to his Fourteenth District House seat. He lost in the primary to Michael Francis Farley, an Irish-born New York liquor magnate.

The news of Levy's change of heart on Monticello made headlines around the nation. It also made Maud Littleton very happy.

"It's the best news I have heard in many days," she told *The New York Times* from her Long Island home. She spoke glowingly of the roles played by Bryan and President Wilson in the matter. "I hope that it can be purchased at a fair price consistent to Jefferson's ideas of democracy," she said.

The *Times* reflected the opinion of many informed observers by saying that Levy's decision to sell would spur quick action in Congress to make Mrs. Littleton's wish come true very soon. "There will be little difficulty in procuring the passage of the necessary legislation," the paper said. The October 7 New York *Herald* contained a similar prediction.

The first hints that those rosy predictions would not come true came within days of Levy's announcement. The Richmond *News Leader* on October 8 reported that several members of Virginia's congressional delegation said it would be impossible for the current Congress to come up with Levy's $500,000 asking price.

The powerful Rules Committee chairman Robert Lee Henry, though, remained optimistic. He called on Congress to appropriate the $500,000 "at once, since Mr. Levy has offered to sell it at this figure." Henry vowed to do his part as Rules Committee chairman and as a member of the House to get the legislation enacted. "I will consider it an honor," he said, "to contribute any effort in the government taking over the property."

On that same day, October 8, Navy Secretary Josephus Daniels sent a letter to Jefferson Levy thanking him for his change of heart and for his stewardship of Monticello. "The country owes you a debt of gratitude for restoring the estate to its original acreage when Jefferson opened it to the throngs of patriots of all nationalities who visited him in his retirement," Daniels said. "It is equally grateful that you have preserved the house, designed by Jefferson, without change. . . ."

An editorial in the October 12 New York *Tribune* questioned Levy's price tag. Using Monticello as a presidents' summer home, the paper said, "seems like a rather slender reason for its acquisition at such a price for such a purpose. If the country is to buy a summer home for the President, undoubtedly some more suitable place could be obtained at much less cost." The editorial said that the "Monticello cult"—i.e., Mrs. Littleton and her allies—should instead "raise funds to purchase and maintain the place as a memorial to Jefferson."

The Staunton (Virginia) *Leader* agreed, recommending on October 14 that the government not purchase Monticello. "We should far rather see Virginia, or a memorial association of Virginians, acquire and preserve the property," the paper editorialized. The *Leader* favored using Monticello as a presidential country retreat rather than a museum

Other observers squarely backed Levy's idea—and price. "We hope that the government by act of Congress will be authorized to accept Jefferson Levy's offer to sell Monticello to the United States to be used as a home for our presidents," the Fredericksburg (Virginia) *Free Lance* said in an October 13 editorial. The Knoxville (Tennessee) *Sentinel* that day took the occasion to honor the Levy family. "Commodore Levy and his descendants have earned national gratitude for preserving this national shrine," the editorial said. The October 14 Charlottesville *Daily Progress* favored making Monticello a government-run "second White House" because it "would be in the best interest of Charlottesville."

Under the prodding either of Republicans or enterprising newspaper reporters, the Albemarle County tax commissioner's office announced on October 15 that Jefferson Levy's Monticello and its surrounding acreage was assessed for tax purposes at less than $30,000. That figure, real estate experts said, was as low as one-fifth the amount of Monticello's actual sales value, which translated to some $150,000.

The New York *Evening Telegram* used that news to lambaste Levy for asking a half million dollars for Monticello. "He has made no vast improvements—no costly collection of Mr. Jefferson's furniture, no macadam roads or landscape gardening," the paper said. "Also he got the estate through the breaking of his uncle's will upon a legal technicality. Otherwise it would now belong to the government, as his uncle desired. Obviously Mr. Levy has a hard position to defend in asking $500,000. . . ."

Perhaps sensing that his price was generating controversy, Jefferson Levy gave a rare interview on the subject of his ownership of Monticello in Washington, D.C., on October 16 to a reporter from the Brooklyn *Times*. Levy said that he went to Monticello "every Sunday" when he was in Washington on a "railroad journey" that "consumes a little over three hours."

That was one reason, Levy said, it would make sense to use Monti-cello as a presidential retreat. "I think it is entirely fit and proper that I include in the provisions of the sale a stipulation that it shall be main-tained throughout time as a summer home where the President of the United States can spend as much or as little of his time as he desires," Levy said.

Levy took the opportunity to tout his stewardship of Monticello. "Jefferson's bedroom and study stand today exactly as they were left by him," he said with slight exaggeration. "I have restored every detail so far as it has been possible." Levy went on to describe the desecration that occurred at Monticello after the Civil War and his efforts to gather "together the relics which had been widely scattered."

He ended the interview with an explanation of sorts of why he had for so many years steadfastly refused to sell Monticello. "The property has been the Levy home for over eighty years, almost continuously since the days of Jefferson," he said, so "is it to be wondered that I have been slow in deciding to part with it?"

In December, James Hay, a Virginia Democrat and the chairman of the House Committee on Military Affairs, introduced a bill directing the government to buy Monticello for $500,000 and turn it into a resi-dence for the President and his family. The bill called for the govern-ment to make a $100,000 down payment and pay off the balance in $50,000 annual increments.

It seemed that 1915 would be the year in which Mrs. Littleton's wish came true. Support appeared strong among Senate and House leaders and in the White House. Mrs. Littleton had ended her anti–Jefferson Levy rhetoric. For his part, Levy had abandoned his strong insistence on not letting Monticello go, and seemed resigned to selling it.

There was one big sticking point, though: the half-million-dollar asking price—a large sum in 1914 and one that a significant number of members of Congress thought was too much to pay.

Representative Henry's Rules Committee met on February 23 to consider two different resolutions to purchase Monticello for $500,000. The first was the one introduced by James Hay in December, which called for turning Monticello into the president's Virginia residence.

The other envisioned transforming Monticello into a museum and archive stocked with Thomas Jefferson's manuscripts and other writings, "especially those connected with his public acts and the public history of the times in which he lived." Monticello also would hold "the relics associated with [Jefferson's] private life and public services," the resolution said.

The committee heard from only two witnesses, Jefferson Levy and Maud Littleton. Levy led off the session with a brief, subdued presentation.

"It had never been my intention or wish to sell Monticello," he said, "but a sense of patriotic duty urged me to do it by the call of the administration, and by various states of this union, which seemed almost imperative." At what he called "a great personal sacrifice, both from a sentimental and monetary standpoint," Levy said, "I have yielded to what appears to be the wishes of the country and I am ready and willing to accept the government's offer of $500,000."

That was the extent of his remarks. Then it was Mrs. Littleton's turn. She also was brief—at least in comparison to her previous hours-long congressional testimony. She reintroduced the 1915 letter from President Wilson, and went on to make a case for Levy's $500,000 price, saying Monticello was "priceless." She cited the $2 million projected cost of the Lincoln Memorial, then under construction at the west end of the Mall. "Surely Congress, which has always been more than generous in honoring the memory of our illustrious dead, will not refuse this small sum for Jefferson," Mrs. Littleton said. "It is a fourth of what is now being expended to build the handsome memorial to Lincoln on the Mall."

She invoked Jefferson's legacy, and defended Jefferson Levy against those who said he was "taking advantage of a national sentiment for private gain." It was a lukewarm defense, however. Mrs. Littleton implied that Levy was doing the right thing for the wrong reasons and—in a roundabout way—impugned his morals, generosity, and patriotism.

"In business agreements or real estate transactions, the moral qualities, or generosity or patriotism of the parties concerned do not matter," she said. "If the owner is willing to convey the property to the government for a certain sum, his motive, whatever it is, should not be considered a reason for not buying the place."

The next day, February 24, the Rules Committee approved the resolution that would turn Monticello into a government-run Jefferson museum and reported it to the House. The following day the Charlottesville *Daily Progress* came out in favor of the deal.

"Half a million dollars is a big sum to pay," the paper conceded. "But when we take into consideration the principle involved and the great value that Monticello as government property will prove for coming generations, we reach the decision that half a million is a small sum and that the United States can well afford to pay it."

University of Virginia president Edwin Alderman endorsed the House resolution in a February 12, 1915, letter to James Hay. On February 26, President Wilson lobbied Senate and House leaders for passage of the resolution. Support on Capitol Hill, though, was tepid, at best. Despite the high-level lobbying from the White House, it appeared that the resolution would not even come up for a vote in the House because there weren't enough votes for passage. House leaders, the New York *Herald* reported that day, "state privately that a gentlemen's agreement had been reached to let the proposal slumber in the Rules Committee." Hay said the strong opposition caused him to abandon hope that Congress would enact the resolution in the current session.

On March 4, 1915, in the waning days of the Sixty-third Congress, Jefferson Levy gave his valedictory speech in the House. "I have distinct views and strong convictions arrived at from a long legal and business experience in contact with men of affairs," Levy said in that day's Extension of Remarks period. "I have endeavored to use this experience for the welfare of the country, and to express these convictions when matters of moment were under consideration which did not appear to me to be conducive to this welfare."

He then set out a long, detailed list of what he considered his accomplishments in his six-year career in the House of Representatives—a "general resume," he termed it, "of the part I have taken in the deliberations and legislative actions of this body." Levy spoke about his opposition to congressional investigations of the Steel Trust. He went on at length about the Federal Reserve Act of 1913, which created the federal reserve system ruled by a new a federal reserve board of presidential appointees. Levy had been a sponsor of the original legislation establishing the system.

He spoke about what he called a pattern in Congress of "unjust attacks" against New York City, particularly in regard to laws dealing with currency and finances. "New York is characterized as the abiding place of all the evils that ever afflicted or ever will afflict this Government," Levy said, "and as the home and refuge of all the enemies who seek to destroy the welfare of our nation." He strongly defended the city in which he was born and raised and where he lived most of his life.

Levy went on to explain why he opposed the imposition of an income tax and why he opposed additional antitrust legislation. He noted that he had been a consistent exponent of a strong U.S. military. He explained how he had worked to streamline Interstate Commerce Commission procedures on railroad regulation and how he proudly helped defeat a bill that would have abolished dealing in cotton futures options.

He spoke with pride of the fact that he was the author of an amendment that limited loan interest rates to a maximum of twelve percent per year and an amendment that increased pay for watchmen, messengers, and laborers employed by U.S. post offices. He touted his unsuccessful efforts to get the government to sell $240-million worth of Panama Canal bonds and his successful effort to block legislation depriving New York State of its territorial rights to the Niagara River.

Levy ended his congressional farewell with another complaint about the "slurs which have . . . ignorantly been sometimes made upon my great city." He allowed, however, that he had "no hard feelings on the matter," and said he would "cherish" the "many strong friendships" he had made in Congress.

In his remarks, Jefferson Levy made no mention of Monticello.

. . .

NOTHING noteworthy occurred on the Monticello front in Washington after the flurry of activity in February 1915 until late July of 1916. Aside from the political reasons alluded to by Congressman Hay, another factor delayed things on Capitol Hill: congressional concern about the large-scale war that had broken out in Europe in August 1914. As an editorial in the Charlottesville *Daily Progress* on September 24, 1915, put it: "It seems that the European situation has for the time being quieted the discussion about purchasing Monticello. . . ."

In the spring and summer of 1916, the National Society of the Daughters of the American Revolution became active for the first time in the Monticello movement. Known familiarly as the Daughters of the American Revolution, or DAR, the patriotic society was founded in 1890 and was incorporated by an act of Congress in 1896. With a motto of "God, Home and Country," the DAR had some ninety thousand members in 1916—all of whom could prove they were descended from an ancestor who either fought in the Revolutionary War or otherwise helped in the American independence effort.

Lobbying from Mrs. Littleton was one reason the DAR became involved. Another had to do with one of the organization's goals: historic preservation. Support among DAR leaders for the Monticello movement received a boost in April when seventy-seven of the organization's leaders paid a visit to Monticello.

The group traveled by special train to Charlottesville on its way to Washington to attend the DAR's annual Continental Congress, which is held during the week of April 19, the anniversary of the Battle of Lexington. After a visit to the University of Virginia, the women went to Monticello where they took part in a brief ceremony at Jefferson's tomb followed by a guided tour of the mansion.

On July 26, 1916, a large delegation of DAR members, headed by the organization's president general, Mrs. William Cummings Story, called on President Wilson at the White House. Their mission: to lobby him to help influence Congress to pass the Monticello purchase resolution.

"The President told the delegation he was in favor of the $500,000 called for in the bill to purchase the property," the *Daily Progress* reported, "and would give his influence and aid having the bill passed."

Mrs. Story, accompanied by Mrs. Littleton and several other Monticello activists, officially announced on July 31 that President Wilson was on board and made public a letter he wrote to them on July 27 following the White House meeting. "I sincerely hope that it will be possible for the Government of the United States to become the owner of Monticello," Wilson said in the letter, adding that he would "be glad at any time to do anything I can to assist."

Mrs. Story was optimistic about congressional passage. "One thing which makes me particularly hopeful that this movement will be a success is the fact that there seems to be no factional opposition to it," she said. "All parties seem to favor it and I think it will be considered in a non-partisan manner."

A new resolution was on the table. This one was introduced at the DAR's request by Rep. Charles S. Davis of Minnesota, whose wife chaired the DAR's Committee on Legislation. Davis's resolution, which called for the government to purchase Monticello for $500,000 and for the DAR to operate the property, was considered in a nonpartisan manner at a two-part hearing held on August 8 by the House Committee on Public Grounds. Mrs. Story was the lead witness, telling the panel that she represented more than 92,000 DAR members, "who constitute the greatest patriotic organization in the world."

She had only glowing words for Jefferson Levy, "himself a descendant of distinguished Revolutionary [War] patriots." Levy, Mrs. Story said, had kept Monticello "in a perfect condition," restored it "to its original beauty," and "filled [it] with many of the original pieces of furniture and objects of art that adorned it during Jefferson's time." Levy, as we have seen, did fill Monticello mainly with furniture and art *similar* to what Jefferson had.

After giving a long, laudatory description of Jefferson's Monticello, Mrs. Story lobbied for the pending resolution. Five hundred thousand dollars, she said, "is not too much to pay when one takes into consideration the fact that the present owner was offered a million dollars for it and refused it because he would not part with this priceless treasure except to the Government of the United States."

Mrs. Story went on to make her case for the government to turn the running of Monticello over to the DAR. "We, the Daughters of the American Revolution, would ask that the custody of this precious shrine be entrusted to our loving, reverent care," she said. "In asking this trust we weigh well the responsibility and the privilege. We ask by right of descent from the patriots, and because [the DAR] is an incorporated body, well disciplined and conducted, accustomed to system and business administration. . . ."

She suggested that the DAR could run Monticello, not as a Jefferson museum or shrine, but as a Virginia home for the president of the United States. To do so, Mrs. Story suggested a congressional appropriation of "not less than $12,000 a year."

Some fifty thousand visitors a year came to Monticello, Mrs. Story claimed. That statement brought up the subject of admission fees. Mrs. Story said that although Levy did not charge admission, a fee "might be necessary for its maintenance" after the sale to the government. Committee chairman Frank Clark, a Florida Democrat, said he thought there should be no admission charge because of complaints about such fees at Mount Vernon.

The committee then heard from J. Charles Linthicum, a Maryland Democrat who spoke in favor of the DAR plan. He told the committee that he had spent the previous weekend at Monticello as Jefferson Levy's guest and "found the place in very good condition." Although the roads leading to the mountain were "somewhat washed," Monticello itself "is in an excellent state of preservation for a building of that age," Linthicum said. "Nothing about the building or the grounds has been changed so as to change the effect of it as it was when Mr. Jefferson lived there. Everything seems to have been kept as intact as near as possible."

Mrs. Story was asked by John L. Burnett, an Alabama Democrat, what Monticello's tax assessment was. "I know very little about that part of it," Mrs. Story said. She said for a second time that morning that she'd been told that Levy was offered $1 million for Monticello and had turned it down. Mrs. Story then said she had appealed to "a very rich man in New York who I know has a desire to own Monticello." She asked the unidentified man for "a large donation toward its preservation," but he turned her down, saying he'd rather buy the place for himself. Mrs. Story called the prospect of Monticello being sold to a private individual "very abhorrent."

Richard W. Austin, a Tennessee Republican, read a telegram he had received the day before from Mrs. Littleton. "I have urged this cause so honestly and so repeatedly upon the Members of the American Congress," she said, "that it is unnecessary for me to say or do more now." She expressed the wish that Austin present the telegram to the committee "and tell them I have done all I could."

After Mrs. Story went over details of Jefferson Levy's collection and restoration of Jeffersonian articles, the committee members debated whether or not to add language to the resolution assuring that those items be conveyed with the sale. After some discussion, they agreed that new language would be necessary to insure that Levy included the items in the sale.

Austin asked Mrs. Story if the DAR would object to another amendment to the resolution barring admissions fees to the house and grounds. Mrs. Story replied that she did not think there would be any objection. When asked if the DAR had calculated what the costs to maintain Monticello would be, Mrs. Story confessed that the DAR's fiscal plan envisioned covering maintenance costs with gate receipts, which she estimated to be "about $30,000." She was asked if the DAR would be willing to absorb that cost if there were no admission fee. Mrs. Story replied affirmatively, saying the organization "would be willing to go to any reasonable possible expense."

The Public Buildings and Grounds Committee took no action on the resolution. On Saturday, October 7, 1916, a large DAR delegation made up of members of the national board and many of its state regents came to Charlottesville from Washington following a board meeting and made a pilgrimage to Monticello. The party was greeted by Carl Mayhoff, several prominent women from Charlottesville, including Mrs. R. T. W. Duke, Jr., and twenty members of the DAR Albemarle County chapter.

The group was treated to a luncheon in the mansion. During the meal, telegrams were read from Jefferson M. Levy and Amelia Mayhoff who were in New York City. After lunch the delegation toured the house and grounds.

Two months later, on Wednesday, December 6, the House Public

Buildings and Grounds Committee held another hearing on the purchase of Monticello. This time the price issue was the main focus. Committee members debated the $500,000 sales price at the start of the 10:00 A.M. hearing because Mrs. Story was late in arriving.

"I would like to know whether that price has been ascertained to be a reasonable price for the property," said Hatton W. Sumners, a Texas Democrat.

"I do not think it has been so ascertained," replied Kentucky Republican John W. Langley.

John L. Burnett said that the committee had not taken any steps to determine Monticello's value. Chairman Frank Clark then read the part of Jefferson Levy's October 5, 1914, letter to William Jennings Bryan, in which Levy said he was offered $1 million for Monticello and had spent that same amount on it, but would sell it to the government for $500,000.

"I have a letter here saying it is not worth $150,000," Langley said.

When Mrs. Story arrived, she was asked about Monticello's worth. "I am unable to give a real estate man's estimate of the value of the property," she said. She then spoke of the valuable timber on the property. She told the committee that she had recently learned that Cornelius Vanderbilt II (1843–1899), the grandson of the famed industrialist, had offered $900,000 for Monticello to use for a country residence.

"That would appear to indicate that at least it was safe in assuming that it is fully worth $500,000 now," she said. Mrs. Story also mentioned that she was told Levy spent some $30,000 a year in upkeep and maintenance.

The discussion then turned to whether or not Monticello's furniture and furnishings would convey with the sale to the government. Mrs. Story testified that she had spoken to Jefferson Levy about the matter and he said the sale would include all of the contents of the house except for his Levy family portraits.

Mrs. Story said that since the prior hearing, she had traveled "all over the country," and found that "the feeling is very strong among a great many people that we should carry this proposition through and preserve this place." Representative Langley read a letter from a DAR member, Mrs. Martha O. Adams of Kentucky, who opposed the purchase on fiscal grounds and because buying Monticello would be "the most dangerous precedent to establish." Mrs. Story said that Mrs. Adams's letter was the first case she had heard "where there was any objection among our members."

The topic then returned to the half-million-dollar sales price. Burnett called it "an enormous price for that property."

"I think it is very cheap in view of the fact that he was offered $1 million for it and refused it," Austin rejoined.

"I am talking about the question of real value, not the sentimental value," Burnett replied.

Chairman Clark asked Mrs. Story to look up Monticello's assessed value and bring that information to the committee. Langley asked her to find out what Jefferson Levy had paid for the property and the surrounding land. Sumners asked her to obtain a listing of Monticello's "relics."

When the committee reconvened nine days later, on Friday, December 15, 1916, Mrs. Story showed up with what she said was "proof of the material value of Monticello." She submitted the assessed value of the property by the state of Virginia, but apologized for not having had the time to get a professional appraisal done.

She read from a letter Jefferson Levy had written to her on December 7 in which Levy said he had spent some $100,000 restoring Monticello. He listed the land acquisitions he made around Monticello, but did not include their purchase prices. He estimated that the total cost for the restoration of Monticello, his land purchases, and yearly maintenance "would, with interest, amount to over $1 million." An appraisal of Monticello, he said, "seems incongruous [and] hideously inappropriate" because of Jefferson's immense stature and because of the building's "solid construction."

Levy closed the long letter with a pledge to convey Monticello's Jefferson-associated contents with the sale. "Whatever personal property there was used by him or has associations connected with him . . . may be included in the estate," Levy said.

Mrs. Story then went into more detail on the value question. A nearby landowner, she said, told her that his 236 acres near Monticello were worth $300,000. She estimated that the value of land at the University of Virginia was more than $1,000 an acre.

Mrs. Story then made a surprising announcement. Because of inferences that the DAR had some "selfish interest" in operating a government-owned Monticello, she asked that the resolution under discussion be amended "so that we do not ask for its custody."

If asked to do so, she said, the DAR would, with "the greatest pleasure" operate Monticello. However, she said, the DAR wanted it made clear that it did "not present our plea and our request for the preservation of Monticello with any string tied to it as to the custody being in our organization."

Austin then asked how Virginia's congressional delegation stood on the bill. Representative Harrison of Virginia spoke out, saying he "heartily" favored the bill. As for the Virginia delegation, Harrison said he thought they would be in favor of the acquisition of the property, "although some of them may think the price asked for is exorbitant."

Judge Duke, who said he was not representing Levy and was appearing "at my own expense as a citizen of the State of Virginia," then elaborated in more detail on the value question. He spoke about Jefferson Levy's acquisition of Monticello and the work he did to restore it. The commercial value of Monticello, he said, "would be $150,000 today." He would not put a price on Monticello's sentimental value.

"When you come to the sentimental value," he said, "suppose it was the statue of the Venus de Milo—if it was sold as a piece of marble, I do not think it would bring fifty cents."

Austin took Levy to task for not telling the committee the exact amount of money he had spent on Monticello and for the land acquisitions around it. "I think the proposition . . . would be stronger if Mr. Levy would put all his cards on the table and not conceal anything and not withhold anything," Austin said. "We know this property was bought at a very small price and it hurts the proposition to withhold the information. . . . This makes me mad and makes me feel like voting against the bill."

Mrs. Story, the *Daily Progress* reported the next day, paid a visit to President Wilson at the White House after the House hearing. She told the president that the DAR would continue to work hard for the Monticello purchase resolution, but "does not want or expect to have the estate placed under its charge when the bill becomes law."

President Wilson again came out in favor of the passage of the bill.

The Senate Committee on Public Buildings on Grounds held a hearing on Tuesday, January 9, 1917, on yet another Monticello resolution, this one sponsored by Senator Ellison DuRant "Cotton Ed" Smith, a South Carolina Democrat. Smith's resolution called for the government to purchase Monticello for $500,000 and use it as a Virginia home for the president. It entrusted the care of the house to the Daughters of the American Revolution. The DAR, the resolution said, would "have the general care and control of [Monticello] and make such rules as they may deem proper in regard to keeping the same open to visitors."

Mrs. Story led off with a prepared statement. She asked once again that the language authorizing the DAR to care for Monticello be eliminated from the resolution. She strongly recommended that the government purchase Monticello and maintain it, not as a Virginia White House, but as a Jefferson shrine and museum.

"It is clear," she said, that Monticello "should be thrown open to the people, belong to the people, and be always accessible to the people."

Senator Claude S. Swanson, the committee's chairman, then turned to Judge Duke. On this occasion, Duke said, he was appearing as Jefferson Levy's attorney. After a very brief opening statement, he agreed to answer questions. Senator James W. Wadsworth, Jr., a New York Republican, peppered Judge Duke with questions about Monticello's agricultural potential.

Senator James A. Reed of Missouri, who had tangled with Judge Duke and Jefferson Levy at the 1914 Public Buildings and Grounds hearings, then grilled Duke about Levy's asking price.

Reed wanted to know what raw land was selling for around Monticello.

"Anywhere from $50 to $250 an acre," Judge Duke answered.

Reed asked what it would cost to build Monticello in 1917, and the Judge replied that it "would cost $100,000 to build it today."

Reed asked about the $45,000 mortgage on Monticello. He asked how to measure Monticello's sentimental value. He asked Judge Duke how much money Jefferson Levy "has laid out and expended" on Monticello.

"Oh, my dear sir," Duke replied, "I suppose that property has cost Mr. Levy since 1880 over a half a million dollars."

Reed asked Duke what that half million went for. Duke spoke, in reply, about how Monticello was "a ruin" when Levy acquired it and how Levy repaired and restored it and bought up the land around it.

Reed hammered away at Duke for not providing exact figures. "I am trying to get at the distinction between what Mr. Levy may have said to you in some statement and something that you know of your own knowledge," he said. Judge Duke still would not offer specifics.

"I never saw Mr. Levy's books," he said.

Reed asked whether Levy received any income from the property. Duke said he doubted it. Reed asked if there was an admission fee. Judge Duke explained that there had been, but that Levy ended the practice many years ago. Reed asked about Uriah Levy's will. Judge Duke explained its terms.

Then Reed asked: "How did the Levy family get this property away from the United States Government, or deprive the United States Government of receiving the benefaction of Commodore Levy?"

Duke described the executors' lawsuit, the family partition suit, and the Virginia Supreme Court suit. Reed interrupted.

"What I am trying to get is this," he said. Uriah Levy's "heirs came in and deprived the United States Government of [Monticello] upon the legal technicality that the bequest was too indefinite as to the recipient of the bequest . . . and because of this technicality the heirs of Levy were able to reclaim the property and take it away from the United States."

Reed then went over Jefferson Levy's acquisition of the other heirs' Monticello shares. He asked Judge Duke how much Levy paid the other heirs.

"About $10,000," Duke answered.

"So," Reed replied, "to all intents and purposes he acquired the property for $20,000?"

Duke agreed.

"Since then he has bought about 550 acres and paid on the average of about $50 an acre for it?" Reed then asked.

"I suppose so," Duke replied.

"That is all I desire to ask," Reed said.

Virginia Representative Thomas N. Harrison—called "Judge Harrison" because he had served as a Circuit Court judge before entering Congress in 1916—then testified, saying he favored the government's purchase but had been against government condemnation of Monticello. Reed challenged Harrison on that point, implying again that Jefferson Levy had used a legal technicality to steal Monticello from the government.

"If it is right for him to take by law, regardless of sentiment, why is it not right for the Federal Government to take back by law regardless of the same sentiment?" Reed asked Harrison.

"I do not think the Government would be justified in doing that," Harrison replied, "especially as I understand the [lawsuits] were instituted by this man's father."

Judge Duke jumped in: "Oh yes," he said. "When those proceedings were instituted by his father [Jefferson Levy] was eight years old, I think." (He was ten and a half.)

Harrison and Reed then sparred over the value of Monticello.

"If a man chooses to ask a certain price for [a property] the Government has to pay the price that he puts upon it, in my judgment, or else forgo the acquisition of the property," Judge Harrison said.

To which Reed replied: "Suppose he should put a price of $10 million on it?"

"I would advise the Government not to take it," Harrison said.

The hearing ended a few minutes later with Harrison and Duke offering their thoughts on what use the government would put to the surrounding acreage after it bought Monticello.

"It could be used for demonstrations of forestry," Judge Duke suggested.

"It would be very useful for a public park," Judge Harrison offered.

The committee went into executive session but took no action on the Monticello resolution. Senator Smith officially introduced his Monticello legislation on April 12. Six days later Charles Russell Davis of Minnesota introduced a companion bill in the House of Representatives. Both bills were referred to committees, where no action was taken on either of them.

That represented the last time the Congress of the United States considered purchasing Thomas Jefferson's Monticello.

.   .   .

IN THE weeks following the committee hearing there still seemed to be fairly widespread sentiment in Congress for the government purchase of Monticello. In an effort to keep the momentum for a sale alive, Mrs. Story and the DAR arranged for a large group of congressmen to make a personal inspection of the house and grounds.

On Sunday morning, January 28, 1917, a party of forty men and twenty-seven women—including many members of the House Committee on Public Buildings and Grounds and their wives—boarded two special Southern Railway cars for the trip from Washington to Charlottesville. The train pulled into Charlottesville shortly after noon.

The party—which also included Mrs. Story and several members of the DAR's national board of directors—was met at the station by a delegation from the local Chamber of Commerce and whisked up to snow-covered Monticello in two dozen automobiles. The lead vehicle was decorated with two huge American flags, donated by the DAR.

The group gathered on Monticello's east lawn to take in the mountain views and then proceeded to the front steps where Jefferson M. Levy, assisted by his Charlottesville neighbor, Miriam Boocock, greeted them. The guests took a guided tour of all of Monticello's rooms before sitting down to a lavish lunch in the dining room. Levy brought in a phalanx of black waiters and maids for the occasion.

"The spread set out by the genial host of today was in keeping with the traditional hospitality of the famous mansion," the Charlottesville *Daily Progress* reported. "An elegant menu was served the many guests, whose appetites had been whetted by the three-mile drive in the bracing mountain air, and they did full justice to the elegant and toothsome viands which had been provided." Several newspaper and newsreel photographers were on hand, although the images they took have not survived.

The visit was not a success, however. The problem—of all things—was Jefferson Levy's refusal to serve wine with lunch. When the thirsty congressmen and newspapermen asked to see Jefferson's wine cellar, Levy "said he had left the keys in New York," the Roanoke *Times* reported.

"'Oh well, that's all right,' said some of the leading committee members. 'We'll just break in the door and make a hole in the floor.'

"But Levy said, 'No' and would not budge from the decision."

That brought about "much grumbling" from the distinguished guests, the paper said, "and it was freely rumored that Mr. Levy would have to materially reduce his offer below $500,000 if he expected Congress to buy the old Jefferson home."

Whether or not the lack of wine had any impact on Congress, the fact remains that the Sixty-Fourth Congress adjourned on March 3, 1917, without taking action on any of the Monticello resolutions.

Later that month the DAR made what Charles Hosmer called its "last great endeavor to help Mrs. Littleton." The endeavor took the form of a decidedly upbeat article in the March 1917 issue of the *D.A.R. Magazine* calling the organization's Monticello effort "the noblest project that has ever engaged the interest of the Society." The article went on to endorse the pending congressional resolution and to praise Monticello as "the most artistic home in America in its time" and "a noble historic shrine of which any Nation can be proud."

In April the DAR made what proved to be the organization's last effort on behalf of Monticello. At its annual Congress in Washington some three thousand pro-Monticello acquisition petitions were distributed to delegates. They were instructed to take the petitions home, fill them with signatures and send them to members of Congress. There is no record of how many petitions were forwarded to Capitol Hill.

Jefferson Levy, meanwhile, seemed to be trying to reactivate his public affairs career. A year earlier, newspaper reports said he was one of two men being given serious consideration by President Wilson to be named postmaster of New York City. The appointment never came.

In February of 1917, Levy let it be known that he would not say no if Tammany Hall asked him to run for mayor of New York City in the upcoming election. Levy was not asked. Tammany Hall instead picked John F. Hylan, who defeated incumbent mayor John Purroy Mitchel in November.

Levy also announced in the spring of 1917 that he wouldn't rule out running for the presidency of New York City's Board of Aldermen, what is now called the City Council. He did not run.

On April 6, 1917, the United States declared war on Germany, and the Sixty-fifth Congress, which began work later that month, was preoccupied with war matters for the rest of that year. At one point the movement to purchase Monticello intersected with Congress's overriding war concerns.

On October 4, Stanley H. Dent, Jr., an Alabama Democrat who chaired the House Committee on Military Affairs, introduced a resolution calling for the government to purchase Monticello for $500,000 and use it as a "convalescent hospital for the soldiers and sailors of the existing war." The bill directed that Monticello be turned into a national park after the war.

The Monticello war hospital resolution received the endorsement of Secretary of War Newton D. Baker and there appeared to be strong support for the measure in Congress. The Charlottesville Chamber of Commerce favored the proposal and set up a committee to lobby Congress for passage of the resolution. To that end, the committee in November invited U.S. Surgeon General W. C. Gorgas to visit Monticello to see if it would be suitable for a wartime hospital.

Observers expected the resolution to pass when Congress began its second session early in December 1917. But, once again, no action was taken.

. . .

ALL WAS quiet on the Monticello front during the war year of 1918. And no one in Congress seemed in a hurry to revisit the Monticello acquisition business after the war ended on November 11. In the spring, when it became apparent that Congress would take no action, Jefferson Levy decided to put Monticello up for public sale. He chose H. W. Hilleary, a real estate broker in Washington, D.C., who specialized in selling large Virginia estates.

In April 1919, Hilleary sent a prospecting letter to upper-crust individuals around the country. It read:

> You are familiar, I am sure, with "Monticello," in the beautiful County of Albemarle, near the University of Virginia, also designed by Thomas Jefferson.
>
> This historic home, this architectural gem, this most picturesque estate, I have the privilege of offering.
>
> The present owner, for sentimental and other reasons, has never consented to part with it. I am allowed now to bring it to the attention of those who can appreciate and are able to own a property of such distinction and merit.
>
> If interested, I shall be glad to give you detailed information and to quote the authorized price.

The "other reasons" Hilleary referred to were financial. Although the news did not come out at the time, during World War I Jefferson Levy suffered the fate of many boom-and-bust stock and real estate speculators. He lost enormous amounts of money in the stock market and was forced to sell virtually all of his vast New York and Virginia real estate holdings to pay his mounting debts.

Hilleary sent one of the letters to William Sumner Appleton, the founder of the Society for the Preservation of New England Antiquities in Boston. Appleton replied to Hilleary on April 4, saying he was "sorry to hear that 'Monticello' is on the market" and asking for more details about the property.

In his April 12, 1919, reply to Appleton, Hilleary, thinking Appleton was interested in buying Monticello, let it be known that it could be had for $400,000, but left room for price negotiation. "I am authorized to quote $400,000 for the property but, if after examination, you deem it to your interest to submit an offer, I shall be most happy to bring it to the attention of Mr. Levy, the owner."

Appleton replied April 14, telling Hilleary he had no personal interest in buying Monticello, but would pass on the information to the society's members.

"I hope," Appleton said, "that 'Monticello' will fall into the very best of hands, as it so richly deserves to do."

Hilleary received another reply on April 19 from Sidney Fiske Kimball (1888–1955), a Massachusetts-born architectural scholar who was a professor of architecture and fine arts at the University of Michigan and the chairman of the Archaeological Institute of America's Committee on Colonial and National Art. Kimball, who had taught architecture at the University of Virginia, was nationally recognized as the foremost expert on Thomas Jefferson's architecture.

In his writings, including *Thomas Jefferson, Architect*, a 1916 folio volume of Jefferson's architectural drawings for which he wrote the text, Fiske Kimball—as he was known—lionized Jefferson's architectural talents. In his reply to Hilleary, Kimball said that it was possible that the Archaeological Institute would purchase Monticello if the price were right.

"I am desirous of further particulars regarding the sale of Monticello, with a view to possible purchase by this and related organizations," Kimball wrote. "At what price does Mr. Levy now hold the estate, and what concessions might he be willing to make to insure its sale to a public body which would hold it in the interest of the nation?"

Kimball added that he knew Jefferson Levy well and had helped him "two years ago at a time when he hoped to effect a sale to the Coolidge family of Boston."

In his reply to Kimball, dated April 29, 1919, Hilleary said that he had talked to Jefferson Levy about possible "concessions," and Levy thought it best that Kimball come to Monticello where the two could meet to discuss the matter. Levy, Hilleary said, "is more than anxious that some organization like yours should hold 'Monticello' in the interests of the Nation."

Hilleary said that Levy would accept $500,000, the price that "the

Government practically decided to purchase the property" before World War I. "At one time," Hilleary said, Levy "had been offered more but did, at the request of many prominent men, consent to deliver the property" to the government.

When he wrote back to Hilleary on May 3, Kimball said the Institute would not consider purchasing Monticello because Jefferson Levy was asking far too much. "I fear we shall have to be counted out of any effort to purchase the place in the public interest," he said. "Leaving aside the question of the reasonableness of the price suggested for a property assessed at about $25,000 and heavily mortgaged, I believe it is entirely impracticable to raise any such sum as half a million by subscription for such an object at this time."

That is an interesting response, especially considering Kimball's intimate knowledge of Monticello's history. He must have known that the $25,000 assessment was an extreme undervaluation, and that the small, partial mortgage Jefferson Levy had on the property could in no way be construed to mean that the property was "heavily mortgaged." Kimball also must have known that Jefferson Levy had spent hundreds of thousands of dollars on Monticello's upkeep during the four decades he had owned it.

Nevertheless, Kimball restated his objections to Levy's $500,000 price tag in a May 15, 1919, letter to Seth Gano, acting secretary of the Harvard Class of 1907. Gano had written to Kimball two days earlier asking—"as a Harvard man"—if he was "still interested" in buying Monticello. Gano said that he had "personal friends who are in a position to possibly deliver the entire estate at a fixed sum," and wanted Kimball's input because "a fairly large sum of money will be required to purchase the estate."

Kimball told Gano he was "greatly interested that Monticello shall be purchased either by some quasi-public body like several with which I am connected, or by some private individual who will not exploit it but treat it with suitable care and public spirit." Then he mentioned his correspondence with Hilleary and Levy's $500,000 asking price.

It appears that Hilleary received no offers for Monticello as a result of his 1919 letter.

. . .

THE SECOND organized movement to purchase Monticello—the
Thomas Jefferson Memorial Association—was formed in June 1920
by Ruth Read Cunningham of Richmond, Virginia, who claimed to be
a direct descendant of Ann Pamela Cunningham, the founder of
the Mount Vernon Ladies Association, which successfully purchased
George Washington's home.

"Miss Ruth Cunningham is said to be inspired with the idea of acquiring the Jefferson home by the work of her relative," *The New York
Times* reported June 29.

Ruth Cunningham's association, based in Richmond, was made up
primarily of socially prominent women. Around the same time another
women's group, the National Monticello Association, was formed in
Washington, D.C., for the same purpose. That group was founded by
the socialite, painter, and writer Marietta Minnegerode Andrews
(1869–1931), who used her social connections in Washington to draw a
well-heeled crowd to a series of receptions, theatricals, and historical
tableaux to publicize the association's work. The co-founder was the
suffragist and Democratic Party activist Rose de Chine Gouverneur
Hoes (1860-1933), a great-granddaughter of President James Monroe.
In 1927 she founded the James Monroe Museum and Memorial Library
in Fredericksburg, Virginia.

The Thomas Jefferson Memorial Association's secretary, Charles W.
Swan, announced in late June that Jefferson Levy had offered Monticello to the association for $500,000, with the stipulation that Monti-
cello be converted into a national memorial to Thomas Jefferson. Levy
said that all of Monticello's Jefferson relics would be part of the purchase price. The association, Swan said, expected to raise the money
from "influential citizens"—not from the general public—for the purchase in the next two to three months.

Among the financial heavy hitters onboard, Swan said, was James
Watson Gerard (1867–1951), a former New York State supreme court
judge, large Democratic Party financial backer, and former ambassador
to Germany who was named the association's president. Also onboard

were Halles Rhinehard, president of the Charlottesville National Bank, and John L. Livers, president of the Charlotte and Albemarle Railway.

Jefferson Levy told *The New York Times* that the actual purchase price was $1 million, but he was willing to "pay" half that amount. He also said the offer was open to any other organization willing to turn Monticello into a Jefferson memorial house. Levy justified the $1-million purchase price as "reasonable," the *Times* said, "because he had been offered $1,200,000 by individuals who desired the property for their private use." Levy refused those offers, he said, "because he wanted the estate to go to the nation."

Jefferson Levy was sixty-eight years old in 1920. His public career had ended ingloriously when he lost in the New York Democratic primary for his own House seat in September 1914. His business career was devolving in a sea of debt. That distressed state of affairs was not evident, however, in Jefferson Levy's entry in the 1920 edition of *The National Cyclopaedia of American Biography*. That reference book, first published in 1892, based its biographies on questionnaires and other information supplied by its biographees. Jefferson Levy's 1920 entry—for which there is little doubt that he provided the information—was filled with embellishments, mistruths, exaggerations, and omissions, especially with regard to his family history.

The entry mistakenly claimed that Levy's great-grandfather was the Revolutionary War figure Benjamin Levy. It said that both of Levy's grandfathers—Michael Levy and Jonas Phillips—were "officers" in the Revolutionary War. There is no record that Michael Levy ever served in the Revolutionary army and Jonas Phillips, as we have seen, was not an officer, but a private in the Philadelphia militia.

The entry says that Monticello was confiscated by the Confederacy "because its owner [Uriah Levy] was one of the first naval officers to offer his services to Pres. Lincoln and was also the first to subscribe to government bonds at the outbreak of the war." The truth is that Monticello was seized under the South's Sequestration Act. The idea that Uriah Levy was the first federal government bond purchaser when the Civil War started is a gross exaggeration, at best.

The entry gave the impression that Levy earned his living in "real estate law." It contained not a word about the real estate and stock market speculation that earned (and lost) him millions. The entry went into mostly factual detail on the highlights of Levy's congressional career, but turned into hagiography with its description of Levy's ownership of Monticello.

"Mr. Levy represents the highest type of public official," the entry said. "He is a man of intense patriotism and keeps 'Monticello' open to the public year round at a personal expense of between $30,000 and $40,000 a year, believing that visits to this historic home inspire patriotism and inspiration in the minds and hearts of the people."

Not a word was mentioned that Levy was very much trying to unload Monticello and that Ruth Cunningham's association had not come up with any large contributors. In May 1921, the association changed its tactics.

At a meeting held in the law offices of Henry Wickham of Richmond, the group drew up a new charter and incorporated under a slightly new name, The Thomas Jefferson National Memorial Association. A few days later at a meeting at the Charlottesville home of Mr. and Mrs. E. D. Hotchkiss, officers were elected. E. D. Hotchkiss, a Chesapeake and Ohio Railway official, was chosen as president; Edith Hotchkiss was named vice president; Mrs. J. Allison Hodges was named second vice president; Mrs. John Skelton Williams, third vice president and Miss Ruth Cunningham, secretary and treasurer. The group also decided to raise money through popular subscriptions, rather than by soliciting large donations.

Jefferson Levy's younger brother and business and law partner, Louis Napoleon Levy, died at his home on West Seventy-second Street in New York City at age sixty-six of encephalitis after a year-long illness on April 9, 1921. In late July, many newspapers around the country— including *The New York Times, Washington Post,* and *Chicago Tribune*— reported that H. W. Hilleary in Washington was again marketing Monticello for $500,000. Jefferson Levy was widely quoted as saying that he was looking for a purchaser who would maintain Monticello as a memorial to Thomas Jefferson—someone Levy "deemed able and worthy to become the owners of such a shrine."

Hilleary's April 1921 advertising letter said:

The owner, Hon. Jefferson M. Levy of New York, has entrusted to me the sale of "Monticello," the Thomas Jefferson home in Albemarle County, Virginia, and I am only presenting it to a limited and special list of some of those who are deemed both able and worthy to become the owners of such a shrine.

I respectfully submit that this is a unique proposition from every standpoint, possessing as it does, such historic distinction; such positive value in buildings and land; such a splendid location, overlooking the great University of Virginia, which Mr. Jefferson founded, and in a region of so many other historic homes where the best social and climatic conditions exist and so easily accessible to all the principal cities.

I earnestly ask your deliberate consideration of the purchase of this property and in this connection, would invite your careful attention to the illustrated pamphlet I am sending you under separate cover, which will give you some idea of this wonderful place and beautiful country.

I trust "Monticello" will appeal to you for your individual use as an elegant and dignified country home of which any man might well be proud. The ownership of such a property by one able and so inclined will make its consecration as a memorial to the great American, Thomas Jefferson, and his works an ever present possibility and inspiration.

I would indeed be gratified to have the privilege of showing you this property at your convenience.

The pamphlet Hilleary referred to was an elaborate one that contained the text of Thomas Jefferson's first Inaugural Address, an essay on Jefferson's political career, and Fiske Kimball's "Thomas Jefferson as Architect" essay. On the last page of the brochure Hilleary made a dis-

creet sales pitch, quoting an "eminent Frenchman," who said: "It is infi-
nitely superior to any of the houses in America from point of taste and
convenience and deserves to be ranked with the most pleasant memories of France and England."

There also was a quote from Jefferson, after his return from Europe,
saying: "How grand, how magnificent, how entrancing. No where have
I seen anything to excel the beauty of this country." Monticello, the
brochure said, "is preserved with thoughtful and patriotic solicitude by
Hon. Jefferson M. Levy, of New York, the owner." Hilleary then listed
some of the "historic homes" he had sold in Virginia—including
George Mason's Gunston Hall in Mason Neck in Fairfax County and
James Monroe's Oak Hill in Loudoun County—and concluded with the
fact that he was now offering Monticello "with confidence."

Jefferson Levy told reporters that he was selling Monticello because
he could no longer afford to maintain the house and grounds. "The
place has become a great care and expense to me," Levy told *The New
York Times*, "and I am getting too old to stand the burden. It had long
been my wish to see [Monticello] set apart as a great national shrine and
I regret that I am not able myself to make this gift to the nation."

"I only wish I was in a position to give it to the Government out-
right," he told the New York *Morning World* July 28. "I have spent more
than $1,000,000 on it myself since I was a boy. The annual cost of up-
keep is tremendous and of late the burden has become so onerous that I
am afraid I will have to dispose of it."

Levy also told the *Morning World* that he had changed his mind in
1914 about selling Monticello after "conferences" he had had with
President Wilson and with William Jennings Bryan. At that time Levy
said he wanted Monticello to be used as the president's Virginia home
and not as a museum. He said in 1921 that he still wanted to sell Monticello to the government for that purpose, rather than to a private person
who might pay him more for the property.

Levy repeated his contention that several wealthy individuals had offered to buy Monticello. In the past he had either refused to identify the
men who made such offers or named Cornelius Vanderbilt II. This time
Levy named other names and gave a few details.

He had received one offer, Levy said, from the famed industrialist and philanthropist Andrew Carnegie. Several years before his death in 1919, Levy said, Carnegie "expressed a desire to buy Monticello and present it to the government, but failing health prevented him from carrying out his plan," the *Morning World* reported.

Levy told *The New York Times* that he met with Carnegie in Washington during Mrs. Littleton's campaign for the government purchase of Monticello. Carnegie, Levy said, had contributed financially to Mrs. Littleton's movement, but also understood why Levy was opposed to her plan. Carnegie said he would purchase Monticello and turn it into a Jefferson shrine if Jefferson Levy decided he wanted to sell it to an individual. A similar offer, Levy said, was made during World War I by Jacob Schiff (1847–1920), the powerful and wealthy banker, financier, and American Jewish community leader.

An editorial that appeared on July 28, 1921, in *The New York Times* called Monticello "a work of art" and as "original as few buildings ever have been." The editorial concluded: "That the first and in many ways the greatest of [Jefferson's] creations should continue in private hands is unthinkable."

An August 14 *Richmond Times-Dispatch* editorial called for the state of Virginia to purchase Monticello and turn it into a Jefferson shrine. The Commonwealth of Virginia, however, did not step forward and buy Monticello. And neither of the two private women's associations had much success raising money in 1921. In April of 1922, Ruth Cunningham's Thomas Jefferson National Memorial Association launched a new drive to raise Jefferson Levy's $500,000 asking price. Cunningham came to New York City on April 12—the day before Jefferson's birthday—to organize the drive in the Northeast.

She arrived in the city armed with endorsements in the form of letters from former presidents Woodrow Wilson and William Howard Taft (who was then Chief Justice of the Supreme Court), Governor E. Lee Trinkle of Virginia, former treasury secretary and future California senator William Gibbs McAdoo (Woodrow Wilson's son-in-law), and Dr. Henry Van Dyke, an influential Princeton University professor and Presbyterian clergyman.

"I hope that the efforts of the association will meet with complete success," Wilson said in his letter. "Monticello ought long ago to have become public property."

"Jefferson M. Levy, the owner of the estate is willing to sell only if Monticello is made a public memorial," Ruth Cunningham said. "He has kept the historic mansion and the 690 acres of land in first-class condition. The Jefferson relics in the mansion alone have been appraised at $292,000. These will be included in the sale of the estate."

In Richmond, Cunningham announced on November 2, 1922, that her association had reached an agreement with Jefferson Levy to purchase Monticello for his $500,000 asking price. Levy gave the association three weeks to come up with a $50,000 down payment, at which time he would sign a contract to sell. According to newspaper reports, Levy and two other New York financiers would underwrite the purchase price—providing the association raised the down payment.

Mrs. Hotchkiss was named to head a committee to raise the $50,000 at a meeting of the association in Richmond on November 8. Among those who addressed the group and endorsed the purchase was Thomas Jefferson Randolph IV, the editor of the Charlottesville *Daily Progress* and a great-great grandson of Thomas Jefferson.

Jefferson Levy, the *Richmond Times-Dispatch* reported on November 23, agreed to reduce the down payment to $25,000 after meeting with Ruth Cunningham. However, the group could not raise even the lower figure and no contract was signed.

In March 1923 Marietta Minnegerode Andrews's Washington-based National Monticello Association made what turned out to be its last effort to raise significant funds to purchase the house. Mrs. Andrews sent out letters asking prominent Americans to serve as sponsors of her association.

Henry Cabot Lodge, the Massachusetts Republican who chaired the Senate Foreign Relations Committee, turned her down, saying in a March 28 letter that he "always made it a rule never to join any organization or association which is likely in any way to have matters come before Congress for action." Treasury secretary Andrew Mellon, secretary of state Charles Evans Hughes, and Maryland governor Albert C.

Ritchie also respectfully declined. Samuel Gompers, the president of the American Federation of Labor, agreed to lend his name.

. . .

A MONTH earlier, in February 1923, Gregory Doyle of Mountain Lakes, New Jersey—a member of Ruth Cunningham's association—had set up a meeting at the Vanderbilt Hotel in New York City to discuss the formation of a new private, nonprofit group with interested parties. Thomas Jefferson Randolph IV, representing Virginia Governor Trinkle, came north for the meeting. Several wealthy and influential New York City lawyers, all of them Wilsonian Democrats, also showed up, including Virginia-born Stuart Gatewood Gibboney, who had been a member of the executive committee of Mrs. Littleton's Jefferson-Monticello Memorial Association.

A follow-up meeting was held March 3, 1823, at the Lawyers' Club at 115 Broadway in New York City. It was at that meeting that the Thomas Jefferson Memorial Foundation was born.

The outline for the foundation was drawn up over lunch at the club by three lawyers: Gibboney, Moses H. Grossman, and John Henry Ranger. Gibboney had moved to New York City after graduating from the University of Virginia Law School in 1903. He was an influential supporter of President Wilson in his 1912 presidential campaign and of William G. McAdoo in his unsuccessful 1920 campaign for the Democratic presidential nomination.

Grossman, a New York City native, was a judge and a founder and executive director of the American Arbitration Society. John Henry Ranger was Jefferson Levy's New York attorney, a Wall Street broker, and an associate of Judge Grossman.

At the meeting Ranger told Gibboney and Grossman that his client was deeply in debt and desperate to sell Monticello. Rumors were circulating that Levy was planning to subdivide Monticello into lots, although it is not known if Ranger brought that prospect up at the meeting. Gibboney and Grossman nevertheless went away from the meeting determined to waste no time in putting together a nonprofit patriotic corporation that would buy Monticello, restore it, and operate it as a shrine.

Soon after that meeting Gibboney and Grossman recruited four influential new members into the organizing committee: George Gordon Battle, a New York City lawyer; Alton B. Parker (1851–1926), the former chief judge of the New York Court of Appeals who was the unsuccessful Democratic Party candidate against Theodore Roosevelt in the 1904 presidential election; Dr. Edwin A. Alderman, the president of the University of Virginia; and Thomas Jefferson Randolph IV of Charlottesville.

Gibboney assumed the presidency of the fledgling group. Theodore Fred Kuper, a young New York City lawyer who had immigrated to this country from Russia as a young boy in 1891, was made national director with a promised salary of $50 a week. Gibboney dispatched Kuper to Washington, where he secured the cooperation of Mrs. Andrews and Mrs. Hoes. Kuper went on to Richmond where Governor Trinkle, Ruth Read Cunningham, and Mrs. Hotchkiss also gave their blessings to the new organization.

The foundation announced early in April that an agreement had been reached with Jefferson Levy to purchase Monticello and that it would soon launch a nationwide movement to raise $1 million to purchase and administer Monticello. "Difficulties which heretofore have prevented the change of ownership of Jefferson's Virginia home have been overcome," the foundation announced April 7. The first donation, a $100 check, had been sent to Ruth Cunningham by Bishop D. J. O'-Connell of Richmond on April 6.

On April 13, 1923, the 180th anniversary of Jefferson's birth, the certificate of incorporation, or charter, of the Thomas Jefferson Memorial Foundation, Inc. was filed in the office of New York's secretary of state in Albany. A certified copy also was filed that day in the County Clerk's Office in New York City where the foundation would set up its offices in Room 607, at 115 Broadway, the same building that housed the Lawyers Club.

Gibboney journeyed to Charlottesville, where he made the public announcement of the foundation's incorporation at a large celebration at the University of Virginia. Charlottesville's Mayor John R. Morris declared the day a half-holiday and called on all of the city's businesses to mark the occasion by closing from noon to 6:00 P.M. Guests from New York and Virginia began arriving several days before the big day. The group included Maud Littleton, Amelia Mayhoff, and Jefferson M. Levy, who arrived in Charlottesville on April 12 and chose to spend the night at the Hotel Gleason.

A spring downpour forced officials to change the venue of the ceremonies from Monticello's lawn to Cabell Hall at the university. Stuart Gibboney, the main speaker, also served as master of ceremonies. The other speakers included Virginia's lieutenant governor Junius E. West (Governor Trinkle was traveling on state business), Mrs. Andrews, Mrs. Hotchkiss, and Virginia state senator Henry T. Wickham. During the program a group of dancers in period costume performed a minuet and the University Glee Club performed. After the ceremonies some of the guests braved the rain and held a brief ceremony at Jefferson's grave.

The crowd greeted the news of the formation of the new association enthusiastically. Gibboney, the Charlottesville *Daily Progress* reported the next day, "set the 500 men and women assembled into tumultuous applause as he read the strong array of names comprising the Board of Governors [of the foundation] and letter after letter and telegram after telegram, pledging support in work and funds to the Foundation's Treasury."

The ceremonies, the paper said, "were dignified, appropriate and uplifting to a degree. When Mr. Gibboney closed his statement reviewing the efforts made to launch the movement and secure necessary contributions by announcing that the success is now assured, the large audience arose en masse and gave a ringing round of cheers."

The list of the foundation's board of directors was long and impressive. It included most of the people who had been active in trying to purchase Monticello in the early 1920s such as Edwin Alderman, Marietta Minnegerode Andrews, Ruth Read Cunningham, Gregory Doyle, James W. Gerard, Stuart Gibboney, Moses Grossman, Rose Gouverneur Hoes, Edith Hotchkiss, Maud Littleton, John H. Ranger, and Mrs. J. Skelton Williams.

It also included a raft of New York City lawyers and several notables of the day, such as Nancy Langhorne Astor, better known as Lady

Nancy Astor (1879–1964), a native Virginian who was the first woman to serve in the British House of Commons, and her sister Irene Langhorne Gibson (1873–1956) of Richmond, better known as the original "Gibson Girl" of the 1890s—the famously beautiful model for hundreds of drawings by her equally famed artist husband Charles Dana Gibson.

Former President Theodore Roosevelt, Governor Trinkle of Virginia, Georgia secretary of state Guy T. McLendon, former Wilson administration secretary of state Bainbridge Colby (1869–1950), and future California senator William McAdoo also were on the board, as was John W. Davis (1873–1955), the former West Virginia congressman, U.S. solicitor general, and ambassador to England who would be Calvin Coolidge's Democratic opponent in the 1924 presidential election. Will H. Hayes (1879–1954), a prominent lawyer who was the president of the Motion Picture Producers and Distributors of America, and Charles D. Hilles, a New York Republican National Committee member, were two of the few Republican Party activists in the group.

Felix M. Warburg (1871–1937), the extremely wealthy German-born Jewish New York banker and philanthropist, also was named to the board. Several years before the foundation was created, Warburg had tried to purchase Monticello for the nation, according to Fred Kuper.

"Judge Jonah Goldstein told J. M. Levy that if he would donate Monticello to the U.S. as a memorial to Jefferson, that on that same day, $500,000 in cash would be deposited in J. M. Levy's account, as a gift to him from Warburg and Julius Rosenwald [the president of Sears]," Kuper wrote in 1976. "J. M. Levy's answer was that he had refused $1,000,000 and laughed."

Fortunately, Kuper said, Levy's dismissal of that offer did not stop Warburg from enthusiastically working with the newly formed Thomas Jefferson Memorial Foundation. Kuper himself helped recruit Warburg to the cause.

"He understood from me that when Jefferson wrote his epitaph . . . he wanted that to be a beacon light for the future: civil liberty, religious freedom and universal education," Kuper said. "I explained that our campaign would be geared on an educational basis and that that would keep on inculcating those ideas. He gave $10,000 originally and he persuaded [Pennsylvania industrialist William H.] Woodin to match it. He said that these ideals and . . . education were what he wanted."

The foundation was well stocked with rich, influential members. But the fund-raising success Gibboney spoke of was slow in coming and difficult in achieving. The foundation held its first meeting at the Lawyers Club on April 24. Officers were elected and an executive committee was empowered to transact business, subject to the approval of the board of governors. Gibboney was named president; another Virginia-born lawyer living in New York, Henry Alan Johnston, was named secretary. Jefferson Levy announced that he was fully in support of the foundation, but then proceeded to throw up a series of roadblocks during negotiations that were held with Gibboney, Kuper, and other TJMF representatives in April and May.

According to Kuper, Levy tried to raise the price from the $500,000 the Foundation was willing to pay. He also wanted to be paid totally in cash. After several meetings, Levy agreed on the $500,000 purchase price and was convinced to accept a down payment of $100,000 in cash, payable in December, at which time he would turn the title of Monticello over to the foundation.

On May 31, 1923, the foundation and Levy signed an option for the purchase of Monticello, the 640 acres around it, and the furniture and furnishings inside. On that same day the foundation was "domesticated" in Virginia, giving it the legal right to transact business in that state. Under terms of the purchase agreement Levy would receive $10,000 in cash immediately to be applied to the purchase price. He gave the TJMF until June 15 to finalize the deal. Gibboney wrote a personal check for $7,000 of that amount and Grossman added $3,000 of his own money.

The contract stipulated that $100,000 would be paid in cash upon the closing of the title and receipt of the deed; $100,000 would be paid subject to the foundation accepting a free and clear title; and the balance of $300,000 would be paid off over several years through the sale of TJMF bonds. The foundation discussed the terms at a June 4 meeting.

Thomas Jefferson Randolph IV presented the foundation with a detailed abstract of Monticello's title he had researched. It showed that Levy's Monticello consisted of 683 acres. Also at that meeting three of the original board of governors resigned: Mrs. G. T. W. Kern, Guy T. McLendon, and Mrs. Martin W. Littleton.

The foundation unanimously approved the contract at its June 8 meeting. The deed of trust was executed on June 30. On that same day Jefferson Levy gave the Monticello Association—the organization of Jefferson descendants that had been formed in 1913 and owned the family graveyard at Monticello—an additional one-half acre of land adjacent to the graveyard to be used as a graveyard for other Jefferson descendants. Levy agreed to donate the land after being lobbied to do so by Thomas Jefferson Randolph IV. The foundation set up a campaign committee at the June 8 meeting to take charge of the fund-raising. The goal was to raise $1 million for the purchase and maintenance of Monticello

This proved to be extremely difficult. Despite its stellar (and well off) list of supporters, no large donors stepped forward. The foundation tried several fund-raising schemes, including what was called a "spiritual pilgrimage" from New York to Monticello, which the foundation kicked off at a dinner in private Pullman dining cars at Grand Central Terminal on June 15. The idea was that people would buy "tickets" for a penny a mile. New York Senator Royal S. Copeland donned a ticket seller's hat inside a "ticket booth" at the event.

New York City movie theater owners agreed to redeem the "tickets" for free performances to selected films. *The New York Times* reported on June 16 that $60,000 worth of tickets was sold at the dinner, but judging by the foundation's continued scramble for funds, that figure was highly inflated.

Kuper led a twenty-six-city, thirty-one-day national fund-raising tour that summer. In Detroit and Chicago he was accompanied by several other foundation members, including Governor Trinkle and Stewart Gibboney. The tour was only moderately successful. The foundation was forced to ask a group of wealthy businessmen to act as underwriters and agree to pay the difference between whatever the foundation raised and the $100,000 that was due to be paid in cash to Jefferson Levy in December. Gibboney himself and Felix Warburg signed on. Herbert Lehman (1878–1963), the New York City financier who later was New York's governor and a U.S. senator, agreed to underwrite some $11,000.

On May 9, 1923, during Jefferson Levy's negotiations with the foundation, he granted a rare interview in his East Thrity-seventh Street New York City brownstone to Raymond G. Carroll of the Philadelphia *Public Ledger.* For one of the few times in his life the seventy-one-year-old Levy spoke passionately for publication about his personal life, and his ownership of Monticello. The article, which appeared on May 11, 1923, provides a rare glimpse of Jefferson Levy's thoughts about his family, his religion, and his reasons for selling Monticello.

Carroll found Levy, whom he described as six feet tall and weighing 180 pounds, living with his younger brother, Mitchell Levy, also a bachelor. Jefferson Levy, Carroll wrote, was pacing "up and down in the drawing rooms" when he arrived. The brownstone was packed with works of art, Carroll reported, including "priceless vases from Sevres, crystal candelabra mounted upon costly bronze bases from Venice, a green malachite table worth $10,000 owned by a Czar of Russia, a bronze head done by the immortal David, a silver carving from the hands of the famous Benvenuto Cellini and other wonderful treasures and paintings."

Levy began by talking about his family, claiming incorrectly—as he had done in the past—that he and his brother were the last Levy descendants of Asa Levy, who came to New York City in 1654.

"Yes, we are the last of our line, my brother and I," Jefferson Levy said, ignoring the fact that his sister Amelia was alive, as were his brother Louis's four children and Amelia's son Monroe.

When the interviewer asked about Monticello, Levy claimed that he and "members of my family" had invested a whopping $2.4 million in the property. "This huge expenditure," Levy said, "includes the original cost of Monticello, the expenses of keeping it up, its restoration after the Civil War and the interest on the money sunk in the property."

Levy told Carroll, disingenuously, that he had "always said [he] would sell Monticello to the Commonwealth of Virginia or to the United

States or to an organization similar to that in control of Mount Vernon, George Washington's home. . . . But I was not going to be driven to do what I wanted to do all the time and had proposed doing from the very first." As we have seen, Levy steadfastly refused to listen to any suggestion that he sell Monticello for such a purpose from the time he gained control of it in 1879 until the fall of 1914.

Levy told Carroll that Cornelius Vanderbilt II once approached him with an offer on Monticello's front lawn, saying: "Cannot I tempt you to sell with a million dollars? If not enough, name your price."

Levy said that Andrew Carnegie came to him in Washington and said: "Any time you want to sell Monticello I'll buy it and present it to the country."

He also said he had had "scores" of other offers for Monticello and had rebuffed them all.

Levy offered the startling—and hitherto publicly unmentioned—news that at the 1912 Democratic National Convention in Baltimore he was offered the vice presidential nomination if he would agree, after the election, to give Monticello to the government. Levy turned that offer down, he said, as well as a similar previous one made by William Jennings Bryan.

"What they failed to recognize—all of them—was the fact that perhaps there might be a pride in my own family connected with the ownership," Levy said. "Once there was a time when I was wealthy enough to have stood the strain of an absolute gift of Monticello to the country. Then they fought me. Now, when I am approached in a different spirit under conditions which I laid down from the start, it is financially necessary for me to allow others to share in the great gift of the historic landmark to the nation."

Jefferson Levy then showed Carroll his right hand, "upon which was a pigeon-blood ruby ring of antique pattern," the reporter wrote. Levy said the ring had belonged to Uriah P. Levy, and then launched into an exegesis on his uncle's naval career and his purchase of Monticello.

"Monticello was never looked upon by my uncle as an investment," Jefferson Levy said. "He bought it out of deep admiration for the great Democrat."

Levy went back again into his family history, once more mistakenly claiming that Asa Levy was his forebear, that the Philadelphia Revolutionary War patriot Benjamin Levy was his great-grandfather, and that his grandfather Michael Levy was in the Revolutionary Army.

"The Levys of that time in my family were all soldiers," Jefferson Levy said.

He then returned to the situation at hand.

"The whole trouble started when they tried to force me to sell Monticello," he said, "and I fought them and beat them. I am proud of my country, my family and my race. We Levys were the first Jews to land in the New World, and as the republic was founded and expanded, we did our share of the fighting. That should entitle our family at least to some consideration."

. . .

On July 14, 1923, the foundation issued a statement making a public appeal for funds. "The American people will now understand that the public appeal of the Thomas Jefferson Memorial Foundation for $1,000,000 has a two fold significance," the statement said. It went on to explain that $500,000 was for the purchase price and $500,000 would be needed for "the proper and effective maintenance of Monticello as a national memorial throughout all time."

It called on Americans to respond to the "twin appeals" because of the "incalculable and eternal" debt owed by all Americans to Thomas Jefferson. "The Monticello for which our appeal is now made will not only atone for the nation's long neglect of Jefferson's memory and peerless patriotic service," the statement concluded, "but will stand as an everlasting inspiration of our whole people."

The fund-raising did not go well during the summer. Early in October the foundation announced a second nationwide campaign. "In this movement the active aid of every loyal American is solicited with all the earnestness that can be put into words and with every confidence of its outcome," the foundation said. The plan this time was for a "country-wide pilgrimage in which all may take part," to be held at Monticello on Jefferson's birthday, April 13, 1924.

The foundation sponsored other fund-raising events in the fall of

1923, including "Monticello Week," the first week in November, in Charlottesville. That event included a benefit bridge and Mah-Jongg party at the Dolly Madison Inn with donated prizes to winners, a benefit showing of a movie, and a Monticello dinner at The Coffee Shop. The bridge and Mah-Jongg party netted $104.95; the movie brought in $264.70. Altogether, including donations, the week's event added a total of $1,473.65 to the foundation's coffers.

The Charlottesville Chamber of Commerce set a goal of $15,000 in fund-raising by the end of November. It closed the effort with $12,881. The Charlottesville total was significant. Still, the foundation was forced to borrow a significant portion of the first $100,000 it paid to Jefferson Levy from several banks based on the underwriters' pledges.

Fred Kuper was among the foundation representatives present when Levy was given the first payment and signed the title of Monticello over to the foundation in New York City on Saturday, December 1, 1923. Kuper described the scene in an interview in the 1970s with Charles Hosmer.

"The cash and the bonds and mortgage were delivered to Levy, and Levy signed the deed conveying full title to the property and all belongings to the Foundation," Kuper said. "This was a very emotional scene and he burst out crying. He said that he never dreamt that he would ever part with the property."

Judge Duke filed the deed of conveyance in the Albemarle county clerk's office on Monday morning, December 3. The news made the front page of the next day's *New York Times*. At the same time Jefferson Levy, with the foundation's consent, officially conveyed the half-acre of land next to the Jefferson family burial site to Thomas J. Randolph and his brother Hollins N. Randolph on behalf of the Jefferson heirs.

On December 5, 1923, a delegation of foundation officials, including Gibboney and Kuper, drove to Monticello, accompanied by Thomas Jefferson Randolph, to inspect the premises and institute some changes. They met with Thomas Rhodes and set out new regulations. There would be a fifty-cent admission fee. Several longtime Monticello employees—all of whom were black—would be hired as guides and would use a short script Kuper wrote. Kuper told Rhodes to take down the

Confederate flag he flew in front of his house at Monticello and to do away with the separate rest rooms for blacks and whites.

"I am very proud to add that, on my instructions to Rhodes . . . all visitors to Monticello were to be received and treated regardless of color, nationality, religion, etc.," Kuper said in a 1976 letter, "and that there was to be no segregation even in toilet facilities, which were to be solely for 'gentlemen' and 'ladies.'"

Three months later, on March 6, 1924, at his home on East Thirty-seventh Street in New York City, Jefferson Levy died of heart disease, five weeks short of his seventy-second birthday. He was buried in Cypress Hills Cemetery in Brooklyn in the Levy family plot near his illustrious uncle. Jefferson Levy was eulogized in a long, five-paragraph *New York Times* obituary that emphasized his congressional accomplishments and briefly mentioned the pending sale of Monticello.

At his death, Levy was insolvent. The entire sum he received for Monticello did not come close to paying off his debts, which included more than $1 million to the brokerage firm of Albert J. Elias & Co.

Jefferson Levy's death, the Thomas Jefferson Memorial Foundation was quick to point out, did not change the fate of Monticello. "The passing of Mr. Levy, of course, makes no difference in our plans," Stuart Gibboney announced on March 7. "The first payment of $100,000 for the property was made on December 1 last, when possession was taken of the property by the Foundation, and we are now proceeding with our plans to raise the necessary money to complete the partial payments as they fall due."

Jefferson Levy left his entire estate to his sister Amelia Mayhoff in a will he had executed on September 28, 1923, less than six months before he died. Within days after her brother's death Mrs. Mayhoff announced that she would not stand in the way of the transfer of Monticello to the foundation.

"It was my brother's wish that it be sold to the Thomas Jefferson Memorial Foundation," she said on March 10. "Arrangements for its purchase of the property had been almost completed when my brother died. I will carry out his wish in that respect."

The foundation continued to concentrate on fund-raising activities after Jefferson Levy's death. One well-publicized event was a two-day fund-raiser held at Monticello on April 12–13. Hundreds of people from around the nation came to Charlottesville for the occasion. Many joined a procession that began at the Rotunda at the University of Virginia and marched in double file across the university's famed lawn before heading up to Monticello.

Once they arrived on top of Jefferson's mountain, the large crowd sat in chairs arrayed on the front lawn and listened to a series of patriotic speeches, songs, and reports on the progress being made to complete the purchase and turn the house into a Jefferson shrine. The speechmakers included Stuart Gibboney, Marietta Minnegerode Andrews, Rose Gouverneur Hoes, Edith Hotchkiss, and Virginia Governor Trinkle, who predicted that the foundation would pay off the mortgage by June 1.

Eight local high school students dressed in period costumes performed a minuet on the lawn. A concert pianist, Germaine Schnitzer of New York, played classical selections. Fifty New York City schoolchildren, ages thirteen to sixteen—winners of a Jefferson essay contest—entertained the audience with patriotic songs and "cheers which voiced their appreciation of Thomas Jefferson as the patron of popular education and advocate of the principles of freedom and religious liberty," *The New York Times* reported on April 13.

Governor Trinkle's prediction proved to be extremely overoptimistic. The foundation struggled mightily in its early years for two main reasons. First, in the early 1920s the idea of historic preservation had yet to take hold widely in the public imagination. Second, the American public had yet to recognize Thomas Jefferson and his many and varied accomplishments, including designing and building Monticello.

"Thomas Jefferson," Fred Kuper said, "was the forgotten man then. People had inherited hatred. There was no interest in saving public places. I witnessed marvelous historic places going to ruin."

The foundation barely managed to come up with the second $100,000 installment on June 30, 1924. And it had great difficulty raising funds after making that payment—so much so that the foundation found itself in default on June 30, 1925, when it was unable to come up with the next $100,000 payment. Mrs. Mayhoff and Jefferson Levy's estate lawyers could have foreclosed on the mortgage, but agreed instead to give the Foundation until December 1, 1930, to pay off the first mortgage.

Levy's "estate and its lawyers were patient with the delays in the payments," Theodore Kuper said, "and even in the default in complying with the terms and conditions of the purchase money mortgage."

The foundation did pay another $100,000 installment in October 1930. Several large contributions helped it meet that goal, including $20,000 from Felix Warburg, the largest single amount the foundation received. Altogether, Warburg donated $35,000. It was not until 1940, however, that the foundation was able to pay off the entire mortgage and free itself of all debt.

The foundation used many types of fund-raising activities. It appealed to the wealthy with a program in which all $1,000 contributors earned the title of "Monticellean" and were given lifetime passes to the mansion. It set up several supporting committees around the country, including a Washington committee headed by Rose Gouverneur Hoes and Marietta Minnegerode Andrews and a Virginia committee headed by Edith Hotchkiss.

On her own, Mrs. Andrews donated silhouette portraits she created of Jefferson and other American historical figures to the foundation, which used them to illustrate programs at its fund-raising events. She also produced a series of historic pageants in the Washington, D.C., area. That included an event at the Lyric Theater in Baltimore on May 20, 1925, in which actors in period costumes presented several "action tableaux" depicting events in Jefferson's life. Mrs. Andrews appeared in colonial garb and served as narrator for several of the tableaux.

"The dances of Thomas Jefferson were shown in the tableau 'The Ball at the White House,'" the Baltimore *Sun* reported May 21. "The girls and men in their costumes of the period presented the minuet, bowed to each other and bowed again until the curtain fell to blot out the quiet revelry."

In 1926 Kuper, the foundation's national director and chief fund-raiser, convinced the New York City Board of Education to set aside one day in which children in that city's public schools would be asked to contribute to Monticello's preservation. On February 17, the city's schoolchildren donated nearly $35,000 to the Foundation—most of it in pennies. A similar event in Chicago netted some $8,000.

Another fund-raising tool the foundation used in the mid-1920s was the exhibition of the body of Thomas Jefferson's Monticello-made one-horse gig. Jefferson had driven the gig on two six-day journeys from Monticello to the Continental Congress in Philadelphia in 1775 and 1776. The gig remained unused and unchanged at Monticello following Jefferson's death. Its wheels and shaft had disappeared, however, by the time Jefferson's great-grandson Thomas Jefferson Randolph IV discovered it in Monticello's attic in 1924.

The gig's first fund-raising gig came in June of 1924 when the foundation shipped it to New York City during the Democratic National Convention and put it on display in the lobby of the Waldorf-Astoria Hotel. The foundation exhibited the gig at other functions, including an April 30, 1925, fund-raising luncheon attended by some four hundred businessmen. Among the luncheon speakers that day was Maud Littleton, who read from Jefferson's letters dealing with the 1826 Monticello lottery.

The foundation used those funds for more than paying off the mortgage. Monticello was in need of restorative work in 1923 when Jefferson Levy sold it. Although he had maintained the mansion well after he took control of it in 1879, because of his precarious financial situation during and after World War I Levy could not afford to lavish attention on its upkeep in the last few years of his life.

The most pressing delayed-maintenance problem with the building in 1923 was its aging roof. Within a year after taking over, the foundation, under the direction of longtime Monticello superintendent Thomas Rhodes, replaced the roof that Jefferson Levy had installed in 1879. The house also needed exterior painting—its terrace roofs especially were in dire need of paint—and many of the outbuildings were in disrepair. The floors of the terrace walks and the stonework underneath also were repaired. The trees around the house received much-needed pruning.

Rhodes continued in his role of overseeing the repairs and restoration work at Monticello—and continued to win praise for his work. "Every bit of work on the buildings, in the rooms or on the grounds was done under the personal direction of Tom Rhodes," Theodore Fred Kuper said. In the years "when the Jefferson Foundation found it difficult to raise the needed funds, Tom Rhodes understood and voluntarily postponed the time for the modest payments due him for his work."

From 1923 to 1928 the foundation spent some $206,000 on repair and restoration. That included—a September 1, 1928, foundation financial report said—"restoration of the exterior and interior of Monticello, road building, restoration of Jefferson trees by modern tree surgery, installation of a complete water system, repairs, upkeep, insurance, interest and maintenance."

In May of 1924 the board of directors unanimously voted to ask Fiske Kimball to chair the foundation's Restoration Committee. The offer was tendered in a May 7 letter from Stewart Gibboney. "We have laid no plans as to how to proceed with the restoration," Gibboney told Kimball. "First, because we do not want to interfere with your present field of work and secondly because our limited finances do not permit any extended program."

Kimball accepted the appointment. He would "be happy to give my professional advice without any compensation," Kimball said in his May 17 acceptance letter. "When more extensive work is undertaken, it will be time enough to consider whether any other basis should be accepted."

At the time, Kimball was the head of New York University's fine arts department. He also was chairman of the American Institute of Architect's Committee on Preservation of Historic Monuments and Scenic Beauties, and—as we have seen—was the preeminent Jefferson architecture scholar in the nation.

"Jefferson's twentieth century reputation as an architect is very largely due to the talent and energy of one man," Jefferson scholar Merrill Peterson said, "the architect, art historian, museum director [at the Philadelphia Museum of Art from 1925 to 1955], and restorer of historic buildings, Fiske Kimball."

For several years after taking over the Monticello restoration Kimball worked on the project with R. T. Haines Halsey, the chairman of the Metropolitan Museum of Art's Committee on American Decorative Art, and Charles Moore, chairman of the Washington, D.C., National Commission of Fine Arts. But after those initial years, Kimball was the sole guiding hand in the restoration efforts, although he worked closely with Charlottesville architect Milton L. Grigg, the founder of the architectural firm, Grigg & Johnson.

The foundation's effort to repair and restore the mansion, its outbuildings and its grounds took decades, during which Kimball also led a nationwide search to collect original Jefferson furnishings through loans, gifts and purchases. The goal was to reshape Monticello so it would appear much as it did during Jefferson's retirement years from 1809 to 1826.

Kimball consulted Jefferson's drawings, letters, and other documents to try to, as he said in 1923, "put the place back exactly in the form which it had in [Jefferson's] lifetime." He restricted his acquisitions strictly to items that had belonged to Thomas Jefferson—no reproductions or similar period pieces would be allowed in the house.

That effort, by necessity, included erasing all traces of the nearly ninety-year ownership of Monticello by the Levy family. "The Foundation did not want [Monticello] to be a Levy shrine," Fred Kuper told Charles Hosmer. Therefore, as Hosmer put it, "everything having to do with the Levys was removed." That included bathrooms, a bathtub and a stairway installed by Jefferson Levy, along with the roof dormers he added, and an enormous amount of furniture and furnishings that Levy conveyed to the foundation with the sale of the property.

Amelia Mayhoff lobbied in 1928 to have portraits she had inherited of her brother Jefferson Levy and her uncle Uriah Levy that had long been hung in Monticello kept on display in the house. "I understand that you are going to dispose, at public auction, of certain of the contents of Monticello which have an historical value," she said in a September 27 letter to the foundation, "in this connection a request has been made of me to give some history and description of some of the articles about to be sold in this way."

Mrs. Mayhoff went on to extol the virtues of Uriah Levy, who, she said, "amid great struggles and the opposition of many enemies, attained a high position in his chosen profession." She mentioned that he was the father of law abolishing flogging in the Navy, and repeated the apocryphal story that President Andrew Jackson ordered him to purchase Monticello. She pointed out that Monticello had been in her family's hands for nine decades, during which time the Levy family "preserved it from destruction, oftentimes at great personal sacrifice."

That said, Mrs. Mayhoff asked that the portrait of Uriah Levy, "which was at Monticello when it was sold to your Foundation, be rehung in the hall where it was when the property was sold."

She made a similar request for the portrait of her brother, Jefferson M. Levy. "He was a representative in Congress from the State of New York for three terms and made a strenuous fight for the cause of sound money and for legislation which finally culminated in the Federal Reserve Act," she said. "He restored the ancient beauties of the place and brought to it many ornaments which were in keeping with the ideals of Thomas Jefferson. I ask that his portrait now at Monticello be rehung. . . ."

Mrs. Mayhoff said that if the foundation rehung the portraits she would "give other relics from Monticello in my possession" to the foundation. "I have a great sentiment for Monticello, which was my home in my childhood, girlhood and womanhood," she said. "I also think that it is only appropriate for some recognition to be given the family that preserved Monticello for ninety-one years [in fact, it was eighty-nine years] and were in possession of it for a longer period than any other owner."

Stewart Gibboney forwarded Mrs. Mayhoff's letter to Fiske Kimball on October 18. The next day Kimball wrote back to Gibboney, recommending that the foundation turn Mrs. Mayhoff down.

"Naturally we sympathize very much with Mrs. Mayhoff's feeling in the matter," he said, "but the request she makes, I am sorry to say, conflicts with the most fundamental principle on which the Restoration Committee has been working."

That principle, of course, was keeping Monticello purely Jeffersonian. "Against every temptation to admit other objects into the mansion which have been offered to us as gifts, we have rigidly adhered to the principle of furnishing it exactly as it was in Jefferson's lifetime, and of accepting nothing except original Jefferson furnishings," Kimball said. "Many other fine objects of his own period have been offered to us, and temptation is sometimes very strong to accept these, but we have felt that only Jefferson things should be taken. . . ."

In a November 9, 1928, letter Amelia Mayhoff appealed directly to Fiske Kimball. "I have not had the pleasure (one I have wished for) of meeting you at Monticello," she said, "but I realize that you are the one person who has a great interest in that wonderful old place and also a deep understanding of its traditions and history. . . . Is what I ask not an act of justice to the men who restored and preserved Monticello for 97 years? I put myself completely in your hands and stand by my offer in my letter sent to the Foundation."

Kimball wrote back to Amelia Mayhoff on November 12, once again turning down her request. Mrs. Mayhoff then donated the full-length Uriah Levy oil portrait to the U.S. Navy. It is on display today at the Naval Academy Museum in Annapolis. She presented the life-sized oil painting of Jefferson Levy to the New York Democratic Club. Jefferson Levy was one of that New York City organization's founders.

On Saturday, November 17, 1928, the foundation held a public auction of Jefferson Levy's former furniture at Monticello. "We are making room at Monticello for more of the original relics and furnishings which belonged to Thomas Jefferson," Gibboney said the day before the sale. "This sale will be a happy contrast to the sale that was held 100 years ago at Monticello. At that time, Jefferson's daughter, Martha Jefferson Randolph, was compelled to sell the furnishings which her illustrious father had gathered and used at Monticello throughout his life."

When Gibboney explained what furnishings were going up for auction, he did not mention Uriah Levy or Jefferson Levy.

"At the present sale," he said, "only those furnishings which did not belong to Jefferson but which were placed there during the years when Monticello was in private hands will be sold."

The long list of Jefferson Levy's items the foundation ridded itself of included many tables and chairs, sofas, carpets, chandeliers, clocks, vases, statuary, paintings, lamps, beds, bureaus, dressers, chests, and a pair of twin beds. Some of the larger items were shipped to New York City where they were sold at auction at the Plaza Hotel early in December. On each item foundation officials pasted a label that said that the piece had come from Monticello during the Levy period.

The largest items Jefferson Levy had added to the house were two pairs of white marble lions. Levy placed two of them, each with a capital letter "L" carved on its chest, on the brick retaining walls beside the steps leading up to the house from Mulberry Row. Another pair of large lions—without the "L"—adorned the west front entrance. All four "Levy lions" were auctioned off at Monticello with the other Levy items on November 17, 1928.

That year the U.S. Treasury Department, under the prodding of Fred Kuper, came up with a new design for the two-dollar bill. The front featured a portrait of Thomas Jefferson based on a painting by Gilbert Stuart. The design on the back centered on an engraving of Monticello by J. C. Benzing, in which the Levy lions may be seen sitting on either side of the west portico steps.

The newly designed two-dollar bills were printed and distributed for the first time in 1929. On July 12, 1929, Gene Oglivie, the manager of the University Branch of the Charlottesville's People's National Bank, made the front page of the *Daily Progress* with the news that he was the first person to discover a "defect, or at least a discrepancy" in the recently introduced two-dollar bill. Oglivie, the newspaper said, pointed out that the Levy lions "were not on the grounds at Monticello. Nor were they there during the regime of Jefferson."

The Treasury Department denied that the bill contained any sort of defect or error. Alvin Whall, the director of the Treasury's Bureau of Engraving and Printing in Washington, announced on July 17 that the engraving was intended to represent Monticello as it appeared in the present day, not in Jefferson's time. The design, he said, was copied from a photograph of Monticello taken before the bill's design was started—in other words, before the Foundation auctioned off the Levy lions in 1928.

The two-dollar bill was modified slightly in 1953 and 1963, but the Levy lions remained on the back. In 1976, the back of the bill was completely redesigned. A scene depicting the signing of the Declaration of Independence replaced Monticello. As for the four Levy lions themselves, one adorned with the letter "L" sits in front of a private house on Canterbury Road in Charlottesville. The whereabouts of the other shielded lion is unknown. The other pair of lions was acquired by the family of Mrs. Meredith Caldwell and donated to the Cheekwood Botanical Garden and Museum in Nashville where they are on display today.

After jettisoning Jefferson Levy's furnishings, the Thomas Jefferson Memorial Foundation—as Jefferson Levy had done—added significantly to the acreage at Monticello. Jefferson Levy had conveyed some 640 acres to the foundation with the sale in 1923. During the next four decades the Foundation purchased more than one thousand contiguous acres for just over $1,028,000. Today, the foundation owns Monticello, its dependencies and 2,060 acres, including the former Jefferson holdings of Tufton and Shadwell.

Large numbers of visitors came to Monticello in the years after the foundation took over. In 1924, some 20,000 visitors paid the fifty-cent admission fee. Three years later, the number jumped to nearly 50,000. In 1929, more than 75,000 people came to Jefferson's mountain. The number of visitors has not been under 500,000 annually since 1984.

The foundation temporarily closed Monticello in 1953 and 1954 while the house was completely structurally renovated. The floors were reinforced with steel joists and a new heating and air-conditioning system was installed. The foundation, which moved its headquarters from New York City to Monticello in 1969, also added educational programs to its mission.

The foundation took a leading role in the movement to build a national memorial to Thomas Jefferson in 1926. Eight years later, in June

1934, Congress created the Thomas Jefferson Memorial Commission and appropriated $3 million for a Jefferson Memorial in Washington, D.C. Stuart Gibboney was named chairman of the commission in 1938. On April 13, 1943, the two-hundredth anniversary of Thomas Jefferson's birth, the Jefferson Memorial on the Tidal Basin in Washington was dedicated by President Franklin D. Roosevelt. Gibboney died a year later.

A Long Time Coming: Recognizing the Levys

At two crucial periods in the history of Monticello, the preservation efforts and stewardship of Uriah P. and Jefferson M. Levy successfully maintained the property for future generations.
PLAQUE AT RACHEL PHILLIPS LEVY'S MONTICELLO GRAVESITE,
DEDICATED JUNE 7, 1985

W hile the Thomas Jefferson Memorial Foundation was restoring Monticello, preserving Jefferson's legacy, and erasing the physical changes made by the Levys, it also all but ignored the family's invaluable stewardship. Until 1985, the millions of visitors who came to Monticello learned only the barest details about what happened to the house after Jefferson's death in 1826 until the Foundation purchased it in 1923.

Volunteers from the Albemarle County DAR chapter replaced the former servants the Foundation first hired as tour guides, and in 1951, the first paid "hostesses" began giving tours. None of them, though, mentioned the Levy family's role in preserving Jefferson's mansion. The foundation's brochures and guidebooks made only the briefest of references to the family's eighty-nine-year ownership.

Levy family members felt less than welcome when they visited, according to Harley Lewis, the grandniece of Jefferson Levy and great-great-granddaughter of Uriah Levy's mother, Rachel. When Harley Lewis's parents—Jefferson Levy's niece Frances Wolff Levy Lewis and her husband Harold Lewis—visited Monticello in the 1930s, "they would ask for the key to the gravesite of Rachel Levy, which was behind a little iron fence," Harley Lewis says. "The people there said no one was buried there by that name. Then eventually someone would come up with the key and they would go in and take care of the grounds."

Harley Lewis also reported that her parents discovered a less-than-flattering plaque near Monticello's gate. "In so many words, it said: 'Uriah Phillips Levy, a Jew, purchased Monticello for $2,500 and later sold it,'" she says.

She attributes the slights to anti-Semitism. "There was tremendous anti-Semitic feeling because of the fact that a Jew owned the house," Lewis says.

Susan Stein, who has been Monticello's curator since 1986, agrees. "There was a leitmotif, if you will, of anti-Semitism here just as it is everywhere at the upper reaches of American society," she says. "I see the attitude here being reflective of our culture."

Daniel Jordan, who has headed the Thomas Jefferson Memorial Foundation since 1985, points to the participation of Jews in the foundation's earliest days as evidence that Monticello's silence on the Levys may not have been solely motivated by anti-Semitism. "The founding board in the 1920s included some very prominent people in the New York Jewish community," Jordan notes. "My sense is that they were trying to figure out how to advance Thomas Jefferson and maybe the Levy story got pushed to the side, almost inadvertently, in an unthinking way. If there had been anti-Semitic overtones early on, surely people like Felix Warburg would not have been associated with the foundation."

The plaque that Harley Lewis spoke of turned out to be the catalyst for a marked change that took place in 1985 in the foundation's recognition of the Levy family stewardship of Monticello. The plaque has long since disappeared and its exact wording has not been recorded. However, there exists an eyewitness description of the plaque written by Malcolm H. Stern, who was the rabbi at Congregation Olef Shalom in Norfolk, Virginia, from 1947 to 1964. In the early 1950s, Stern learned about what he called "a new signpost" that had been placed at Monticello's entrance.

The sign, labeled "The Story of Monticello," said, in part, according to Stern: "After Jefferson's death in 1826, Monticello was occupied by his daughter for two years. When her husband, Governor Thomas Mann Randolph, died in 1828, she felt that [she] could no longer afford to remain at Monticello. The estate was then advertised in the 'Herald' of Alexandria, Va., as being worth $71,000, and contained 409 acres. It was sold, however, to James T. Barclay for $7,000. Four years later it was acquired by Uriah Phillips Levy, of New York City, for $2,500.

"In 1912, a movement was started to bring Monticello under public ownership as a national shrine. Eleven years later, on Dec. 23, 1923, the Thomas Jefferson Memorial Foundation purchased the property from Jefferson Monroe Levy for $500,000. . . ."

Stern and others interpreted that sign as a backhanded, anti-Semitic slap at the Levy family. They pointed out that the plaque said nothing about the Levys' saving of Monticello from ruin, nor did it take note of the large amounts of money both Uriah and Jefferson Levy spent to repair, renovate, and restore the house and grounds. It also implied, Stern felt, that Jefferson Levy made a huge profit on the sale.

The plaque set Malcolm Stern on a mission to investigate the Levys' role in Monticello. Once he found out the facts, Stern—working with several others, including Fred Kuper, Saul Viener and Virginius Dabney of Richmond, and Irving Lipkowitz of New York—led a long and ultimately successful effort to have the foundation acknowledge the Levys' stewardship.

Malcolm Stern (1915–1994) was born in Philadelphia. He was ordained as a rabbi at Hebrew Union College in Cincinnati and in 1941 became assistant rabbi at a Philadelphia synagogue. He served as a U.S. Army Air Corps chaplain during World War II, then went to Norfolk. In 1964, Stern moved to New York City and became the first director of rabbinic placement for Reform Judaism for the Central Conference of American Rabbis.

Known as the founder of American Jewish genealogy, Stern served as the American Jewish Archives' genealogist from 1949 until his death in 1994. He also was a founder of the Jewish Historical Society of New York and a trustee of the American Jewish Historical Society.

The first fruit of Malcolm Stern's research into the Levys and Monticello was "Monticello and the Levy Family," an article he wrote that appeared in the October 1959 issue of the *Journal of the Southern Jewish Historical Society*. In it, Stern gave a history of the Levy family's ownership of Monticello. He noted that the foundation had done very little to recognize the Levy's stewardship, and mentioned the offensive plaque. That same year saw the renaming and dedication of the Jewish chapel at the Norfolk Naval base in honor of Uriah Levy.

It wasn't until the mid-1970s, however, that momentum began to build for recognition of the Levys at Monticello. Saul Viener, a Richmond businessman, biblical scholar and historian, and the founder of the Southern Jewish Historical Society, set things in motion when he sent a copy of Stern's article to Fred Kuper in April 1976.

Kuper, who had just turned ninety, said that there was no such sign at Monticello when he was the foundation's national director from 1923 to 1935. "I should have regarded" such a plaque, he said, "not only erroneous as to some vital facts, but vicious in its innuendo."

Two years earlier, in 1974, Irving Lipkowitz, a retired lawyer who lived in Richmond where he had represented the Reynolds Metals Company, had visited Monticello and was distressed that no mention was made of the Levys' stewardship. "I find that what the visitor is told during the guided tour and what he reads in the descriptive folder do not convey a proper understanding of the Levys' relationship to Monticello," Lipkowitz wrote in an August 21, 1974, letter to James A. Bear, Jr., Monticello's first full-time resident director. Lipkowitz asked Bear to make a "compact summary" of the Levy period "readily available to visitors."

In his reply to Lipkowitz, Bear—who had done some research on the Levys and Monticello that included contacting Levy descendants in 1956 and 1957—explained that the foundation believed that its exhibition of Monticello, its house and grounds "should be restricted to Thomas Jefferson and his family." That policy, he said, had been in effect since the foundation purchased the property from Jefferson Levy in 1923. Bear said that the foundation did not believe that the Levy ownership was "of enough interest to those who come here to reduce what we say about Jefferson, or to lengthen the tour by including the Levy lore."

He also noted that the foundation had erected a plaque on the enclosure of Rachel Levy's gravesite. It said, in part: "Except for a short period during the Civil War when it passed into the hands of the Confederate Government, the estate remained in the hands of the Levy family until 1923 when Jefferson M. Levy, one of Uriah's nephews, sold it to the Thomas Jefferson Memorial Foundation. The Trustees of the Foundation acknowledge a debt of gratitude to the Levy family without whose care Jefferson's beloved home might not have survived the ravages of time."

Bear and his co-author Frederick D. Nichols also had given qualified credit to the Levys in a foundation-published guidebook sold at Monticello at the time. "It appears," they wrote, that Uriah Levy "and especially his nephew Jefferson Monroe Levy . . . maintained it extremely well. Without the efforts of this family, which actually owned the house for eighty-nine years—a far longer period than did Jefferson—Monticello might not be today on top of its 'little mountain.'"

Irving Lipkowitz wrote back to Bear, asking him to find a way to add "a reasonable and fair reference" to the Levys because the wording on the plaque at Rachel Levy's gravesite was "appropriate as far as it goes, but is too limited in scope." Bear wrote to Lipkowitz on October 21, telling him that he was about to begin work on a manuscript dealing with the post-1826 history of Monticello, and asking Lipkowitz to send him "meaningful material." Bear sent a similar letter to Malcolm Stern.

On July 19, 1976, Malcolm Stern wrote to Bear and enclosed a research paper he and Lipkowitz had written detailing the Levys' role in preserving Monticello. The following day Stern wrote to Saul Viener in Richmond, filling him in on the lobbying he and Lipkowitz were doing on behalf of the Levys. The time had come, he said, "to set the record straight with due regard to the facts."

Stern believed that one reason the foundation seemed unwilling to recognize the Levys was a feeling of animosity left over from Jefferson Levy's resistance to opening Monticello to the public. "Even Mr. Kuper's letters reflect this," Stern said.

Theodore Fred Kuper, in fact, did not have a high regard for Jefferson Levy. "His years of fighting and defeating every attempt to buy Monticello from him and establish it as a patriotic shrine were not heart warming," Kuper wrote in a 1975 letter.

The fact that Jefferson Levy finally agreed to sell Monticello, Kuper said, "was no credit to him." It was fairly well known, Kuper said, "that his ventures in Wall Street forced him to get cash. Then and only then did he advertise Monticello for sale, and when this brought no results he had a friend [presumably his lawyer, John H. Ranger] get people in New York to create the Jefferson Foundation, with the Washington and Virginia committees and buy Monticello."

Bear did in fact write a brief history of Monticello, post 1926. The foundation did not publish it, but the typewritten manuscript is in the foundation's research department files in Charlottesville.

Nothing of consequence occurred on the Levy-Monticello lobbying front until 1981 when Irving Lipkowitz again visited Monticello and was distressed with what he read in the newly written brochure given to visitors. The brochure, he said in a November 23 letter to Stern, has "three times the text it previously had, but the reference to the Levys has been eliminated." Lipkowitz also reported unhappily that the foundation was using one wall of the Rachel Levy gravesite as an observation platform to overlook excavations that were going on along Mulberry Row.

Around that time Viener, who was the president of the American Jewish Historical Society, enlisted the help of his friend Virginius Dabney (1901–1995) of Richmond, the Pulitzer Prize–winning former editor-in-chief of the Richmond *Times-Dispatch*. Dabney, a member of an old Virginia family, was born in Charlottesville and had graduated from the University of Virginia where his father taught history. He went to work as a reporter for the *Times-Dispatch* and made his reputation as an editorial writer. He was regarded as a liberal for advocating integrated seating on city streetcars in Richmond in the early 1940s.

Dabney began lobbying foundation board members to recognize the Levys. That prompted a letter from Bear to Dabney on September 2, 1982, defending the foundation's position on the issue. "With the exception of the [Sally] 'Hemings' affair, no issue is addressed more by our staff and guides than this one," Bear said.

No one at the foundation, Bear said, "willfully denigrates the Levy family's association or contribution to Monticello." He then went on to praise Jefferson Levy's repairs of Monticello and spoke of the "failure of the Levy family to look after the property following Uriah P. Levy's death . . . until the 1870s when Jefferson M. Levy assumed sole title to the property." That alleged failure, Bear said, "contributed greatly to the near ruin of the building."

Bear disputed the contention that Jefferson Levy's sale of Monticello for $500,000 was a money-losing proposition. He said no historical evidence had come to light proving Jefferson Levy's oft-repeated claims that he had turned down more than $1 million for the house, or that the Jefferson furnishings he conveyed with the property were worth some $250,000, as some of his supporters claimed.

Until historical evidence proving those claims came to light, Bear said, he saw "no reason to change the presentation of Monticello as established by Stuart Gibboney, Kuper and Fiske Kimball. If such evidence was available, we would include it in our presentation, even if it meant editing out one of Jefferson's many facets."

After seeing a copy of the letter, Irving Lipkowitz took issue with Bear's measuring "Jefferson Levy's contribution to Monticello's survival and preservation" by the "market value" of the items he conveyed to the foundation. "What has been sought all these many years," he said in an October 25, 1982, letter to Viener, "is an accurate, adequate and forthright acknowledgment, in foundation literature and at Monticello, of Uriah and Jefferson Levy's indisputable contributions to Monticello's survival and preservation."

Lipkowitz spoke of Bear's "animus against Jefferson Levy and the 'Levy Family' collectively" as "disconcerting." Despite the fact that Jefferson Levy "was difficult to deal with," and that he "held Monticello privately for 44 years," Lipkowitz said, "it is beyond dispute that he rescued Monticello from extinction and rehabilitated it, especially after he put Thomas Rhodes in charge."

Lipkowitz also took issue with Bear's description of Monticello's sad state of repair in 1879 as a "failure" of the Levy family to look after the property. "Actually," he said, "a multiplicity of disasters [the Civil War, for example, and the three lawsuits] befell Monticello during those years." Bear's "statement of the Levy family's 'failure' to care for Monticello," he said, "is much too simplistic and one-sided."

Malcolm Stern visited Monticello around that time and met with Bear. He "assured me that the Levys *were* being recognized in the literature," Stern said in a September 22 letter to Viener. "But it remains evident that little has been done. It is certainly not in the spirit of Thomas Jefferson that the Thomas Jefferson Memorial Foundation has consistently ignored, and at times has given the impression of being inimical to, the record of the Levy family."

James Bear retired in 1984 after nearly thirty years of service to Monticello. In February of that year, the foundation's board of trustees chose his successor: Daniel P. Jordan, a Virginia Commonwealth University history professor who specialized in colonial American history. Jordan, a native of Mississippi who had been teaching at the Richmond university since 1969, had been a Thomas Jefferson Memorial Foundation fellow at the University of Virginia, where he earned a Ph.D. in history. He would begin his official duties on January 1, 1985.

"A wonderful choice. V. Dabney and I are very pleased," Saul Viener told Stern in a February 24 letter. "When I phoned him congratulations, he brought up the Levy family!"

Viener, Lipkowitz, Stern, and Dabney soon thereafter "began working on Jordan," in Stern's words. Lipkowitz sent the detailed notes he and Lipkowitz had written on the Levy family and Monticello to Dabney, who forwarded them on to Jordan.

"Almost immediately after the announcement in February I started to hear from various Jewish friends—some were eminent scholars and some just had an interest in history—as well as from Virginius Dabney," Jordan says, "all with the same message: namely, that an important story was not being told at Monticello."

The foursome convinced Jordan.

"I looked into it. What I was told was correct," Jordan says. "I went to the Board and asked about it. The Board, I think, was genuinely naive.

No one could recall, in their opinions as trustees, any issues or controversies. But all agreed that we needed to find a way to tell an important story."

With the blessing of the foundation's trustees, Jordan in April 1984 began an effort to have the Levys' role officially recognized at Monticello. The first step was refurbishing the Rachel Levy gravesite and placing a plaque there honoring the family.

"It was clear that one opportunity was the gravesite," Jordan says. "It's along Mulberry Row, one of the main modern pathways and one on which most of our visitors walk. It also is a lovely site with a great vista."

"I received a joyous call in April from Saul Viener," Malcolm Stern said, "announcing that a formal dedication of the Rachel Levy gravesite would be held in June [1985] and I would be invited by Jordan to present a paper on the Levy role at Monticello."

Stern helped the foundation contact several Levy descendants, including Harley Lewis, in Westchester County, New York, who had taken a strong interest in her family's Monticello legacy. On June 7, 1985, family members and several dozen guests took part in a commemorative ceremony at Monticello. Jordan welcomed the guests, saying the occasion marked the beginning of the foundation's recognition of the Levys' "good stewardship" of Monticello.

"This morning," he said, "we are pleased to honor the Levy family who, for the better part of a century, owned and preserved this priceless estate, which is perhaps unique in our land for its combination of historic significance and scenic beauty."

Saul Viener spoke next, saying: "We are restoring the name 'Levy' to its rightful place in this shrine." Viener then read Malcolm Stern's paper on the Levys and Monticello because Stern was unable to attend the ceremonies.

Edgar Bronfman, the head of World Jewish Congress and CEO of Joseph E. Seagram & Sons, made the principal address. Bronfman, who owned a large estate in Albemarle County, had agreed to speak at the behest of Saul Viener and Daniel Jordan. In his remarks, Bronfman focused on Thomas Jefferson and Uriah Levy.

Monticello, Bronfman said, "was rescued from destruction by a Jewish-American naval officer whose own fiery independence led him through a highly successful but storm-tossed career in the service of his country."

Following a scripture reading by Bernard Honan, the rabbi of Charlottesville's Temple Beth Israel, and a prayer by Louis C. Gerstein of New York City's Congregation Shearith Israel, Harley Lewis unveiled the new plaque at her great-great-grandmother's grave.

It reads in toto:

This is the grave of Rachel Phillips Levy (1769–1839), daughter of Jonas and Rebecca Machado Phillips of Philadelphia, and mother of Commodore Uriah P. Levy (1792–1862), who purchased Monticello in 1836.

An ardent admirer of Thomas Jefferson, Commodore Levy believed that the houses of great men should be preserved as "monuments to their glory," and he bequeathed Monticello in his will to the "People of the United States." The government relinquished its claim to the estate, however, and litigation over the will deprived Monticello for seventeen years of an owner to care for it.

In 1879 Jefferson Monroe Levy (1852–1924), who shared his uncle Uriah's admiration for Jefferson, gained clear title to Monticello and began to make badly needed repairs. After adding considerable land from the original Monticello tract, he sold the house and 662 acres to the Thomas Jefferson Memorial Foundation in 1923.

At two crucial periods in the history of Monticello, the preservation efforts and stewardship of Uriah P. and Jefferson M. Levy successfully maintained the property for future generations.

Since 1985, the foundation has taken many other steps to recognize the Levy family's important role at Monticello. The visitors' center, at the foot of Jefferson's mountain, for example, contains a permanent exhibit called "Monticello After Jefferson." That exhibit tells the full story of the Levy family's ownership, complete with photographs of Uriah and Jefferson M. Levy and of Monticello in the late 1870s before it was repaired and restored. The foundation sponsors lectures on the Levy family, and its latest official guidebook contains a photograph of Uriah and a summary of the family's stewardship.

The foundation also supported a six-year effort by the National Museum of American Jewish Military History to document the life of Uriah Levy. That effort culminated with an exhibit, "An American, a Sailor, and a Jew," which was on display at the Washington, D.C., museum in 1997–1998. The exhibit contained a great deal of material on Uriah Levy's ownership of Monticello.

"Commodore Uriah P. Levy is a major American hero who needs to be returned to his rightful place in our country's history," Jordan said in a June 26, 1991, letter announcing the foundation's support for the museum's efforts.

Jordan has subsequently spoken out strongly in support of the Levys' contributions to Monticello. On April 13, 1994, when the foundation announced the beginning of its first large-scale public fund-raising effort since the early 1920s, for example, Jordan said the occasion marked "perhaps the third most significant event in the post-Jefferson era." He said the other two were Uriah Levy's 1834 purchase of the house and the foundation's acquisition of it from Jefferson M. Levy in 1923.

"We've tried to do as much as possible," Susan Stein, Monticello's curator, said in an interview. "The guides are fully informed about the Levy family [but] we can only give the barest hint of the restoration of Monticello as part of the tour. We only have about thirty minutes with each tour group [and] there's so much to say about Jefferson."

Uriah Levy and Jefferson M. Levy were—in essence—the guests of honor at the foundation's official seventy-fifth anniversary celebration held on December 2, 1998, at the Pierpont Morgan Library in New York City. In his remarks, Jordan termed the transformation of Monticello from its sad state when Uriah Levy bought it to the present time "one of the towering stories in American preservation."

Levy, Jordan said, "stepped in at a critical juncture in 1834 to purchase and protect the deteriorating home. The Commodore's farsighted conviction that the houses of great men should be preserved as 'monuments to their glory' guided his family's efforts to safeguard the home—for the benefit of generations of Americans—until it was sold to the Thomas Jefferson Memorial Foundation in 1923."

The event's program includes a historical essay by Susan Stein on Uriah and Jefferson M. Levy that highlights their stewardship of Monticello. Jefferson M. Levy, Stein said, "shared his uncle's commitment to Monticello, which had fallen into disrepair [when he purchased it in 1879]." Jefferson Levy, she said, preserved "Jefferson's legacy over more than four decades."

In his essay on Monticello's restoration, William L. Beiswanger, the foundation's longtime director of restoration, also had words of praise for Jefferson Levy. "The saving grace," Beiswanger said of the house's condition in 1923 when the foundation bought it, "was that its seller, Jefferson Monroe Levy, had resisted, as had his uncle before him, the common urge of Americans to remodel. For the most part the nephew's efforts were directed toward stabilization of the building and making only those changes necessary for the house to function as a summer residence."

"The entire evening felt like a tribute to the Levy family," said Harley Lewis, who was among the family members at the event.

Harley Lewis also said that—in marked contrast to the situation a half-century ago—she and other members of the Levy family are warmly welcomed when they visit Monticello today.

"Ever since we had such a royal welcome by Dan Jordan [in 1985], we've gone down every couple of years," Mrs. Lewis said. "They have really treated us well. They have been very interested in talking to the Levy family."

It took until the mid-1980s, but the Levy family is once again at home at Thomas Jefferson's Monticello.

APPENDIX I

NUNEZ, PHILLIPS, LEVY FAMILY GENEALOGY

Diogo Nunes Riberio (anglicized to: **Dr. Samuel Nunez**) (1668–) married Gracia (Rebecca) De Siquera (1678, Portugal–?)
> Arrived Savannah, Georgia, July 11, 1733
> Seven children: including **Maria Caetana (Zipporah)** born 1714 in Portugal

Maria Caetana (Zipporah) Nunez (1714–1799, Phila.) married **Rev. David Mendes Machado** (born 1695, Portugal; died 1747, N.Y.C.) in 1733
> Two daughters: first born **Rebecca Machado,** born November 21, 1746, Reading, Pa.

Jonas Phillips (1735–1803) born in Busek, Germany, arrived in Charleston, S.C. in 1756; married **Rebecca Machado (Nunez)** (1746–1831) in 1762 near Phila.
> Children: 21, Including twins Sarah and **Rachel,** born May 23, 1769

Michael Levy (1755–1812) married **Rachel Phillips** (1769–1839) June 1787 in Philadelphia; 10 children survived infancy:
> Elizabeth (?–?)
> Louis (?–?)
> Benjamin (?–?)
> **Uriah Phillips** (April 22, 1792–March 22, 1862)
> Amelia (1793–1867)
> Morton Phillips (?–?)
> Joseph M. (?–?)
> Isaac (1800–?)
> Frances (Fanny) (1804–1857) married Abraham Lopez; youngest of three children: **Virginia Lopez** (Sept. 25, 1835, Kingston, Jamaica-May 3, 1925, N.Y.C.)
> **Jonas Phillips** (1807–1883) married Frances (Fanny) Mitchell, Nov. 22, 1848; Four children:
>> Isabella (1849–1925) married Clarkson Potter (1881–?)
>> **Jefferson Monroe** April 15, 1852 (N.Y.C.)–March 6, 1924 (N.Y.C.)
>> Louis Napoleon (1854–1921) married Lillian Hendricks Wolff
>>> Four daughters, including Frances (Fanny) Wolff (1893–?) married Harold Lewis; children: Evelyn, Philip, **Harley**
>> Amelia (1862–?) married Charles Mayhoff (1852–1923) in 1890
>>> son: Monroe (1897–1941) unmarried
>> Mitchell Abraham Cass (1863–1928) unmarried

Source: Malcolm H. Stern, *First American Jewish Families: 600 Genealogies, 1654–1988*, 3rd ed., Ottenheimer Publishers, Baltimore, 1991.
Note: The names highlighted in bold figure prominently in this book.

APPENDIX II

GRANDCHILDREN OF THOMAS JEFFERSON

Children of Martha Jefferson (September 27, 1772–October 10, 1836) and Thomas
Mann Randolph (May 17, 1768–June 20, 1828):

Anne Cary (January 23, 1791–February 11, 1826)
    Married Charles Lewis Bankhead, September 19, 1808—4 children
Thomas Jefferson (September 12, 1792–October 8, 1875)
    Married Jane Hollins Nicholas, March 10, 1815—13 children
Ellen Wayles (August 30, 1794–July 26, 1795)
Ellen Wayles (October 13, 1796–April 21, 1876)
    Married Joseph Coolidge, Jr., May 27, 1825—6 children
Cornelia Jefferson (July 26, 1799–February 24, 1871)—Unmarried
Virginia Jefferson (August 22, 1801–April 26, 1882)
    Married Nicholas Philip Trist, September 11, 1824—3 children
Mary Jefferson (November 2, 1803–March 29, 1826)—Unmarried
James Madison (January 17, 1806–January 23, 1834)—Unmarried
Benjamin Franklin (July 14, 1808–February 18, 1871)
    Married Sarah Champe Carter, November 13, 1834—3 children
Meriwether Lewis (January 31, 1810–September 24, 1837)
    Married Elizabeth Martin, April 9, 1835—1 child
Septemia Anne (January 3, 1814–September 14, 1887)
    Married David Scott Meikleham, August 13, 1838—5 children
George Wythe (March 10, 1818–April 13, 1867)
    Married Mary E. Adams Pope April 1852—no children

Children of Maria Jefferson (August 1, 1778–April 17, 1804) and John Wayles Eppes
(April 7, 1772–September 15, 1823):

Infant (December 31, 1799–January 25, 1800)
Francis (September 20, 1801–May 30, 1881)
    Married Mary Elizabeth Cleland Randolph, November 28, 1822—6 children
    Married Susan Margaret Ware Couch, March 15, 1837—7 children
Maria (February 15, 1804–July 1807)

Source: Dumas Malone, *Jefferson and His Time: The Sage of Monticello* (1981), pp. 502–503.

NOTES

INTRODUCTION: JEFFERSON'S HOUSE

1   Jefferson rarely was sick: This account of Jefferson's final illness is based on the following works: Merrill D. Peterson, *The Jefferson Image and the American Mind* (Oxford University Press, 1962), pp. 3–8; Dumas Malone, *Jefferson and His Times: The Sage of Monticello* (Little, Brown, 1981), pp. 447–448 and 496–498; Elizabeth Langhorne, *Monticello: A Family Story* (Algonquin, 1987), pp. 247–251; Henry S. Randall, *The Life of Jefferson III* (Lippincott, 1865), pp. 543–548; and Samuel X. Radbill, ed., *The Autobiographical Ana of Robley Dunglison, M.D.* (American Philosophical Society, 1963).

1   "My own health is very low": Thomas Jefferson letter to Frances Wright, August 7, 1825, Library of Congress, "Thomas Jefferson Papers," Series 1, General Correspondence, 1651–1827.

2   "It is agony to leave her in the situation she is now in": Jefferson quoted by Jane Hollins Randolph (Thomas Jefferson Randolph's wife) letter to Cary Ann Smith, June 27, 1826, "Randolph Family Papers, 1790–1864," University of Virginia Library, Special Collections Department.

CHAPTER ONE: STEALING MONTICELLO

7   "I am happy": Thomas Jefferson letter to George Gilmer, Aug. 12, 1787.

8   Jefferson spent many years: An excellent, concise description of Jefferson's plans for Monticello can be found in "Monticello: A Guidebook," published by the Thomas Jefferson Memorial Foundation, 1997. Especially useful is Susan Stein's essay, "Jefferson's Monticello." Also see James A. Bear, Jr.'s essay, "Monticello," in Merrill D. Peterson, ed., *Thomas Jefferson: A Research Biography* (Scribner's, 1986), pp. 437–452; the Thomas Jefferson Memorial Foundation website, *www.monticello.org* section "The House"; and Susan Stein, *The Worlds of Thomas Jefferson at Monticello* (Abrams, 1993), pp. 11–33.

8   The result was a 10,660-square-foot, twenty-room Roman neoclassical building: Those figures do not include Monticello's pavilions or the rooms under the terraces. In the main house itself the cellar accounts for 3,200 square feet, the first floor 4,100, the second floor 1,840 and the third floor 1,520 square feet, according to the Thomas Jefferson Memorial Foundation.

8   "The influence was Palladian": Bear, op. cit., p. 437.

8   "shopped for a lifetime": Stein, op. cit., p. 11. See, also, Marie G. Kimball,

"The Furnishings of Monticello," Thomas Jefferson Memorial Foundation, 1946.

9   the Marquis de Chastellux: De Chastellux's description of Jefferson was written on April 13, 1792, at Monticello. Chastellux was a member of the French Academy and was in America fighting with General Rochambeau's army. See *Travels in North America in the Years 1780, 1781 and 1782*, Howard C. Rice, Jr., translator and editor (University of North Carolina Press, 1963), pp. 389–396.

9   an "ornamental working farm": Joseph Giovannini, "The Restoration of Garden and Grove at Monticello," *The New York Times*, July 7, 1983, p. C10.

10   Jefferson built a thousand-foot-long: On Jefferson's gardens, see Dumas Malone, *Jefferson and His Times, Vol. VI: The Sage of Monticello* (Little, Brown 1981), pp. 45–48. Also, Cullen Murphy, "Eminent Domains," *The Atlantic Monthly*, August 1996, and Robert Wernick, "At Monticello, a Big Birthday for the Former Owner," *Smithsonian*, May 1993.

10   "an artistic achievement of the first order": Merrill D. Peterson, *The Jefferson Image in the American Mind* (Oxford University Press, 1960), p. 380.

10   owed his creditors about $11,000: Malone, op. cit., p. 3. Malone covers Jefferson's life at Monticello from 1809 to 1826 in depth. For an abbreviated version of Jefferson's post-presidency life at Monticello see Jack McLaughlin, *Jefferson and Monticello: The Biography of a Builder* (Holt, 1988), pp. 375–385.

10   He also owned the 157-acre Natural Bridge: In a July 1, 1809, letter to William Jenkins, Jefferson called Natural Bridge "undoubtedly one of the sublimest curiosities in nature."

13   At his death, Jefferson owed: For a thorough discussion of Jefferson's final estate and his will see Malone, op. cit., pp. 511–512.

14   "His house is rather old": Samuel Whitcomb, Jr., "An Interview with Thomas Jefferson," May 3, 1824, University of Virginia Library, Special Collections Department. See, also, Merrill D. Peterson, ed., *Visitors to Monticello* (University of Virginia Press, 1993), pp. 95–96.

15   "You may suppose how unwilling we are to leave": Mary Jefferson Randolph to Ellen Wayles Randolph Coolidge, October 1, 1826, "Correspondence of Ellen Wayles Randolph Coolidge," University of Virginia Library, Special Collections Department.

15   the sale brought in $47,840: *Niles' Register*, July 19, 1828. Also see Stein, op. cit., pp. 118–120.

16   Virginia Randolph Trist and her husband Nicholas also left Monticello: Details about the Trist family from the Nicholas Philip Trist Papers, Southern Historical Collection No. 2104, Manuscripts Department, Library of the University of North Carolina at Chapel Hill. See also: Gerald Morgan, Jr., "Nicholas Trist and Virginia Jefferson Randolph Trist," in *Collected Papers to Commemorate Fifty Years of the Monticello Association of the Descendants of Thomas Jefferson* (Princeton University Press, 1965), pp. 100–109.

19   Edgehill Plantation six miles from Monticello: William Randolph had named

the property in honor of the Battle of Edgehill, the first large battle of the English Civil War on October 23, 1642, which was a victory for King Charles I. See Sarah N. Randolph *The Domestic Life of Thomas Jefferson* (University Press of Virginia, 1978), pp. 436–437.

22    $15,000 to $20,000: Thomas Jefferson Randolph letter to J. H. Cocke, November 17, 1928, "Papers of Betty Page Cocke," University of Virginia Library, Special Collections Department.

22   "low prices": Thomas Jefferson Randolph letter to J. H. Cocke, December 7, 1928.

23   "offered for sale for $12,000": Francis Tuckett, *A Journey in the United States in the Years 1829 and 1830*, Hubert C. Fox, ed., (St. Nicholas Books, 1976).

23   "We found a great coarse Irish woman": Anne Royall, *Mrs. Royall's Southern Tour* (Washington, D.C., 1830), p. 88; see also, Peterson, *Visitors*, op. cit., p. 116.

23   Poindexter introduced a bill: U.S. Congress, Documents and Debates, 1774–1873, Senate, 21st Congress, 2nd Session, Library of Congress, p. 180.

26   He had purchased it the year before: Details of the exchange of the Hatch house and the Monticello purchase from Rev. Edgar Woods, *Albemarle County in Virginia* (C. J. Carrier, 1964), p. 141, Cornelia Jefferson Randolph letter to Ellen Coolidge, June 29, 1831, and Martha Jefferson Randolph letter to Ellen Coolidge, August 15, 1831.

26   "We are none of us in very good spirits": Cornelia Jefferson Randolph letter to Ellen Coolidge, June 29, 1831.

26   "There is some prospect of selling Monticello": Martha Jefferson Randolph letter to Virginia Trist, July 5, 1831, Nicholas Philip Trist Papers, Southern Historical Collection, Wilson Library, University of North Carolina at Chapel Hill, Reel 3.

26   "which continued some weeks": Martha Jefferson Randolph letter to Ellen Coolidge, August 15, 1831.

27   "a Charlottesville druggist": Peterson, *The Jefferson Image*, op. cit., p. 380.

27   a recent resident of Charlottesville: Paul Wilstach, *Jefferson and Monticello* (Doubleday, Page & Company, 1925), p. 214.

28   "had no interest in preserving Monticello": Donovan Fitzpatrick and Saul Saphire, *Navy Maverick: Uriah Philips Levy* (Doubleday, 1963), p. 136.

28   "a bitter opponent of the late President": Samuel Sobel, *Intrepid Sailor* (Cresset Publishers, 1980), p. 29.

28   "an intimate and cherished friend": J. T. Barclay, "Dr. James T. Barclay," in *Churches of Christ: A Historical, Biographical and Pictorial History of the Churches of Christ in the United States, Australasia, England, and Canada*, John T. Brown, ed. (Norton and Co., 1904), p. 440.

28   "Dr. Barclay never cut down a tree": Decima Campbell Barclay, "Jefferson's First Successor at Monticello," abstracted by Mrs. Leslie R. Smith, 1976, photocopy of section on James T. Barclay in the files of the Thomas Jefferson Memorial Foundation Research Department. A version of the article ap-

peared in *Discipliana*, the Disciples of Christ Historic Society publication, Vol. 49, No. 1, 1989.

29 Cornelia Randolph referred to Julia Ann Stowers as "an heiress": Cornelia Randolph letter, June 29, 1831, to Ellen Coolidge.

30 "There was never a day": quoted by John Levin, "Her Home Reflects Jefferson Connection," *Currents* (Portsmouth, Va.), January 4–5, 1978.

30 "I have often heard one of my aunts": Letter from R. T. W. Duke, Jr. to Jefferson M. Levy, quoted in address delivered by Jefferson Levy to the Empire State Society, Sons of the American Revolution in New York City, April 15, 1913. From Jefferson Monroe Levy, *1852–1924*, Collection, American Jewish Historical Society, New York.

30 "too much visited to be a private residence": quoted in Leroy Garrett, *Alexander Campbell and Thomas Jefferson: A Comparative Study of Two Old Virginians* (Wilkinson Publishing, 1963).

31 "The late residence of Mr. Jefferson": William Barry letter, August 16, 1832, in "Letters of William T. Barry," *William and Mary College Quarterly*, Vol. 14, 1906, p. 234.

31 "The first thing that strikes you": John E. Semmes, *John H. B. Latrobe and His Times, 1803–1891* (Norman, Remington Co., 1917), p. 248. Also see Peterson, *Visitors*, op. cit., p. 121.

32 Barclay "asked $10,000": Martha Jefferson Randolph to Ellen Coolidge, October 27, 1833.

32 "Both the manner in which Levy came to own Monticello": Charles B. Hosmer, Jr., *Presence of the Past: A History of the Preservation Movement in the United States Before Williamsburg* (Putnam's, 1965), p. 153.

33 One of the earliest published versions: Amos J. Cummings, "A National Humiliation: A Story of Monticello, reprinted in *Rare Virginia Pamphlets*, Vol. 70, University of Virginia Library, Special Collections Department.

33 Merrill Peterson, the Jefferson historian: Peterson, *Visitors to Monticello*, op. cit., p. 174.

34 Maud Littleton repeats the story: "Monticello." The author is indebted to Susan Stein, the curator at Monticello, for providing him with a copy of the booklet, which was published privately in 1913.

35 Around the same time, the widely read advice columnist: Dorothy Dix, "Monticello: Shrine or Bachelor's Hall," *Good Housekeeping Magazine*, April 1914, pp. 538–541.

35 Jefferson Levy spoke out strongly: Testifying on March 19, 1914, before the U.S. Senate Committee on Public Buildings and Grounds.

35 The same story, minus the overimbibing: Paul Wilstach, *Jefferson and Monticello* (Doubleday, Page, 1925), p. 216.

35 Judge R. T. W. Duke, Jr., a Charlottesville lawyer: Letter from R. T. W. Duke, Jr. to Jefferson M. Levy, quoted in address delivered by Jefferson Levy to the Empire State Society, Sons of the American Revolution in New York City, April 15, 1913, op. cit.

36 "That man Hart was here": Martha Randolph to Ellen Coolidge, October 23, 1833, "Thomas Jefferson Memorial Foundation Deposits," University of Virginia Library, Special Collections Department, Box 3. See, also, Martha Jefferson Randolph to Ellen Wayles Coolidge, October 27, 1833, and Ellen Wayles Coolidge to Virginia Trist, April 15, 1834, "Correspondence of Ellen Wayles Randolph Coolidge, 1810–1861," University of Virginia Library Special Collections Department.

38 "the spring of 1836": Donovan and Saphire, op. cit., p. 133.

39 The evidence—presented here for the first time: Albemarle County Circuit Superior Court records, Library of Virginia, Box 41. The following documents were useful in reconstructing the sequence of events beginning with Uriah Levy's April 1, 1834, purchase of Monticello and ending with the filing of the deed on May 21, 1836: "Levy vs. Barclay, Bill and Exhibits, October 6, 1934; Depositions taken of Doctor Hardin Massie and Bernard H. Buckner," October 7, 1834; "The answer of James T. Barclay to a bill exhibited against him . . .," January 12, 1835; "Deposition of Isaac Raphael, October 6, 1835;" "Plot of 218 acres . . .," May 3, 1836. The finding in the court case Barclay vs. Levy of May 18, 1836, may be found in the Albemarle County Virginia Law Order Book for 1831-1837, Library of Virginia, Microfilm Reel No. 125. The author is indebted to Library of Virginia archivist Minor Weisiger for finding the records.

39 "If I remember it right": Jefferson Levy, "Notes Upon the Sale of Monticello," in George Alfred Townsend, *Monticello and Its Preservation Since Jefferson's Death, 1826–1902, Correspondence of George Alfred Townsend,* (Gibson Brothers, 1902), p. 51.

40 "This celebrated seat": *Atkinson's Saturday Evening Post,* October 19, 1833.

41 "Lieut. Levy left here a week since": Thomas Jefferson Randolph letter to Virginia Trist, April 4, 1834, Nicholas Philip Trist Papers, Southern Historical Collection, Wilson Library, University of North Carolina at Chapel Hill, Reel 4.

43 It appears that Levy obtained a judgment: "James T. Barclay versus Uriah P. Levy," Albemarle County, Virginia Law Order Book, 1831–1837, Library of Virginia, Microfilm Reel No. 125, p. 360.

44 "Captain Levi is hear [*sic*]. 'raving'": Virginia Trist letter to Nicholas Trist, January 21, 1835, transcription in the files of Thomas Jefferson Memorial Foundation Research Department.

44 Virginia Trist elaborated on Uriah Levy's marital plans: Virginia Trist lettter to Nicholas Trist, February 3, 1835, Nicholas Philip Trist Papers, Southern Historical Collection, Wilson Library, University of North Carolina at Chapel Hill, Reel 4. Cornelia and Mary Randolph never married. Septimia, the youngest Jefferson granddaughter, married David Scott Meikleham in 1838. They had five children. She died in 1887.

45 Jonas Levy, Uriah's younger brother: Details taken from a transcribed copy of Jonas Levy's unpublished memoir, written in 1877. The author is grateful to

Harley Lewis, a great granddaughter of Jonas Levy, for kindly providing a copy of the memoir.

CHAPTER TWO: THE COMMODORE'S HOUSE

47   "We Levys were the first": Jefferson M. Levy, quoted in the *Public Ledger* of Philadelphia, May 11, 1923. For detailed genealogical information on the Levy, Phillips, Machado, and Nunez families, see Malcolm H. Stern *First American Jewish Families: 600 Genealogies, 1654–1988*, 3rd edition (Otten-heimer Publishers, 1991).

47   published in the mid-nineteenth century: See Levi Sheftall, "The Jews in Sa-vannah," *The Occident and American Jewish Advocate*, Vol. I, 1843; George White, *Statistics of Georgia* (1849), Leon Huhner, "The Jews of Georgia in Colonial Times," *Publications of the American Jewish Historical Society*, No. 10, 1902, and Malcolm H. Stern, "Jewish Settlement in Savannah," *American Jewish Historical Quarterly*, Vol. 52, March 1963. An excellent secondary source is Alfred A. Weinstein, "Georgia's First Physician," *Harvard Medical Alumni Bulletin*, Summer 1961, pp. 25–27.

48   Dr. Marcos Fernan Nunez: quoted in Emily Coffin, "Nunez Family Spans Over Two Centuries in Medicine," *The Bulletin of the Georgia Medical Society*, undated, copy in the files of the Jacob Rader Marcus Center of the American Jewish Archives at the Hebrew Union College in Cincinnati.

48   lived as a crypto-Jew, or *marrano*: Perhaps the best-known *marrano* was the philosopher Baruch Spinoza (1632–1677) whose Spanish and Portuguese an-cestors were forced to convert to Christianity.

48   underwent the rite of ritual circumcision: Dr. Malcolm H. Stern, "The Levys and Monticello," address given June 7, 1985, at the rededication of the grave of Rachel Levy at Monticello.

49   pleasure "with the Behaviour": *The Colonial Records of the State of Georgia*, Vol. 26, *Letter Books of the Trustees, Orders, Rules Regulations &c*, 1732–1738, p. 42.

50   Congregation Shearith Israel: see David and Tamar de Sola Pool, *An Old Faith in the New World: Portrait of Shearith Israel, 1654–1954* (Columbia University Press, 1955).

50   "She was a woman of many accomplishments": N. Taylor Phillips, "Family History of the Reverend David Mendez Machado," *Publications of the American Jewish Historical Society*, No. 2, 1894, p. 50.

51   He was born in 1735: See David de Sola Pool, *Portraits Etched in Stone: Early Jewish Settlers, 1682–1831* (Columbia University Press, 1953), pp. 290–297, and Samuel Rezneck, *The Saga of an American Jewish Family Since the Revolu-tion: A History of the Family of Jonas Phillips* (University Press of America, 1980), pp. 7–17.

51   His most famous public religious act: Jonas Phillips' letter, "Jonas Phillips to the President and Members of the Convention," is published in *Farrand's Records*, CIV, September 17, 1787.

52   the first Jew to own a house in North America: Edwin G. Burrows and Mike Wallace, *Gotham: A History of New York City to 1898* (Oxford University Press, 1999), p. 60.

52   "The Levys I belong to": Jefferson M. Levy, quoted in the *Public Ledger* of Philadelphia, op. cit.

53   In 1910, Jefferson Levy: New York *Evening Telegram*, October 29, 1910; New York *Herald*, November 10, 1912. *New York Times* obituary of Jonas Levy, September 15, 1883. *New York Times* obituary of L. Napoleon Levy, April 11, 1921.

53   As for Michael Levy: *First American Jewish Families*, op. cit., p. 159. See also Edwin Wolf 2nd and Maxwell Whiteman, *The History of the Jews of Philadelphia* (Jewish Publication Society of America, 1957).

53   is further evidence that he: Rev. Dr. Henry Berkowitz, "Notes on the History of the Earliest German Jewish Congregation in America," *Publications of the American Jewish Historical Society*, No. 9, 1901, p. 124.

53   Advertisements in the . . . *Maryland Gazette*: cited by Ira Rosenwaike, "The Jews of Baltimore to 1810," *American Jewish Historical Quarterly*, Vol. 64, June 1975.

54   Jefferson wrote to Noah on May 28, 1818: Library of Congress, Thomas Jefferson Papers, Series 9, Collected Manuscripts, 1783–1822.

54   That letter was sold October 29, 1986: "Jefferson Letter Brings Record Price," *The New York Times*, October 30, 1986.

55   "My parents were Israelites": "Defense of Captain Uriah P. Levy, U.S. Navy Before a Court of Inquiry, Convened in Washington, D.C. in November 1857, Defense Statement," Levy, *Uriah Phillips, 1792–1862*, Library of Congress Miscellaneous Manuscripts Collection, p. 13. See also Jacob Rader Marcus, *Memoirs of American Jews, 1775–1865* (The Jewish Publication Society of America, 1955), p. 84.

55   His biographers: Donovan Fitzpatrick and Saul Saphire, *Navy Maverick: Uriah Phillips Levy* (Doubleday, 1963); Abram Kanof, "U.P. Levy: The Story of a Pugnacious Commodore" in Abraham J. Karp, ed., *The Jewish Experience in America* (American Jewish Historical Society, 1969); Samuel Sobel, *Intrepid Sailor* (Cresset Publishers, 1980).

56   "good-sized for his age": Fitzpatrick and Saphire, op. cit., p. 2.

57   "Uriah Levy never set foot in Dartmoor": Author interview with Ira Dye, February 6, 2000. Dye is the author of *The Fatal Cruise of the Argus: Two Captains in the War of 1812* (Naval Institute Press, 1994).

58   "They spoke at some length": Fitzpatrick and Saphire, op. cit, p. 114.

59   "Especially after the Christopher Street pier": Burrows and Wallace, op. cit., p. 475.

59   He came close to marriage: The Koch-Messchert Family Papers, 1784–1914, Manuscript Collection No. 329, Special Collections Department, University of Delaware Library.

60   Levy proposed marriage to Elizabeth McBlair: Michael McBlair Correspondence, McBlair Papers, 1797–1849, Manuscripts Department, Maryland Historical Society Library, Baltimore.

60   "I consider Thomas Jefferson": Uriah Levy letter to John Coulter, November 1832. Quoted in Fitzpatrick and Saphire, op. cit., p. 128. Levy did not leave a journal or a memoir; nor are his letters collected in any archive. They are widely scattered among private individuals, archives and library special collections. In the 115-page defense statement Levy gave at his November 1857 Navy Court of Inquiry, he provided some details on his early life and naval career, but nothing about his ownership of Monticello. Fitzpatrick and Saphire provide no information about the whereabouts of the November 1832 letter quoted above, nor do they give the letter's exact date. Attempts by the author and other researchers to find the letter have been to no avail.

61   On July 4, 1833, Levy was involved in a public incident: "Defense of Captain Uriah P. Levy, U.S. Navy Before a Court of Inquiry . . . ," op. cit., pp. 102–103.

62   "symbolically the most important public space": Author interview with Deborah Bershad, March 24, 2000.

62   "I beg leave to present": *Journal of the House of Representatives*, March 25, 1834.

63   "It is every way fit and proper": *Journal of the Senate*, May 6, 1834, pp. 246–247.

63   The Senate passed a resolution on May 12: *Journal of the Senate*, May 12, 1834. The Marquis de Lafayette died eight days later on May 20, 1834, in Paris, between the time the Senate and House passed the resolutions accepting the David sculpture of Jefferson.

63   Uriah Levy was breaking new ground: See Hank Burchard, "Hidden in Plain Sight," *The Washington Post*, January 21, 2000, an article on the history of Washington, D.C.'s monuments.

64   "I desire to honor the name of Jefferson": Jonas P. Levy, February 15, 1874, letter to Hon. Justin Morrill, chairman, U.S. Senate Committee on Public Buildings and Grounds. Letter published in U.S. House Committee on Rules, "Hearing on Public Ownership of Monticello," Appendix B, 62nd Congress, 2d session, on S. Con. Res. 24, July 9, 1912, p. 56.

65   The David Jefferson is considered to be: Charles E. Fairman, the Capitol's then art curator, characterized the statue as "a valuable accession to the art works of the Capitol" in *Art and Artists of the Capitol of the United States of America* (U.S. Government Printing Office, 1927), p. 68.

65   "strolling around the public grounds": Townsend, op. cit., p. 55.

66   When Jefferson had learned: Gilbert Chinard, ed., *Letters of Lafayette and Jefferson* (Johns Hopkins University Press, 1929), p. 423.

66   "Silence fell as the carriages neared the house": Malone, op. cit., p. 404.

67   Jefferson M. Levy believed that his uncle: letter to Martin W. Littleton, February 3, 1912, American Jewish Historical Society archives.

67   Navy Lieutenant Levy, his nephew said in 1914: Jefferson M. Levy testifying March 19, 1914, before the U.S. Senate Committee on Public Buildings and Grounds.

67   "I think he just went down there": author interview.

68   Theodore Fred Kuper, the national director: see Theodore Fred Kuper letter to Saul Viener, April 10, 1976, in the files of the American Jewish Archives at the Jacob Rader Marcus Center at the Hebrew Union College in Cincinnati and article by James A. Bear, Jr. and Susan Kalffky in the Charlottesville *Daily Progress*, November, 7, 1971, p. B11.

68   In 1836, Joseph Martin: Joseph Martin, *A New and Comprehensive Gazetter of Virginia and the District of Columbia* (Charlottesville: J. Martin, 1836), pp. 116–117.

69   In October 1837 Levy added significantly: Albemarle County Deed Book, 35, p. 351, October 31, 1837.

69   Uriah signed a document in which he named George Carr: George Carr Papers, University of Virginia Library, Special Collections Department.

69   "The commodore delighted in donning an old hat": Quoted in B. W. Blandford, "Commodore Uriah P. Levy," *The American Hebrew*, April 10, 1925, p. 739.

71   "the long years of Uriah's discontent": Fitzpatrick and Saphire, op. cit., p. 163.

71   "he cut something of a swath in the social life.": Ibid., pp. 175–176.

71   "With the exception of the terraces": quoted in "Jefferson's Grave," *Niles' National Register*, September 22, 1838, p. 50.

72   "We were overrun with sightseers at Monticello": Blandford, op. cit., p. 739.

72   the July 1839 issue of *The Collegian:* "Monticello," *The Collegian*, Vol. I, July 1839, pp. 367–368.

72   The Reverend Stephen Higginson Tyng . . . of Philadelphia: Letter dated May 27, 1840, in the *Episcopal Recorder*, June 13, 1840. See also Peterson, *Visitors*, op. cit., pp. 124–128.

73   Buckingham, in his account of the visit: James S. Buckingham, *The Slave States of America* (Fisher Son & Co., London, 1842) pp. 400–402. See also Peterson, *Visitors*, op. cit., pp. 129–135.

74   "I don't think Uriah Levy owned [any] of Thomas Jefferson's paintings": author interview, June 1, 2000.

74   Levy reported that he was "hard at work in the field": Letter to David Coddington from Monticello, December 1, 1842, transcribed photocopy from the files of the Thomas Jefferson Memorial Foundation Research Department, Charlottesville, Virginia.

75   Lossing described a visit he paid to Monticello: Benson J. Lossing, "Monticello," *Harper's New Monthly Magazine*, July 1853, pp. 145–155.

76   It is not certain exactly when and where: Fitzpatrick and Saphire, op. cit., p. 195. The author and others have searched several likely archives to try to find records of the Uriah Levy–Virginia Lopez marriage, to no avail. A search conducted for the author by the New York City Department of Records and Information Services' Information Archives came up empty, as did a search of the marriage records in Albemarle County, Virginia. Military historian Ira Dye, while doing research for a book on Uriah Levy's naval career, also was unable to locate a record of the marriage at the clerk of the court's office in Albemarle County; among the official records of New York City, Richmond, and Norfolk; or in the records of Shearith Israel, the synagogue Uriah Levy belonged to in New York City; the Beth Ahaba synagogue in Richmond; and the Ohef Shalom synagogue in Norfolk. A search of the marriage indexes of the *Brooklyn Eagle, New York Evening Post,* and *New York Herald* newspapers by the New York City Public Library Research Division found no listing of the marriage.

76   Other secondary sources say: see, for example, "An American, a Sailor, and a Jew: The Life and Career of Commodore Uriah Phillips Levy, USN (1792–1862)," National Museum of American Jewish Military History, July 1997, p. 31 and Sobel, op. cit., p. 100.

76   Levy's biographers describe Virginia Lopez: Fitzpatrick and Saphire, op. cit., pp. 195–196.

77   many of whom "were resentful and regarded the Levys as intruders": Anna Barringer, "Pleasant It Is," *Magazine of Albemarle County History,* Vol. 27/28, 1970, p. 52.

77   "Capt. Uriah P. Levy, a Capt. in the U.S. Navy": Memoirs of George Walter (Clements) Blatterman (1820–1910), University of Virginia Library, Special Collections Department.

77   "How I did enjoy galloping over those hills": B. W. Blandford, "Commodore Uriah P. Levy," *The American Hebrew,* May 15, 1825, p. 58. Virginia Levy, who was born on September 25, 1835, died at her home, 420 W. 121st Street in Manhattan, on May 3, 1925. She had survived her first husband, Uriah Levy, by sixty-three years.

78   Two unidentified visitors, who reported: "A Visit to Monticello," transcribed by John Barnwell in "Monticello: 1856," *Journal of the Society of Architectural Historians,* Vol. 34, 1975, pp. 280–285.

80   Naval historian James Tertius de Kay described the scene: James Tertius de Kay, *Chronicles of the Frigate Macedonia, 1809–1922* (Norton, 1995), p. 266.

80   A British diplomat: The diary of James Finn, British consul to Jerusalem, in "Levy, Uriah P." files of the American Jewish Archives.

80   "I had a most enjoyable stay" in Boston: quoted by B. W. Blandford, "Commodore Uriah P. Levy," *The American Hebrew,* May 8, 1825, p. 835.

80   "less like a military cruise than a social saga": Fitzpatrick and Saphire, op. cit., p. 229.

81   Rothschild . . . who, she said, had a synagogue in his home: quoted in Blandford, op. cit., p. 32.

81   In a letter he wrote to George Carr: a copy of this letter is in the files of the TJFM Research Department.

82   in a September 17, 1858, letter he wrote to Carr: from George Carr Papers, University of Virginia Library, Special Collections Department.

84   Markens said he had had three mistakes about Uriah Levy: Letter to the editor, *Hebrew Standard*, January 27, 1911.

84   Jefferson M. Levy made a case that Uriah was: *Hebrew Standard*, February 3 and 24, 1911.

84   "He had every right to it after 1860": author interview, February 6, 2000.

85   "place his entire fortune at [Lincoln's] disposal": Isaac Markens, "Lincoln and the Jews," *Publications of the American Jewish Historical Society*, Vol. 17, 1909, p. 158. Markens did not provide a source for this grandiose claim.

CHAPTER THREE: SAVING MONTICELLO

87   His funeral, which was held in New York: *New York Times*, March 25, 1862, and *New York Herald*, March 26, 1862.

87   escorted the body from Levy's St. Marks Place house: *The New York Times* reported that Levy was interred at Salem Fields Cemetery in Brooklyn. In fact, Uriah Levy is buried at the nearby Cypress Hills Cemetery. The epitaph on his enormous tombstone reads: "In memory of Uriah P. Levy, Father of the Law for the abolition of the barbarous practice of corporal punishment in the Navy of the United States."

88   According to an article in the *Richmond Examiner*: *Richmond Examiner*, October 11, 1861.

88   Monticello "has been confiscated": "Monticello, Once the Residence of Thomas Jefferson," *Frank Leslie's Illustrated Newspaper*, February 8, 1862.

89   Charlottesville, however, played an important support role: see Ervin L. Jordan, Jr., *Charlottesville and the University of Virginia in the Civil War* (H.E. Howard, 1988) and "Monticello During the Civil War," TJMF Research Department unpublished monograph, July 5, 1990.

89   "The place was once very pretty": quoted in "Monticello During the Civil War," op. cit., p. 2.

90   *The New York Times* account of that day's events reported: "The Sale of Monticello," *The New York Times*, December 1, 1864.

90   We know that Jonas Levy opened up a chandlery: See the well-documented account of this period of Jonas Levy's life in Samuel Rezneck, *The Saga of an American Jewish Family Since the Revolution: The History of the Family of Jonas Phillips* (University Press of America, 1980), pp. 118–120.

90 These offers included building a twenty-gun ironclad ship: in Europe . . .": *Journals of the Confederate Congress*, April 15, 1862, Library of Congress.

90 On April 16, 1862, Jonas presented a petition: Ibid., April 16, 1862.

91 In *Monticello and Its Preservation:* Townsend, op. cit., p. 182.

92 Ficklin, the new owner of Monticello: For overviews of Benjamin Ficklin's life, see Rick Britton, "Thrillseeker: The Amazing Life of Benjamin Franklin Ficklin," *Albemarle Magazine*, December 1998–January 1999 and B. M. Read, "Ben Ficklin 1849 and the Pony Express," *VMI Alumni Review*, Summer 1973.

93 According to Ficklin family lore: See C. Grove Smith, Letters, Documents bearing on the Ficklin and Hardesty Families, in the files of the TJMF Research Department.

94 he owned more than two dozen properties in New York: A New York City tax receipt for October 1862 indicated that Uriah Levy paid $1,199.60 for twenty-four properties he owned on Duane, Division, Canal, Houston, Macdougal, Thompson, Greenwich, and Rivington Streets. The receipt can be found in the Uriah P. Levy files at the American Jewish Historical Society in New York. A city tax receipt for October 1863 for his estate lists thirty-three properties owned on Broome, Crosby, Prince, Bowery, Thirteenth, Thirty-ninth, Duane, Division, Canal, Houston, Macdougal, Sullivan, and Thompson Streets and on First Avenue. Uriah Levy's tax bill that year totaled $1,484.50. That document can be found in the TJMF Research Department. Assessors placed a value on his New York properties of $331,606.15 during the lawsuit over the terms of his will.

94 bequeathed all of his city property to his wife: "The Last Will and Testament of Uriah Phillips Levy," admitted to probate June 9, 1862, Surrogate Court of the County of New York. A photocopy of the will is in the Uriah P. Levy files at the American Jewish Historical Society in New York. A transcribed copy may be found in Kanof, op. cit., p. 66.

94 one of eight executors Uriah Levy named: The others were Benjamin F. Butler, Uriah Levy's friend and lawyer; David V. S. Coddington, another lawyer friend; Joseph H. Patten, a third New York City lawyer; the brothers Dr. Joshua Cohen and Jacob I. Cohen of Baltimore; George Carr, Uriah Levy's Charlottesville lawyer; and Dr. John B. Blake of Washington.

95 James A. Bear, the former curator at Monticello: Merrill Peterson, ed., *Thomas Jefferson: A Reference Biography* (Scribner, 1986), p. 447.

95 Thomas L. Rhodes . . . offered the theory: See Thomas L. Rhodes and Frank B. Lord, *The Story of Monticello* (Pridemark Press, 1947), pp. 85–86.

96 On April 6, 1858—the year Uriah Levy wrote his will: The association paid John Augustine Washington, Jr. $18,000 as a down payment and agreed to pay him an additional $57,000 within a year. The balance of the purchase price was paid in three annual installments. Mount Vernon, like Monticello in 1834 when Uriah Levy purchased it, was in dire need of repair when the

association acquired it. Repair and restoration work began in February 1860 after the last Washington family members moved out of Mount Vernon. See: Gerald W. Johnson, *Mount Vernon: The Story of a Shrine* (Random House, 1953), pp. 14–26 and James C. Rees, "Preservation," in Wendell Garrett, ed., *George Washington's Mount Vernon* (Monacelli Press, 1998), pp. 220–226.

96   "A matter of family interrelations": John S. Patton and Sallie J. Doswell, *Monticello and Its Master* (Michie, 1925), p. 58.

97   The debate in the Senate was short: Congress of the United States, 37th Congress, 3rd Session, 1863, *Congressional Globe*, p. 1495.

97   In his transmittal letter, Smith said: U.S. Department of Justice, *Records of the Attorney General's Office, Letters Received, 1809–1870*, Entry 9, Box 4, National Archives.

98   The government completely opted out: Bates's letter is not included in the *Opinions of the Attorneys General*. It is quoted in J. G. Randall, "When Jefferson's Home Was Bequeathed to the United States," *The South Atlantic Quarterly*, Vol. 23, January 1924, p. 37.

98   Again, the will was declared invalid and void: For details on the lawsuit, see "Asahel S. Levy and David S. Coddington, acting executors &c. of Uriah P. Levy, deceased, vs. Virginia Levy and others," Oliver Barbour, *Reports of Cases in Law and Equity Determined in the Supreme Court of the State of New York*, 1864, pp. 585–626 and Levy *et al.* v. Levy *et al., Reports of Cases Argued and Determined in the Court of Appeals of the State of New York* (1866), pp. 187–188.

98   The original 1863 decision: Quoted in Blandford, op. cit., May 15, 1925, p. 59.

98   described by Uriah Levy's biographers as: Fitzpatrick and Saphire, op. cit., p. 247.

98   According to the Ketubah . . . at Shearith Israel synagogue: Shearith Israel, Register, Volume 3, *Ketubah*, Vol. I, No. 129.

98   a group of Levy family members: In a partition suit, a judge usually is asked to order property sold and to divide the net proceeds among those who are party to the suit. Partition suits are most commonly used in divorce matters.

100   In a letter dated December 18, 1868: Jonas Levy: Carr Papers, University of Virginia Library, Special Collections Department.

100   "I have seen Mr. Wheeler," Carr said: George Carr to J. P. Levy, December 23, 1868, Papers of Jonas Phillips Levy, 1807–1883, American Jewish Historical Society, New York.

101   Carr notified Jonas Levy that he had placed ads: A copy of the advertisement from an unidentified newspaper—probably the *Richmond Dispatch* or the *Richmond Examiner*—is in the Carr papers, op. cit. The other letters to and from George Carr cited in this chapter also may be found in the Carr papers.

105   "The Bill authorizes the President of the United States": *Congressional Record*, 1874, p. 761.

105   "We have no desire to part with the property": Jonas Levy letter to Rep. Mil-

ton Speer, January 21, 1873. In the files of the TJMF Research Department.

106 By 1865, the house was "an absolute ruin": testifying March 17, 1914, before the U.S. Senate Committee on Public Buildings and Grounds, hearings on the "Purchase of Monticello," 63rd Congress, 2nd Session.

107 "I can remember my first years as a student": testifying December 15, 1916, before the U.S. House Committee on Public Grounds and Buildings hearings on the "Purchase of Monticello," 64th Congress, 1st Session.

107 Another University of Virginia student of that era, David M. R. Culbreth: David M. R. Culbreth, *The University of Virginia* (Neale Publishing, 1908), pp. 222–223.

107 Monticello "is in a semi-ruinous state": Letter to Mary Woodman, May 2, 1875, University of Virginia Library, Special Collections Department. See also "The Home of Thomas Jefferson," Evansville *Journal*, May 4, 1877.

107 "Desolation and ruin mark everything": *Congressional Record*, April 13, 1878, 45th Congress, 2nd Session, p. 2494. See also Wilstach, op. cit., p. 217.

107 Thomas Rhodes, Jefferson Levy's Monticello superintendent: Rhodes, op. cit., pp. 87, 91–92.

108 "a man of great distinction in appearance": Anna Barringer, "Pleasant It Is," *Magazine of Albemarle County History*, Vol. 27/28, 1970, p. 53.

109 Levy is a "reminder of Jefferson's figure": Townsend, op. cit., p. 34.

109 described his father's employer: Frederick H. Rhodes interview with Annabelle Prager, notes, June 1976. The author is indebted to Ms. Prager for kindly allowing him to quote from the interview.

109 Family lore holds that he began dabbling: photocopied and transcribed letter to Louis Napoleon Levy from Jefferson Monroe Levy, September 5, 1875, courtesy of Harley Lewis.

109 According to the deed books in Albemarle County: See Deed Book, 69, 1875, p. 661 and p. 693; Deed Book 71, pp. 171–172; Deed Book 74, pp. 298–299. The author gratefully acknowledges the assistance of Joan Graves of the Albemarle County Historical Society Library for her search of the records at the Albemarle County Courthouse.

109 "I own about one half of Monticello": Jefferson Levy letter to George Carr, April 2, 1877. Carr papers, op. cit.

110 Jefferson Levy bought "about five of the seven interests": Testifying December 6, 1916, before the House Committee on Public Buildings and Grounds, hearings on the "Purchase of Monticello," op. cit.

111 Wheeler "had been in charge so long": Patton and Doswell, op. cit., p. 59. See also testimony of Judge R. T. W. Duke, Jr., March 17, 1914, Senate Committee on Public Buildings and Grounds, "Purchase of Monticello," 63rd Congress, 2nd Session.

111 the new owner "has done a great deal": quoted in Merrill Peterson, ed., *Thomas Jefferson: A Reference Biography*, op. cit., p. 449.

112 Monticello, she said in a July 4 letter: Fanny Levy letters from Monticello, courtesy of Harley Lewis.

113   "Possibly the only business in Charlottesville": William Edward Webb, "Charlottesville and Albemarle County, Virginia, 1865–1900," Ph.D. dissertation, University of Virginia, undated copy in Albemarle County Historical Society Library.

113   "The whole establishment has been put in excellent order": Stockton, op. cit., p. 657.

113   Jefferson Levy, whose goal, he later wrote, was to restore Monticello: December 17, 1916, letter to Mrs. William Cumming Story, president-general of the Daughters of the American Revolution, printed in "Purchase of Monticello," hearings, December 6 and 15, 1916, U.S. House of Representatives, Committee on Public Buildings and Grounds, 64th Congress, 1st Session, p. 17.

113   He purchased a seventy-six-acre parcel: see Deed of Trust, Thomas Jefferson Memorial Foundation, Inc., to Robert L. Harrison, June 30, 1923.

114   George Blatterman, in his handwritten memoir: Blatterman, op. cit.

114   "Monticello profited for over half a century": Theodore Fred Kuper, "Collecting Monticello," *Manuscripts*, Vol. 7, Summer 1955, p. 223.

114   Thomas Rhodes was born on June 11, 1863: Biographical information from P. A. Bruce, *History of Virginia* (1924), Vol. 4, p. 319.

115   he received an offer for Monticello from a Jefferson great-great-grandson: See Robert F. Byrnes, *Awakening American Education to the World: The Role of Archibald Cary Coolidge, 1866–1928* (1982), pp. 13–27.

115   There has long been a debate: See, for example, Hosmer, op. cit., p. 158.

116   In 1916 Levy said: December 7, 1916, letter to Mrs. William Cumming Story, op. cit.

116   Another Levy ally, W. K. Semple: W. K. Semple, "The Care of Monticello by Its Owner," American Scenic and Historic Preservation Society *Annual Report*, 1914, p. 528.

117   One was an eighteenth-century coffee urn: Stein, op. cit., p. 182.

117   He replaced the broken tiles: Rhodes, op. cit., p. 92.

118   "Mr. Levy had the mansion done over by Sloan's of New York": Anna Barringer, "Pleasant to Remember: The Last Years of the Chairmanship of the Faculty of the University of Virginia," privately printed, 1970, University of Virginia Library, Special Collections. See also: *The Magazine of the Albemarle County Historical Society*, Vol. 27/28, 1970.

118   Levy, "mindful of the tastes of [Jefferson]": John S. Patton, "Monticello," *University of Virginia Alumni Bulletin*, Vol. 7, 1914, p. 645.

121   "Half a dozen English spaniels sport": Edward C. Mead, *Historic Homes of the South-West Mountains, Virginia* (C. J. Carrier, 1898), p. 33.

122   "most complex of any dwelling": Quoted by Jeanne Nicholson Siler, "Razing the Roof at Monticello," *The Observer Magazine*, May 16–22, 1991.

122   "Except for the painted surfaces": Author interview, October 13, 1997.

122   according to William M. Thornton: Testifying December 15, 1916, before the U.S. House Committee on Public Buildings and Grounds, "Purchase of Monticello," 64th Congress, 1st Session.

123   "He put it in pretty good shape": Author interview with James A. Bear, Jr.,
      May 6, 2000.

           CHAPTER FOUR: CLAIMING MONTICELLO

125   where he had a large staff of servants: Anna Barringer, who was a frequent
      guest at Monticello in the late 1890s and early 1900s, described Levy's Mon-
      ticello staff as "substantial" in her memoir, op. cit., p. 56. According to Fred-
      erick Rhodes, the son of Jefferson Levy's Monticello superintendent, Levy's
      New York servants who accompanied him to Monticello included his valet
      Willie McGushin and his brother Jack, the butler, and laundress Maria Mc-
      Manus. From "Notes on Visit to Mr. Rhodes," June 1976, unpublished notes
      by Annabelle Prager, used by permission.
125   "bachelor hall and summer estate": Peterson, *The Jefferson Image and the
      American Mind*, op. cit., p. 381.
126   "Upon presentation to the person in charge": photocopy of the admission
      ticket, which is undated, is on file at the TJMF Research Department.
127   The Levy Opera House hosted: see Richard E. Waddell, "The Theatre in
      Charlottesville," *The Magazine of the Albemarle County Historical Society*, Vol.
      31, 1973.
127   An addendum to the lease stipulated: Duke Family Papers, Box 38, No. 9521-
      h,-m, Jefferson Levy Legal Papers, University of Virginia Library, Special
      Collections Department.
127   the Redlands Club: for details on the Levy Opera House and Redlands Club,
      see City of Charlottesville, Department of Community Development, "His-
      toric Landmark Study," 1976.
127   In April 1893, the *Daily Progress* reported: Charlottesville *Daily Progress*, April
      8, 1893.
128   A few days later he sent $100: reported in the Charlottesville *Daily Progress*,
      February 11, 1895.
128   Levy also contributed financially: Charlottesville *Daily Progress*, January 12,
      1895.
129   Fanny Levy "came down from New York": Barringer, op. cit., p. 59.
130   In October 1904, for example: Unsigned article in the Ironton, Ohio, *Ironton-
      ian*, October 6, 1904.
130   "The President wore riding britches": Barringer, op. cit., p. 99.
132   "One was an elegant fringed landau": Annabelle Prager, "Notes on the Levy
      Family and Monticello," unpublished manuscript. Used by permission.
132   "This morning we racked the hay": photocopy of letter courtesy of Harley
      Lewis, Frances Wolff Levy Lewis's daughter.
133   By the turn of the twentieth century, Merrill Peterson noted: Peterson, *The
      Jefferson Image in the American Mind*, op. cit., pp. 381–382.

134   Levy celebrated in London by buying: New York *Mail and Express* article cited in the Charlottesville *Daily Progress*, September 13, 1897.

135   "I have received," he told the Fredericksburg *Free Lance:* reprinted in the Charlottesville *Daily Progress*, November 15, 1898.

136   greeted Fossett at the front door: Quoted by Lucia Stanton, "The Hemings Family and Charlottesville," *The Magazine of Albemarle County History*, Vol. 55, 1997, p. 120.

136   In the summer of 1902, *Jewish World* magazine: reported in the *New York Tribune*, July 27, 1902.

137   "late frivolous biographies": Townsend, op. cit., p. 1.

138   "one of the most conspicuous bachelor hosts": *Washington Post*, September 8, 1902.

138   "The Honorable Jefferson M. Levy": *Washington Post*, September 5, 1902.

138   "the same agreeable gentleman": *Washington Post*, January 21, 1903.

138   "getting to look more and more like Monticello": *Brooklyn Eagle*, January 27, 1903.

139   On the Fourth of July 1903: Charlottesville *Daily Progress*, July 3, 1903.

140   "Nothing remarkable about it": *The New York Times*, September 30, 1904.

140   the largest diamond ever discovered: The stone that became known as the Hope diamond, which probably was unearthed in India, by comparison, was 112 3/16 carats.

142   Thomas Jefferson, whom Levy called "the greatest statesman": quoted in City of Angers, "Statue of Thomas Jefferson, the Third President of the United States, Work of David d'Angers offered to the City of Angers by the Hon. Jefferson M. Levy, American Citizen," program dated September 16, 1905, p. 16.

142   Jefferson Levy was on the Riviera: According to an article in the *Daily Telegram*, an English language French newspaper, quoted in the Charlottesville *Daily Progress*, March 22, 1906.

143   the countess's "legal adviser": Charlottesville *Daily Progress*, October 1, 1907.

144   the playboy millionaire Harry K. Thaw: Thaw, the playboy son of a Pittsburgh railroad magnate, murdered the nation's top architect, Stanford White, on June 25, 1906, on the rooftop restaurant of Madison Square Garden in New York City. White had been having an affair with Thaw's wife, the famous showgirl, Evelyn Nesbit. Thaw's first murder trial ended in a mistrial. Martin W. Littleton represented Thaw at his second trial and used an insanity defense. Thaw was convicted, but served only a few years at a New York state hospital for the criminally insane. The sensational case was heavily covered in the newspapers and became known as the "Trial of the Century." The events are told in fictionalized form in the novel, film, and Broadway musical *Ragtime*.

144   Mrs. Littleton said three years later: testimony on July 24, 1912, before the House Rules Committee, "Hearings on Public Ownership of Monticello," 62nd Congress, 2nd Session, on S. Con. Res. 24, pp. 35–36.

145   "their ejectment from the premises": Charlottesville *Daily Progress*, July 10, 1909.

146   "President Taft freely expressed his indignation": Memphis, Tennessee *Commercial Appeal*, May 27, 1911.

146   "a patriotic labor of love": *Congressional Record*, House of Representatives, April 13, 1912, p. 4714.

147   "What a precious gift to the South!": Mrs. Martin W. Littleton, "One Wish," 1911. The text of the pamphlet was printed in the *Congressional Record*, op. cit.

148   Levy first responded: Letter from Jefferson Monroe Levy to Hon. Martin W. Littleton, Monticello, February 3, 1912, copy in the files of the American Jewish Historical Society, New York City.

149   On March 19, 1912, Sen. James E. Martine: *Congressional Record*, 62nd Congress, 2nd Session, p. 3599.

149   written on the stationery of the House Committee on Claims: copy of letter in the American Jewish Historical Society archives, New York City.

151   In an April 6 letter to Martin Littleton: copy of letter in the American Jewish Historical Society archives, New York City.

152   On Jefferson's birthday, April 13, 1912: *Congressional Record*, House of Representatives, April 13, 1912, p. 4714.

152   Mrs. Littleton began her testimony: "Proposed Name for House Office Building," House Committee on Public Buildings and Grounds, U.S. House of Representatives, 62nd Congress, 2nd Session, June 21, 1912, p. 3.

154   "I feel a trifle nervous": "Public Ownership of Monticello," hearing before the Committee on the Library, U.S. Senate, 62nd Congress, 2nd Session, July 9, 1912.

155   The family donated the old monument: Robert H. Kean, "History of the Graveyard at Monticello," The Monticello Association, 1965, p. 15.

157   she said in a 1904 family letter: Ibid., p. 16.

157   W. N. Ruffin of Danville, Virginia: quoted in *The New York Times*, December 10, 1912.

161   She once again lionized Thomas Jefferson: "Public Ownership of Monticello," hearing before the Committee on Rules, U.S. House of Representatives, 62nd Congress, 2nd Session, July 24, 1912.

162   "Every stone and every brick": quoted in *The New York Times*, August 8, 1912, and the *Washington Post*, August 8, 1912. A transcript of the hearing is not among the congressional documents at the Library of Congress.

165   He ran a modest campaign: *New York Times*, October 29, 1912.

170   Judge Duke, at a Senate hearing in 1916: "Purchase of Monticello," hearings before the U.S. House of Representatives Committee on Public Buildings and Grounds, 64th Congress, 1st Session, December 6, 1916.

171   He sent a telegram to Governor Mann: printed in the *Washington Post*, December, 12, 1912.

171   "I assure you that the most friendly feelings": quoted in the Charlottesville *Daily Progress*, December 12, 1912.

171 "I have been informed": a copy of the letter is among the Jefferson Levy papers at the American Jewish Historical Society archives in New York City.

172 In her letter to association members: undated transcribed copy of the letter in the files of the TJMF Research Department.

173 In a letter dated December 31, 1912: Ibid.

177 If Levy did not come up with a proposal, Sen. Reed said: "Purchase of Monticello," hearings of the Committee on Public Buildings and Grounds, U.S. Senate, 63rd Congress, 2nd Session, March 17, 1914.

CHAPTER FIVE: SELLING MONTICELLO

188 Between 1890 and 1920 the Jewish population: statistics cited in Jacob Rader Marcus, *The American Jew, 1585–1990: A History* (Carlson, 1995), p. 385.

188 Levy, like other acculturated American Jews: see Howard M. Sachar, *A History of the Jews In America* (Alfred A. Knopf, 1992), p. 275, and Patricia West, *Domesticating History: The Political Origins of America's House Museums* (Smithsonian Institution Press, 1999), pp. 104–105.

188 "The unfortunate lasting effect": Theodore Fred Kuper letter to Saul Viener, April 10, 1976, American Jewish Archives at the Jacob Rader Marcus Center, Cincinnati.

188 a strong anti-Semitic subtext: see, for example, the analysis of the Littleton campaign in Eliza R. L. McGraw, "The Country of the Heart: Twentieth-Century Representations of Southern Jewishness," Ph.D. dissertation, Vanderbilt University, 1999, UMI Dissertation Services, Ann Arbor, Michigan, Chapter I.

189 says their daughter Harley Lewis: author interview, January 12, 2000.

190 "The federal government has no right to confiscate this property": Danville *Register*, July 17, 1914, reprinted in the Charlottesville *Daily Progress* of the same date.

191 Around that same time Mrs. Littleton announced: quoted in the Charlottesville *Daily Progress*, May 22, 1914.

192 "You will remember that several years ago": Bryan's letter was printed in toto in many newspapers, including the Charlottesville *Daily Progress* of September 23, 1914.

192 "Mr. Bryan's letter makes it an administrative movement": quoted in the Charlottesville *Daily Progress*, October 3, 1914.

193 "I confess to you that your letter": the letter was printed in many newspapers, including *The New York Times*, October 6, 1914.

194 Navy Secretary Josephus Daniels sent a letter: the letter was entered into the record in the House Rules Committee's February 23, 1915, hearings on the "Purchase of Monticello," 63rd Congress, 3rd Session.

195   the Albemarle County tax commissioner's office announced: see articles in the October 15, 1914, New York *Evening Telegram* and Richmond *News Leader.*

197   "It had never been my intention": U.S. Congress, House Committee on Rules, "Purchase of Monticello," Hearings, 63rd Congress, 2nd Session, February 23, 1915.

201   "I sincerely hope that it will be possible": quoted in *The New York Times,* August 1, 1916.

201   Mrs. Story was the lead witness: U.S. Congress, House Committee on Public Buildings and Grounds, "Purchase of Monticello," Hearings, 64th Congress, 1st Session, August 8, 1916.

204   "I would like to know whether that price has been ascertained": U.S. Congress, House Committee on Buildings and Grounds, "Purchase of Monticello," 64th Congress, 1st Session, December 6, 1916.

210   "The spread set out by the genial host": "Gay Party at Monticello," Charlottesville *Daily Progress,* January 29, 1917.

211   Levy "said he had left the keys in New York": Roanoke *Times,* January 30, 1917.

211   what Charles Hosmer called its "last great endeavor": Hosmer, op. cit., p. 177.

211   "the noblest project that has ever engaged the interest: Fanny Harnit, "Monticello," *D.A.R. Magazine,* vol. 50, 1917, p. 158.

212   one of two men being given serious consideration: see New York *Morning World,* January 24, 1916.

212   In February of 1917, Levy let it be known: see Brooklyn *Eagle,* February 12, 1917.

213   "The present owner, for sentimental and other reasons": quoted in Hosmer, op. cit., p. 178. Also see letter dated April 1, 1919, from H. W. Hilleary to W. S. Appleton, Society for the Preservation of New England Antiquities Archives, Boston.

213   The "other reasons" Hilleary referred to: see "Monticello Owner Insolvent at Death," *The New York Times,* February 27, 1930.

214   "I am desirous of further particulars": Fiske Kimball letter to H. W. Hilleary, April 19, 1919, copy in the TJMF Archives, University of Virginia Library Special Collections Department, Box. 16.

215   Kimball told Gano he was "greatly interested": Ibid., Box 14.

216   writer Marietta Minnegerode Andrews: see West., op. cit., p. 107.

217   Levy justified the $1-million purchase price: *The New York Times,* June 29, 1920.

217   Jefferson Levy's entry in the 1920 edition: Vol. XVII, 1920, p. 432.

219   someone Levy "deemed able and worthy": *The Washington Post,* July 20, 1921.

219   Hilleary's April 1921 advertising letter said: July 19, 1921, letter from H.W. Hilleary to William Sumner Appleton, Society for the Preservation of New England Antiquities Archives. Portions of that letter were quoted in "Monti-

cello, the Famous Jefferson Estate, For Sale; Once Sought as a National Shrine," *The New York Times*, July 27, 1921.

219   The pamphlet Hilleary referred to: a copy is in the files of the TJMF Research Department.

220   "The place has become a great care": quoted in *The New York Times*, July 28, 1921.

222   "I hope that the efforts of the association": quoted in *The New York Times*, April 13, 1922.

222   According to newspaper reports, Levy and two other New York financiers: see *The New York Times*, November 3, 1922, *Richmond Times Dispatch*, November 3, 1922, Charlottesville *Daily Progress*, November 6, 1922.

223   Rumors were circulating: see Patton and Doswell, op. cit., p. 71.

224   Theodore Fred Kuper, a young New York City lawyer: see Thomas Fleming in "Monticello's Long Career—From Riches to Rags to Riches," *Smithsonian*, June 1973, p. 64.

224   "Difficulties which heretofore have prevented": quoted in the Washington *Evening Star*, April 7, 1923.

226   "Judge Jonah Goldstein told J. M. Levy": Theodore Fred Kuper letter to Saul Viener, April 10, 1976, in the Kuper, Theodore, Personal Papers files of the American Jewish Archives in Cincinnati.

226   "when Jefferson wrote his epitaph": quoted in Hosmer, op. cit., p. 181.

227   According to Kuper, Levy tried to raise the price: Ibid.

228   Kuper led a . . . national fund-raising tour: for details, see Theodore Fred Kuper, "Collecting Monticello," *Manuscripts*, Summer 1955, pp. 216–223.

229   Herbert Lehman . . . the New York City financier: Hosmer, op. cit., p. 182.

231   "In this movement the active aid": Thomas Jefferson Memorial Foundation, "Up to the American People," 1923. A copy of the statement may be found in the files of the TJMF Research Department.

232   the week's events added a total of $1,473.65: Charlottesville *Daily Progress*, November 14, 1923.

232   "The cash and the bonds and mortgage": Hosmer, op. cit., p. 183.

233   "I am very proud to add that, on my instructions to Rhodes": Theodore Fred Kuper letter to Saul Viener, April 10, 1976, op. cit.

233   At his death, Levy was insolvent: According to an article in the February 27, 1930, *New York Times*, Levy's estate was so complicated and he owed so much money that it took nearly six years for the New York City Tax Commissioner to file the report on the estate. His net worth at death, consisting primarily of the TJMF bonds, was $220,405. According to the report, at his death Jefferson Levy owed one brokerage firm, Albert J. Elias & Co., $1,041,447. The firm settled for $20,000 from the estate. Levy owed the estate of his brother, L. Napoleon Levy, $120,933. The estate accepted $30,000.

233   "The passing of Mr. Levy, of course, makes no difference": quoted in *The New York Times*, March 8, 1924.

234   "Thomas Jefferson," Fred Kuper said: quoted in the *Los Angeles Times*, September 19, 1976.

235   Levy's "estate and its lawyers": Kuper letter to Saul Viener, April 10, 1976, op. cit.

236   Among the luncheon speakers that day: reported in *The New York Times*, May 1, 1925. Maud Littleton's interest in Monticello seems to have waned considerably following the death of her son, who was killed in France during World War I. Soon thereafter she took a strong interest in religion, visited the Holy Land several times, and began amassing a huge collection of religious-themed books. She built a library to house the collection on the twelve-acre Long Island estate where she lived with her husband. The building also served as a shrine to her son. "The architecture was similar to that of old Palestine, and was surrounded by a high concrete wall on which were painted scenes of Jerusalem," according to a July 24, 1998 article in the *Manhasset (N.Y.) Press.* Mrs. Littleton began lecturing on the life of Christ and opened her library to students interested in the subject. Following the death of her husband in 1934, she moved to a ranch near Cody, Wyoming, with her son Martin W. Littleton, a former Nassau County, N.Y., district attorney and prominent criminal defense lawyer. He later became editor of the Cody *Times.* After her death in 1953, her son donated Mrs. Littleton's collection of some 2,000 books on theological topics to the University of Wyoming, where today they make up the Maud Littleton Collection at the university's American Heritage Center. "Mrs. Littleton started the successful campaign to purchase for the nation Monticello, Thomas Jefferson's home," her February 15, 1953, *New York Times* obituary says. "A zealous fundamentalist, she traveled in the Holy Land and built a Nazarene shrine on the Littleton estate at Plandome, L.I."

237   "Every bit of work on the buildings": Theodore Fred Kuper, "Collecting Monticello," *Manuscripts*, Summer 1955, pp. 222–223.

237   a September 1, 1928, foundation financial report: Thomas Jefferson Memorial Foundation, "Financial Statement as of Sept. 1, 1928," TJMF Research Department.

237   The offer was tendered in a May 7 letter: May 7, 1924, letter from Stewart Gibboney to Fiske Kimball, Thomas Jefferson Memorial Foundation Archives, University of Virginia Library Special Collections Department, Box 14.

237   "Jefferson's twentieth century reputation": Peterson, *The Jefferson Image in the American Mind*, op. cit., p. 397.

238   Kimball consulted Jefferson's drawings, letters, and other documents: writing in the American Institute of Architect's "Report of Committee on Preservation of Historic Monuments and Scenic Beauties," March 14, 1923.

238   "I understand that you are going to dispose, at public auction, of certain of the contents of Monticello": Amelia Mayhoff letter to TJMF, September 27,

1928, Thomas Jefferson Memorial Foundation Archives, University of Virginia Library Special Collections Department, Box 18.

240 "We are making room at Monticello": Quoted in the Charlottesville *Daily Progress*, November 16, 1928.

241 On each item foundation officials pasted a label: See Fiske Kimball letter to Mrs. David Tucker Brown, April 23, 1953, Thomas Jefferson Memorial Foundation Archives, University of Virginia Library Special Collections Department, Box 13.

241 That year the U.S. Treasury Department: Kuper interview in Charlottesville *Daily Progress*, April 14, 1973.

241 Alvin Whall, the director of the Treasury's: *The New York Times*, July 18, 1929.

242 As for the four Levy lions: March 18, 1999, letter from Jack Owen, in the files of the TJMF Research Department. A photocopied newspaper article (that has no date nor identifying newspaper) in the same files reports that the larger marble lions were acquired by the Caldwell family and donated to the Cheekwood Museum.

242 During the next four decades the Foundation purchased: see Susan Klaffy and James Bear, op. cit.

EPILOGUE

245 Until 1985, the millions of visitors: See, for example, James L. Nolan, Jr. and Ty F. Buckman, "Preserving the Postmodern, Restoring the Past: The Cases of Monticello and Montpelier," *The Sociological Quarterly*, Vol. 39, Spring 1998, p. 253.

245 When Harley Lewis's parents . . . visited Monticello: author interview, November 8, 1997.

246 "There is a leitmotif": author interview, November 10, 1997.

246 The founding board in the 1920s: author interview, October 19, 1997.

247 The sign, labeled "The Story of Monticello": Malcolm H. Stern Papers (1982–1994), Jacob Rader Marcus Center for American Jewish Archives.

248 "I find that what the visitor is told": Lipkowitz letter to Bear, August 21, 1974, Malcolm H. Stern Papers, op. cit.

248 Bear . . . explained that the foundation believed: Bear letter to Lipkowitz, October 1, 1974, ibid.

249 Bear"It appears," they wrote, that Uriah Levy: Frederick D. Nichols and James A. Bear, Jr., "Monticello: A Guidebook," Thomas Jefferson Memorial Foundation, 1967, p. 71.

249 Irving Lipkowitz wrote back to Bear: Lipkowitz letter to Bear, October 22, 1974, Malcolm H. Stern Papers, op. cit.

250 "His years of fighting and defeating every attempt": Theodore Fred Kuper letter to Annabelle Prager, December 16, 1975. Used by permission of Ms. Prager.

252 "I started to hear from various Jewish friends": author interview, op. cit.

253 "I received a joyous call in April from Saul Viener": Malcolm Stern, "The Levy Role at Monticello," address delivered October 13, 1985, to the Jewish Historical Society of New York, Malolm H. Stern Papers, op. cit.

253 On June 7, 1985, family members and several dozen guests: See Thomas Jefferson Memorial Foundation, "The Levy Family and Monticello: A Commemorative Ceremony," June 7, 1985.

255 "perhaps the third most significant event": quoted in the Charlottesville *Daily Progress,* April 14, 1994.

255 "We've tried to do as much as possible": author interview with Susan Stein, op. cit.

255 Jordan Levy said: see Thomas Jefferson Memorial Foundation, "Celebrating Seventy-Five Years of Preservation and Education: Thomas Jefferson Memorial Foundation, 1923–1998," 1998.

BIBLIOGRAPHY

Because Uriah Levy did not leave a memoir and because his letters are not collected in any archive, the primary sources dealing with his ownership of Monticello are scattered among the letters he wrote that rest in several collections. Uriah Levy's naval career, however, is extensively documented in the official U.S. Navy records held at the National Archives in Washington, D.C., and College Park, Maryland.

The 1963 biography of Uriah Levy, *Navy Maverick*, is woefully undocumented. It appears that the authors got most of their material from the Navy records. That includes the 115-page, 9,000-word "memorial" Levy wrote as the basis for his defense in his Navy Court of Inquiry hearing that was held in November 1857 in Washington. A copy of Levy's anecdotally autobiographical defense is in the Library of Congress and the document has been reproduced in several secondary sources. It contains the only first-person version that has surfaced in which Uriah Levy explains many of the events in his life.

Jefferson Levy left no memoir or collection of letters. The most extensive collection of material on his life and times is contained in the scrapbooks of newspaper clippings—mostly from the late 1890s to around 1920—in the Jefferson Monroe Levy collection at the American Jewish Historical Center Archives in New York City. The center also has a small amount of primary source material on Uriah Levy and on Jonas P. Levy.

A vast amount of primary source material on the Levys—as well as on the other post-Jefferson Monticello owners James T. Barclay and Benjamin F. Ficklin and on Monticello itself—is housed at the Research Department of the Thomas Jefferson Memorial Foundation in Charlottesville. There also is a good deal of material at the Albemarle County Historical Society library in Charlottesville.

Another treasure trove of information on Monticello is the University of Virginia's Alderman Library. There are many collections of letters in the Special Collections Department, including those of George Carr, Uriah Levy's Charlottesville lawyer; R. T. W. Duke, Jefferson Levy's Charlottesville lawyer; and the Randolph family. Luckily for historians, Jefferson's granddaughter Ellen Wayles Randolph Coolidge married Joseph Coolidge and moved to Boston. There is an enormous amount of correspondence back and forth between Ellen and her mother Martha and her sisters Cornelia, Virginia, and Mary back in Virginia. Special Collections also contains the archives of the Thomas Jefferson Memorial Foundation.

The Charlottesville *Daily Progress* extensively covered events at Monticello during the Jefferson Levy period. The newspaper is available on microfilm at Alderman Library. The author was greatly aided in his search of that newspaper by annotated indexes provided by the Albemarle County Historical Society Library and the Thomas Jefferson Memorial Foundation Research Department.

Also helpful for information on the Levy family ancestry were the archives at the Jacob Rader Marcus Center of the American Jewish Archives housed at the Hebrew Union College in Cincinnati. Among other materials, the center contains the papers of Malcolm Stern, who took a strong interest in the Levys and Monticello and was instrumental in gaining recognition for the family at Monticello.

The author is indebted to those Monticello experts who kindly consented to interviews, both for his article on the Levys and Monticello that appeared in the March–April 1998 issue of *Preservation* magazine and for this book. That group includes James A. Bear, Jr., William Beiswanger, Ira Dye, Dan Jordan, Jeffrey Hantman, Harley Lewis, Susan Stein, Saul Viener, and Patricia West.

BOOKS

Abrahams, Robert D. *The Commodore: The Adventurous Life of Uriah P. Levy.* Jewish Publication Society of America, 1954.

Adams, William Howard. *Monticello.* Abbeville, 1983.

Andrews, Marietta Minnegerode. *My Studio Window: Sketches of the Pageant of Washington Life.* Dutton, 1928.

Barclay, J. T. *The City of the Great King: Jerusalem As It Was, As It Is, and As It Is To Be.* Challen, 1858.

Beach, Moses Y. *Wealth and Biography of New York City,* 12th edition. New York Sun, 1855.

Bear, James A., Jr. and Lucia C. Stanton, eds. *Jefferson's Memorandum Books: Accounts, with Legal Records and Miscellany, 1767–1826,* Vol. II. Princeton University Press, 1997.

Bear, James A., Jr. *Old Pictures of Monticello: An Essay in Iconography.* University Press of Virginia, 1957.

Bear, James A., ed. *Jefferson at Monticello (Memoirs of a Monticello Slave* and *The Private Life of Thomas Jefferson).* University Press of Virginia, 1967.

Betts, Edwin Morris, and James Adam Bear, Jr., eds. *The Family Letters of Thomas Jefferson.* University of Missouri Press, 1966.

Betts, Edwin Morris. *Thomas Jefferson's Farm Book: With Commentary and Relevant Extracts from Other Writings.* Princeton University Press, 1953.

Birmingham, Stephen. *The Grandees: America's Sephardic Elite.* Harper & Row, 1971.

Brown, John T. *Churches of Christ: A Historical, Biographical, and Pictorial History of Churches of Christ in the United States, Australasia, England, and Canada.* John P. Morton and Company, 1904.

Buckingham, James S. *The Slaves States of America.* Fisher, Son & Co. (London), 1842.

Burrows, Edwin G., and Mike Wallace. *Gotham: A History of New York City to 1898.* Oxford University Press, 1999.

Chambers, S. Allen, Jr. *Poplar Forest and Thomas Jefferson*. Corporation for Jefferson's Poplar Forest, 1993.

Culbreath, David M. R. *The University of Virginia*. Neale Publishing, 1908.

Daniels, Jonathan. *The Randolphs of Virginia: America's Foremost Family*. Doubleday, 1972.

De Kay, James Tertius. *Chronicles of the Frigate Macedonian, 1809–1922*. Norton, 1995.

De Sola Pool, David. *Portraits Etched in Stone: Early Jewish Settlers, 1682–1831*. Columbia University Press, 1953.

De Sola Pool, David and Tamar de Sola Pool. *An Old Faith in the New World: Portrait of Shearith Israel, 1654–1954*. Columbia University Press, 1955.

Eiseman, Alberta. *Rebels and Reformers: The Lives of Four Jewish Americans*. Zenith, 1976.

Fairman, Charles E. *Art and Artists of the Capitol of the United States of America*. U.S. Government Printing Office, 1927.

Felton, Harold W. *Uriah Phillips Levy*. Dodd, Mead, 1978.

Fitzpatrick, Donovan, and Saul Saphire, *Navy Maverick: Uriah Phillips Levy*. Doubleday, 1963.

Frary, I. T. *Thomas Jefferson: Architect and Builder*. Richmond, Garrett and Massie, 1931.

Higham, John. *Strangers in the Land: Patterns of American Nativism, 1860–1925*. Atheneum, 1966.

Hosmer, Charles B., Jr. *Presence of the Past: A History of the Preservation Movement in the United States Before Williamsburg*. Putnam, 1965.

Karp, Abraham J., ed. *The Jewish Experience in America*. American Jewish Historical Society, 1969.

Karp, Deborah. *Heroes of American Jewish History*, revised edition. KTAV Publishing, 1972.

Kimball, Fiske. *Thomas Jefferson, Architect: Original Designs in the Coolidge Collection of the Massachusetts Historical Society with an Essay and Notes by Fiske Kimball*. Da Capo Press, 1968.

———. *Domestic Architecture of the American Colonies and the Early Republic*. Scribner's, 1922.

Langley, Harold D. *Social Reform in the United States Navy, 1798–1862*. University of Illinois Press, 1967.

Leuchtenburg, William E., ed. *American Places: Encounters with History*. Oxford University Press, 2000.

Lindren, James. M. *Preserving the Old Dominion: Historical Preservation and Virginia Traditionalism*. University Press of Virginia, 1993.

Lord, Frank B. *The Story of Monticello as Told by Thomas L. Rhodes*. Pridemark Press, 1947.

Malone, Dumas. *The Sage of Monticello: Jefferson and His Time*, Vol. VI. Little, Brown, 1981.

Marcus, Jacob Rader. *Memoirs of American Jews, 1775–1865.* The Jewish Publication Society of America, 1955.

———. *The American Jew, 1585–1990: A History.* Carlson, 1995.

Martin, Joseph. *A New and Comprehensive Gazetteer of Virginia and the District of Columbia.* J. Martin (Charlottesville), 1836.

McLaughlin, Jack. *Jefferson and Monticello: The Biography of a Builder,* Henry Holt, 1988.

Mead, Edward C. *Historic Homes of the South-West Mountains, Virginia.* C.J. Carrier, 1898.

Patton, John S., and Sallie J. Doswell. *Monticello and Its Master.* Michie, 1925.

Peterson, Merrill. *The Jefferson Image in the American Mind.* Oxford University Press, 1960.

———. ed. *Thomas Jefferson: A Reference Biography,* Scribner, 1986.

———. ed. *Visitors to Monticello.* University Press of Virginia, 1993.

Randolph, Sarah N. *The Domestic Life of Thomas Jefferson.* Thomas Jefferson Memorial Foundation, 1947.

Rezneck, Samuel. *The Saga of an American Jewish Family Since the Revolution: The History of the Family of Jonas Phillips.* University Press of America, 1980.

———. *Unrecognized Patriots.* Greenwood, 1975.

Rosenbloom, Joseph R. *A Biography of Early American Jews.* University Press of Kentucky, 1960.

Sachar, Howard. *A History of the Jews in America.* Knopf, 1992.

Semmes, John E. *John H. B. Latrobe and His Times, 1803–1891.* Norman, Remington, 1917.

Sobel, Samuel. *Intrepid Sailor.* Cresset Publishers, 1980.

Stein, Susan R. *The Worlds of Thomas Jefferson at Monticello.* Abrams, 1993.

Stern, Malcolm H. *First American Jewish Families: 600 Genealogies, 1654–1988,* 3rd ed. Ottenheimer Publishers, 1991.

Sternlicht, Sanford V. *Uriah Phillips Levy, The Blue Star Commander.* Norfolk Jewish Community Council, 1959.

Thacker, William. *The Structural Preservation of Monticello.* Jarman, 1973.

Townsend, George Alfred. *Monticello and Its Preservation Since Jefferson's Death, 1826–1902, Correspondence of George Alfred Townsend.* "Gath," Gibson Brothers, 1902.

Tuckett, Francis. *A Journey in the United States in the Years 1829–1830.* St. Nicholas Books (London), 1976.

Urofsky, Melvin L. *The Levy Family and Monticello, 1834–1923: Saving Thomas Jefferson's House.* Thomas Jefferson Foundation, Monticello Monograph Series, 2001.

West, Patricia. *Domesticating History: The Political Origins of America's House Museums.* Smithsonian Institution Press, 1999.

Wilstach, Paul. *Jefferson and Monticello.* Doubleday, 1925.

Wolf, Edwin, 2nd, and Maxwell Whiteman. *The History of the Jews of Philadelphia.* The Jewish Publication Society of America, 1957.

ARTICLES

Adams, William Howard. "Historic Houses: Thomas Jefferson's Monticello," *Architectural Digest*, August 1983.

Aycock, B. L. "Monticello." *Confederate Veteran*, Vol. 34, 1926.

Barclay, J. T. "Culture of Silk." *American Farmer*, No. 21, Vol. 14, August 3, 1832.

Barnwell, John. "Monticello: 1856." *Journal of the Society of Architectural Historians*, Vol. 34, 1975.

Barringer, Anna. "Pleasant It Is." *Magazine of Albemarle County*, Vol. 27/28, 1970.

Bear, James A., Jr. "Accounts of Monticello: 1780–1878, A Selective Bibliography." *Magazine of Albemarle County History*, Vol. 21, 1963.

Blandford, Benjamin W. "Commodore Uriah P. Levy." *American Hebrew*, Vol. 16, April 10, 1925 through May 15, 1825.

Britton, Rick. "Thrillseeker: The Amazing Life of Benjamin Franklin Ficklin." *Albemarle Magazine*, December 1998.

Cable, Mary, and Annabelle Prager. "The Levys of Monticello." *American Heritage*, February/March 1978.

Campbell, Mrs. A. A. "Monticello." *Confederate General*, April 1920.

Cummings, Amos. "A National Humiliation." New York *Sun*, August 24, 1897.

Dix, Dorothy. "Monticello—Shrine or Bachelor's Hall?" *Good Housekeeping*, April 1914.

Eisen, Sylvia K. "The Levys of Monticello." *The Light*, February 1976.

Ferguson, Henry N. "The Man Who Saved Monticello." *American History Illustrated*, Vol. 14, February 1980.

Fleming, Thomas. "Monticello's Long Career—From Riches to Rags to Riches." *Smithsonian*, June 1973.

Gage, Marjorie E. "Inside Monticello." *Country Living*, July 1993.

Gaines, William H., Jr. "From Desolation to Restoration: The Story of 'Monticello' Since Jefferson." *Virginia Cavalcade*, Vol. I, Spring 1952.

Godfrey, Naomi. "Credit—At Last: Jewish Family Finally Acclaimed for Saving Jefferson's Home." *The Jewish Week*, December. 20, 1985.

Harnit, Fanny. "Monticello." *DAR Magazine*, Vol. 50, March 1917.

Healy, Robert M. "Jefferson on Judaism and the Jews." *American Jewish History*, Vol. 73, 1984.

Hosmer, Charles B., Jr. "The Levys and the Restoration of Monticello." *American Jewish Historical Quarterly*, Vol., 53, 1964.

"Jefferson and Madison." *Harper's Weekly*, June 6, 1885.

Judge, Joseph. "Mr. Jefferson's Monticello." *National Geographic*, September 1966.

Kanof, Abram. "Uriah P. Levy: The Story of a Pugnacious Commodore." *American Jewish Historical Quarterly*, No. 39, Part 1, September 1949.

Kimball, Fiske. "Monticello." *Journal of the American Institute of Architects*, Vol. 12, April 1924.

Kimball, Marie. "The Furnishing of Monticello." *Antiques*, Vol. 12, 1927.

Kimball, Marie G. "Jefferson's Furniture Comes Home to Monticello." *The House Beautiful*, August. 1929.

Kuper, Theodore Fred. "Collecting Monticello." *Manuscripts*, Summer 1955.

Leepson, Marc. "The Levys of Monticello." *Preservation*, March/April 1998.

Lewis, Jack P. "James Turner Barclay: Explorer of Nineteenth-Century Jerusalem." *Biblical Archaeologist*, September 1988.

Llewellyn, Robert. "Monticello." *Horizon*, June 1983.

Lossing, Benson J. "Monticello." *Harper's New Monthly*, Vol. 7, 1853.

Lucas, Ann M. "Jefferson's Print Collection." *The Magazine Antiques*, July 1993.

"Monticello, Once the Residence of Thomas Jefferson." *Frank Leslie's Illustrated Newspaper*, February 8, 1862.

"Monticello, the Home of Jefferson, Near Charlottesville, Virginia." *Harper's Weekly*, June 2, 1866.

Morgan, James Morris. "An American Forerunner of Dreyfus." *Century Illustrated Monthly Magazine*, Vol. 58, 1899.

Murphy, Cullen. "Eminent Domains: A Horticulturalist and the Landscape at Monticello That He Brought Back to Life." *Atlantic Monthly*, August 1996.

Nolan, James L., Jr. and Ty F. Buckman. "Preserving the Postmodern, Restoring the Past: The Cases of Monticello and Montpelier." *Sociological Quarterly*, Spring 1998.

Patton, John S. "Monticello," *University of Virginia Alumni Bulletin*, Vol. 7, 1914.

Peterson, Maud Howard. "The Home of Jefferson." *Munsey's Magazine*, January 1899.

Randall, J.G. "When Jefferson's Home Was Bequeathed to the United States." *South Atlantic Quarterly*, Vol. 23, January 1924.

Rezneck, Samuel. "Maritime Adventures of a Jewish Sea Captain, Jonas P. Levy." *American Neptune*, Vol. 37, October 1977.

————. "The Strange Role of a Jewish Sea Captain in the Confederacy." *American Jewish History*, September 1978.

"Saving Monticello." *Literary Digest*, August 27, 1921.

Settle, Mary Lee. "Mr. Jefferson's World." *New York Times Magazine*, March 13, 1983.

Slatin, Peter D. "Dry Technology Fixes Roof at Monticello." *Architectural Record*, August 1991.

Sly, Caroline. "Jefferson's Skylights." *Early American Life*, August 1994.

Sobel, Samuel. "The Levy Who Saved Monticello." *The Jewish Digest*, July 1962.

Stein, Susan R. "Jefferson's Museum at Monticello." *The Magazine Antiques*, July 1993.

Stern, Rabbi Malcolm H. "Monticello and the Levy Family." *Journal of the Southern Jewish Historical Society*, Vol. 1, October 1959.

Stockton, Frank R. "The Later Years of Monticello." *Century Magazine*, Vol. 34, 1887.

Stone, Herbert S. "Buying Monticello." *House Beautiful*, January 1913.

Wamsley, James S., and Kerry Hayes. "Digging for Jefferson." *Geo*, April 1984.

Weinstein, Alfred A. "Georgia's First Physician." *Harvard Medical Alumni Bulletin*, Summer 1961.

Willner, Nancy E. "A Brief History of the Jewish Community in Charlottesville and Albemarle." *Magazine of Albemarle County History*, Vol. 40, 1982.

Wilstach, Paul. "Jefferson's Little Mountain." *National Geographic*, April 1929.

REPORTS, STUDIES, OTHER

Albemarle County Historical Society. "Monticello: Extracts from Charlottesville Newspapers." A. Robert Kuhlthau, compiler, 1992.

American Scenic and Historic Preservation Society. "Annual Report." 1914.

Carr Papers, University of Virginia Library, Special Collections Department.

Correspondence of Ellen Wayles Randolph Coolidge. University of Virginia Library, Special Collections Department.

"Defense of Captain Uriah P. Levy, U.S. Navy Before a Court of Inquiry, Convened at Washington, D.C. in November 1857." Defense Statement, *Uriah Phillips Levy, 1792–1862*, Library of Congress Miscellaneous Manuscripts Collection.

Jefferson Club of St. Louis. "The Pilgrimage to Monticello, the Home and Tomb of Thomas Jefferson." 1902.

Kean, Robert H. "History of the Graveyard at Monticello." *The Collected Papers of the Monticello Association*, Vol. I, 1965.

Kimball, Fiske. "Thomas Jefferson: An Outline of His Life and Service with the Story of Monticello: The Home He Reared and Loved." Thomas Jefferson Memorial Foundation, 1924.

Kimball, Marie. "The Furnishings of Monticello." Thomas Jefferson Memorial Foundation, 1946.

Kuper, Theodore Fred. "Thomas Jefferson the Giant." Thomas Jefferson Memorial Foundation, 1945.

Levy v. Levy, 33 New York 97-138 (Tiffany, 1866). Court report, Levy's estate and will.

Lipkowitz, Irving. "Monticello's Century of Challenge: 1820s to 1920s." Unpublished paper, Thomas Jefferson Memorial Foundation Research Department files.

Malcolm H. Stern Papers (1882–1994). Jacob Rader Marcus Center for American Jewish Archives.

McGraw, Eliza R. L. "The Country of the Heart: Twentieth-Century Representations of Southern Jewishness." Ph.D. dissertation, Vanderbilt University, 1999. UMI Dissertation Services, Ann Arbor, Michigan.

National Museum of Jewish Military History. "An American, a Sailor, and a Jew: The Life and Career of Commodore Uriah Phillips Levy, USN (1792–1862)." 1997.

Papers and Recollection of R. T. W. Duke, Jr. University of Virginia Library, Special Collections Department.

Papers of the Duke Family. University of Virginia Library, Special Collections Department.

Papers of the Meikleham Family. University of Virginia Library, Special Collections Department.

Thomas Jefferson Memorial Foundation. "Celebrating Seventy-Five Years of Preservation and Education: The Thomas Jefferson Memorial Foundation, 1923–1998." December 2, 1998.

———. "Facts & Figures: A Quick Reference Guide to Monticello and the Thomas Jefferson Memorial Foundation." Revised, Spring 1997.

———. "Home of Thomas Jefferson." 1940.

———. "Monticello: A Guidebook." Frederick D. Nichols and James A. Bear, Jr., 1967.

———. "Monticello: A Guidebook." 1997.

———. "Official Souvenir Booklet of Monticello: The Home of Thomas Jefferson." 1926.

———. "The Levy Family and Monticello: A Commemorative Ceremony." June 7, 1985.

ACKNOWLEDGMENTS

In the spring of 1997 Lee and Sally Sherman drove from their home in New York City to visit me and my family in Loudoun County in northern Virginia. As they usually did when they came for a visit, Aunt Sally and Uncle Lee made a side trip, a one-day jaunt to Monticello. When they came back to our house, Lee had news for me.

"Did you know that Jews owned Monticello?" he asked.

Before I could answer, he said, "You have to write a book about them."

He went on to tell me, with cultural pride, how at Monticello he saw the Rachel Levy gravesite, read the plaque and was intrigued with the fact that Uriah and Jefferson Levy owned Monticello longer than the Jefferson family did. He hadn't been aware of what to him was a significant event in Jewish-American history and he wanted to know more. He was sure many other people would want to know more about the Levys as well.

To placate him (and because I had heard about the Levys but knew no details of their Monticello ownership), I said I'd try to write a magazine article first, then maybe I would write a book. A few days later I called Bob Wilson, the editor of *Preservation* magazine, the award-winning publication of the National Trust for Historic Preservation, and pitched the idea. Bob loved it. The result: a terrifically designed front-cover article in the March-April 1998 issue.

I received the galleys for the article in January of that year and mailed a copy to Sally and Lee in New York, thanking Lee for not letting me rest until I told the Levy-Monticello story. He was very ill at the time. He died on February 12, 1998, the day the issue was printed.

I received more feedback—all of it positive—from that article than from anything I had written in nearly twenty-five years of writing hundreds of magazine and newspaper articles. I got letters, phone calls, and e-mails (both *Preservation* and the Thomas Jefferson Memorial Foundation put the article on their web sites along with my e-mail address) from people I knew and from strangers. That's when I realized that Lee was right.

The topic deserved to be fully presented in a book. I knew I had only touched on the highlights of the story in my 3,500-word article. So I wrote a proposal for a book that would, for the first time, tell the complete story of Monticello after Jefferson's death.

I owe a great debt of thanks to Lee Sherman, to Bob Wilson, and to Chad Conway at The Free Press, who has been a dream editor. Chad fought for my book, encouraged me steadfastly every step of the way, and did a wonderful job editing the manuscript. I am eternally grateful to him.

My thanks go, too, to Susan Stein, the curator at Monticello, who has helped me immeasurably in many ways beginning in 1997 when I first interviewed her for the magazine article. Her book, *The Worlds of Thomas Jefferson at Monticello*, is an invaluable and comprehensive source of information about Monticello's furniture and furnishings.

Dan Jordan, the Thomas Jefferson Memorial Foundation's president, also has been a great source of help and encouragement. I also benefited from advice and counsel from William Beiswanger, the Foundation's long-time director of restoration, from former Foundation research historian Rebecca Bowman and from Heather Carlton, Kelly Fearnow, Susanne Lilly, Carrie Taylor, and Chad Wollerton at the Foundation.

Jeff Hantman of the University of Virginia deserves special thanks for his help with the magazine article and with sage publishing advice. Thanks, too, to Robert Shepard in the latter area. David Willson, my friend, colleague, and fellow laborer in the Vietnam War literature world, has been my writing confidant every step of the way. I cherish his advice and counsel. Moses Robbins, my great friend of three decades, provided immeasurable research support on two trips to Charlottesville. Harley Lewis, Jefferson Levy's grandniece, also has helped me since day one. She and her husband Dick have been extremely kind, generous, hospitable and supportive.

I always have been an admirer of libraries and librarians. My admiration for the institution and for those who labor in libraries has increased a thousand fold since I began research for this book. I have benefited tremendously from the help of many librarians and archivists at many libraries. I would like to thank them for their kindness, knowledge and assistance.

I received unstintingly generous help from Sheila Wetzel, Tia Sperduto and Helen Carr at the Middleburg Library (Loudoun County, Virginia's wonderful community library); Robert Boley, the Loudoun Library System's steadfast ILL expert; Regina Rush and her colleagues at the Special Collections Department at Alderman Library at the University of Virginia; Camille Servizzi, Kevin Proffitt, Dorothy Smith (for heroic technical help) and Gary Zola at the Jacob Rader Marcus Center of the American Jewish Archives at the Hebrew Union College in Cincinnati; Abigail Schoolman, Lyn Slome, Michelle Sampson and Abraham J. Peck at the American Jewish Historical Society in New York City; Gaye Wilson and Betty Goss at the Thomas Jefferson Memorial Foundation's Research Department; Margaret M. O'Bryant, the librarian, and Joan Graves, a volunteer researcher, at the Albemarle County Historical Society; and Minor Weisiger at the Library of Virginia Archives Research Service in Richmond.

Also: Joe Mosier, the archivist at the Chrysler Museum in Norfolk; Jeffrey T. Hartley at the National Archives in Washington; Anneliese Taylor at George Mason University's Fenwick Library; Ed Liskey, collections manager at the National Museum of American Jewish Military History in Washington, and former AJMH curator Laura Willoughby; and Judy Trump at the Georgetown University Library.

Also: Steve Mayer at the U.S. House of Representatives Library; Zoe Davis at the U.S. Senate Library; Betty K. Koed at the U.S. Senate Historical Office; Donna

Baker at the Manuscripts Department, Library of the University of North Carolina at Chapel Hill; Linda Seguin at the University of Georgia's Hargrett Rare Book and Manuscripts Library; Lorna Condon at the Society for the Preservation of New England Antiquities's Library and Archives; Steve Mathews and Alex Northrup at the Foxcroft School Library; and Carl Hallberg at the American Heritage Center, University of Wyoming.

I had specialized help from Mark Levy with Levy family genealogy; Jeffrey Kaplan of Mikveh Israel in Washington, D.C.; Neil Blumofe, the Hazzan at Congregation Agudas Achim in Austin, Texas; Rabbi Shmuel Kaplan of Chabad Lubavitch in Maryland; my brother, Evan Leepson; Annabelle Prager, Levy family researcher; Patricia West, who shared her vast knowledge on historic homes; James Bear, the former longtime curator at Monticello; Saul Viener, the Richmond amateur historian who helped the Levy family gain just recognition at Monticello; Kaye Crouch at the Cheekwood Museum of Art in Nashville, and Deborah Bershad, executive director of the Art Commission of New York City.

Special thanks to Ira Dye, retired U.S. Navy captain, University of Virginia professor and naval historian of the first rank. He generously shared his research on Uriah Levy's naval career and kindly reviewed and critiqued the sections in the book on that subject.

I am greatly indebted to Bill Fogarty—former high school English teacher, University of Notre Dame English major, charter member of the Male Book Group, and attorney extraordinaire—for research and advice that helped me unravel the extremely complicated details of the three 1860s and 1870s Levy family lawsuits. Thanks, too, for the steady support of the other MBGers: Bob Carrola, John Czaplewski, Russell Duncan, and Angus Paul.

I owe a great deal to Edith Lewis, the editing supervisor, to Linnea Johnson, the copyeditor, and others at The Free Press, and to a group of excellent editors I've been fortunate to work with in my journalism and free-lance writing careers: Irwin Arieff, Debby Baldwin, Jim Churchill, Alan Ehrenhalt, Gayle Garmise, Hoyt Gimlin, Mike Keating, Wayne Kelley, Dave Loomis, John Moore, Warden Moxley, Mark Perry, Michael Pleasants, Mokie Porter, Michael Pretzer, Bob Rankin, Sandy Stencel, Sharon Thom, Bill Thomas, Jim Wagner, Bob Wilson, Elder Witt, and Dick Worsnop.

Thanks also go to my supportive friends Mark Andrus, Linda and Bernie Brien, Julie Coles, Larry and Gail Cushman, Tommy and Marianne Dodson, Randy Fertel, Fred Geary, Michael Kelley, Treavor Lord, Greg McNamee, Ann and Tom Northrup, Susan and Gray Price, Margie and Dan Radovsky, Barbara and Pat Rhodes, Susan and Fraser Wallace, and Linda and Marvin Watts.

And I would be nothing without the three most important people in the world to me—my wife Janna, my son Devin and my daughter Cara.

Lastly, my special thanks and all my love to my treasured Aunt Sally Sherman.

INDEX